REV. EDWARD GARDINER LATCH, D.D., L.H.D.

𝕻𝖗𝖆𝖞𝖊𝖗𝖘

OFFERED BY THE CHAPLAIN

REV. EDWARD GARDINER LATCH, D.D., L.H.D.

AT THE OPENING OF THE DAILY SESSIONS OF THE

HOUSE OF REPRESENTATIVES OF THE UNITED STATES

DURING THE EIGHTY-NINTH, NINETIETH,

AND NINETY-FIRST CONGRESSES

1966–1971

H. Con. Res. 789   Passed December 2, 1970

CONCURRENT RESOLUTION
(Submitted by Mr. Arends)

Resolved by the House of Representatives (the Senate concurring), That the prayers offered by the Chaplain, the Reverend Edward Gardiner Latch, D.D., L.H.D., at the opening of the daily sessions of the House of Representatives of the United States during the Eighty-ninth, Ninetieth, and Ninety-first Congresses, be printed, with appropriate illustration, as a House document, and that three thousand additional copies be printed and bound for the use of the House of Representatives, to be distributed by the Chaplain of the House of Representatives.

Attest:

W. PAT JENNINGS,
Clerk of the House of Representatives.

Attest:

FRANCIS A. VALEO,
Secretary of the Senate.

II

DEDICATED

TO

JOHN W. McCORMACK

BELOVED SPEAKER

UNITED STATES HOUSE OF REPRESENTATIVES

JANUARY 10, 1962–JANUARY 2, 1971

WHO APPOINTED ME CHAPLAIN

MARCH 14, 1966

Introduction

The U.S. House of Representatives, by a resolution adopted in the 91st Congress, authorized the printing of the prayers offered by the Chaplain, Edward Gardiner Latch, D.D., L.H.D., at the opening of daily sessions during the 89th, 90th, and 91st Congresses.

Dr. Latch was born in Philadelphia, Pennsylvania, raised in Baltimore, Maryland, and all his ministry of 45 years was spent in the metropolitan area of Washington, D.C. Here he served four churches and the last one, Metropolitan Memorial, the National Methodist Church, he served for 26 years. On Monday, March 14, 1966, I had the happy privilege of appointing him Chaplain of the House of Representatives for the remainder of the 89th Congress. He was elected Chaplain in 1967 for the 90th Congress and was reelected in 1969 for the 91st Congress. He gives full time to his work and enjoys it as much as we enjoy having him.

The prayers offered by Chaplain Latch during the last four years have warmed our hearts, increased our faith, made us more conscious of the divine presence, and strengthened our efforts to serve our country and to bring peace to our world. Again and again, he prayed that we may be given courage to walk in God's way, wisdom to make right decisions, strength to devote ourselves to our nation, and love to relate ourselves affirmatively to one another. Here is the mood of moral earnestness, a feeling of deep religious faith, an eager devotion to keep our Republic great and good, and a genuine desire to advance the Fatherhood of God and the Brotherhood of man. May the spirit of this volume awaken in all who make use of it a sense of the presence of God and a stimulation to work for one nation, indivisible, with liberty and justice for all.

JOHN W. McCORMACK,
Speaker, House of Representatives.

v

Foreword

by

THE HONORABLE CARL ALBERT

President Johnson once described the daily prayers in Congress as one of the most important traditions of government. I agree. Like him, I feel that the prayer is as much a part of the legislative process as is the drafting of bills and the taking of votes on them.

I have made it a practice ever since I have been a Member of Congress to be present every possible day for the opening prayer in the House of Representatives. I think this has profited me not only in the personal strength and peace which prayer always engenders but more important in the perspective which the reflections of a man of God bring as I face problems from day to day.

It has been my good fortune to know personally six Chaplains who have served in the Congress. None has been more outstanding than our present House Chaplain, Dr. Edward Gardiner Latch. His prayers have been an inspiration to all of us, lifting our spirits above the dome of the Capitol to the Almighty. I am delighted that many of these prayers are included in this volume and can thus be shared with others of this generation and of generations to come.

It is particularly fitting that this volume should be dedicated to our beloved Speaker, the Honorable John W. McCormack, who has retired after more than 42 years of outstanding service in the Congress.

His tenure has been marked by a recognition of our need for Divine Guidance as individuals and as a nation. His devotion to God has been reflected in his public life and in his service to his fellowman. Perhaps one of his constituents described him best when she said that not only is he a great man but a good man.

The dedication of these prayers to Speaker McCormack is an appropriate tribute to a good man . . . a faithful servant of God.

VI

Foreword

by

THE HONORABLE HALE BOGGS

Dr. Edward G. Latch, the Chaplain of the House of Representatives, is a gifted man.

Each day, when the House is called to order, Dr. Latch steps up to the lectern and offers a prayer. He has done this hundreds of times, and yet each prayer is an original work of a master craftsman.

Dr. Latch's craft, of course, is the art of communicating with God. And, his unique specialty is doing it in behalf of the House of Representatives.

The content of Dr. Latch's prayers—and the enthusiasm which he brings to his work—set the tone for a working day in the House. Each invocation offers a fresh insight and a new perspective of the real business of government: the care and maintenance of human life and happiness.

Dr. Latch's prayers—and counsel—have won him respect and admiration from all four hundred and thirty-five Members of the House. It is therefore fitting that this collection of Dr. Latch's prayers be published and made available for the inspiration and benefit of others.

Foreword

by
THE HONORABLE GERALD R. FORD

Prayer is a power in the lives of all those who believe deeply in a Supreme Being and address themselves to that Being. Prayer heals; prayer comforts; prayer inspires.

There are few who can speak to the Supreme Being in words more inspirational than those of Dr. Edward G. Latch, for nearly five years the revered chaplain of the U.S. House of Representatives.

Dr. Latch clearly and eloquently speaks for all Members of the House when each day he opens the legislative session with words of prayer.

Dr. Latch has a profound sense of knowing—knowing the innermost thoughts of Members of the House, knowing their spiritual needs, and knowing how to speak for House Members in words of prayer. He has counseled many House Members and their staff people.

Having listened daily to Dr. Latch, I can highly recommend this volume of prayers to all potential readers both as to content and inspiration.

As House chaplain, Dr. Latch has the great gift of speaking in phrases which express love of country as well as a deep love of God. He sets forth, therefore, the sense of religious conviction which sustained our forefathers when they settled on these shores.

I commend Dr. Latch's volume of prayers to all who are in need of moral sustenance. His is a book filled with the love of God.

Foreword

by

THE HONORABLE LESLIE C. ARENDS

This is an extraordinary book. It is a compilation of the prayers offered by the Chaplain of the U.S. House of Representatives at the opening of each legislative session. This of itself is not what makes the volume extraordinary. It is that the man—Dr. Edward G. Latch—who as the House Chaplain delivered these prayers is himself so extraordinary.

Perhaps I know Dr. Latch better than most. Before being selected to serve as Chaplain of the House of Representatives, he served as Pastor of the Metropolitan Memorial United Methodist Church, where I have regularly attended services for many years. He has been a continuing source of inspiration to me, as he unquestionably has been to countless others.

This volume of prayers reflects the character of Dr. Latch, who is as close to the image and likeness of God as any man I know. His very presence radiates goodness, coupled with understanding.

Dr. Latch's prayers present a panorama of the problems confronting our country, with which Members of Congress are called upon to deal in their deliberations. He shows us how we can make practical application of spiritual principles in best meeting the many needs of mankind.

The contents of this book could well guide the daily prayers of every man. And they are certain to bring renewed faith and renewed courage in our struggle to realize God's Kingdom on earth.

Foreword

by

The Honorable George Mahon

I have not known a finer man than our Chaplain, Dr. Latch.

I have known him well for a quarter of a century. He has been my good and always helpful friend. He is a friend to all mankind.

Filled to overflowing with love and compassion for his fellow man and blessed with an abundance of that great Christian virtue of charity, he is superbly endowed by his Maker to discharge his appointed commission. I have always thought of him as a "perfect and upright" man of God.

Prayer is our conduit to God. May the House of Representatives never be without this never-failing source of strength. Dr. Latch, in his great understanding of the purposes of God and of man, has blessed the House and the Nation through his spiritual leadership.

The Apostle Paul wrote that it is required of stewards that they be found faithful. I believe I bespeak the sentiments of Members of the House of Representatives generally that we—the people of his pasture and the sheep of his land, so to speak—draw inspiration and comfort from his daily faithfulness in the service of his God, his country, and the House.

I warmly commend this collection of prayers to one and all and express the hope that the House of Representatives may be blessed with the services of Dr. Latch for many years to come.

x

Prayers

OFFERED BY THE CHAPLAIN AT THE OPENING OF THE DAILY SESSIONS OF
THE UNITED STATES HOUSE OF REPRESENTATIVES DURING THE EIGHTY-
NINTH (SECOND SESSION), THE NINETIETH, AND THE NINETY-FIRST
CONGRESSES (1966–1971)

EIGHTY-NINTH CONGRESS
Second Session

MONDAY, APRIL 25, 1966

God is our refuge and strength, a very present help in trouble. Therefore will we not fear.—Psalm 46: 1.

O GOD, OUR FATHER, who art the refuge and strength of Thy people in every age and our refuge and our strength in this present hour, we pause in Thy presence to offer unto Thee once again the devotion of our hearts. Amid all the changes of this life, help us to rest our spirits upon those eternal foundations of truth and love which Thou hast laid for us. Save us from restlessness, from confusion, and from perpetual movement. Draw us unto Thyself that for this moment we may be still and know that Thou art God. With the assurance of Thy Spirit may we accept the responsibilities of this day and fulfill all our obligations with fidelity and honor. Into Thy loving arms we commit ourselves and our Nation—praying that together we may be one in Thee: through Jesus Christ our Lord. Amen.

TUESDAY, APRIL 26, 1966

Let your light so shine before men, that they may see your good works, and glorify your Father who is in heaven.—Matthew 5: 16.

O GOD OUR FATHER, who art the source of light and life, whose glory is in all the world, without whom no one is strong, no one is good—make

1

us one with Thee as we begin this day. May our faith in Thee make us strong, hold us steady, and keep us serene as we face the responsibilities and the tasks which confront us. May we always know that Thou art with us. May we always believe that Thou art leading us. Amid all our differences may we be one in spirit, one in purpose, and one in good will as we give ourselves in deep devotion to the welfare of our beloved country and for the good of all mankind. May the light of Thy spirit shine forever in our hearts. In Jesus' name we pray.   Amen.

WEDNESDAY, APRIL 27, 1966

In solemn truth I can see that God is no respecter of persons, but that in every nation the man who reverences Him and does what is right is acceptable to Him. And Jesus went about doing good.—Acts 10: 34, 38, Phillips Translation.

O God, Creator of the world, sustainer of life and the Father of all men, in quietness and reverence we lift our hearts anew to Thee, praying that Thy grace may cleanse us, Thy power may strengthen us, and Thy love develop in us greater good will. Forgive our selfishness, our narrowness, our prejudices, and our pride. Set us free from the bonds which separate us and draw us together in Thee as one people in spirit and in truth. May we become like Him who went about doing good, always good, nothing but good: even Jesus Christ our Lord.   Amen.

THURSDAY, APRIL 28, 1966

The Lord God is a sun and shield: the Lord will give grace and glory: no good thing will He withhold from them that walk uprightly.—Psalm 84: 11.

> "Spirit of God descend upon my heart;
>   Wean it from earth: through all its pulses move:
>   Stoop to my weakness, mighty as Thou art:
>   And make me love Thee as I ought to love."

Spirit of God descend upon my heart—this is our morning prayer. Make us daily aware of Thy presence and in Thy spirit may we find the attitudes we need for this day. Slow us down, Lord, slow us down; we work too hard, we eat too fast, we hurry too much. Help us to take time to think clearly, time to pray sincerely, and above all time to cultivate the sense of Thy presence in our hearts and in our homes. Then give us the faith and the fortitude to walk uprightly in Thy way, for the good of our Nation and for the glory of Thy Holy Name, through Jesus Christ our Lord. Amen.

WEDNESDAY, MAY 4, 1966

Enter into His gates with thanksgiving and into His courts with praise: be thankful unto Him and bless His name. For the Lord is good; His mercy is everlasting; and His truth endureth to all generations.—Psalm 100: 4, 5.

ALMIGHTY GOD, RULER OF THE UNIVERSE, THE SUSTAINER OF LIFE, AND THE FATHER OF ALL MEN, unto Thee do we lift our hearts in prayer and in praise. We thank Thee for the gift of life ever fresh from Thy hand, for the blessings of home, for work to do and the strength to do it, for friendships which warm our hearts, for a nation that is free and for our faith in Thee which keeps us strong, holds us steady and carries us through every experience with honor.

May Thy wisdom make us wise, may Thy patience help us to be more patient: may Thy love strengthen us to love others and may Thy forgiveness help us to forgive one another.

Sustained by Thy presence may we walk the paths of truth and love this day, harboring no ill will, but filled with good will growing evermore like Thee who hast revealed Thyself in Jesus Christ our Lord. Amen.

THURSDAY, MAY 5, 1966

God who made the world and all things therein, seeing that He is Lord of heaven and earth, dwelleth not in temples made with hands; neither is worshipped with men's hands, as though He needed anything, seeing He giveth to all life, and breath, and all things.—Acts 17: 24, 25.

ETERNAL GOD, from whom cometh all things good and true, in the quiet of this moment we open our hearts unto Thee. Thou art everywhere, Thou art everywhere present, and now in the silence of this moment we would find Thee and would be found by Thee. Breathe on us, breath of God, fill us with life anew, that we may love what Thou dost love, and do what Thou wouldst do.

Strengthen Thou our faith, renew our courage, make us great in goodness and good in greatness that we may triumph over wrong and conquer every evil intention. Put beneath us, the leaders of our beloved land, Thy strong foundation and send us forth our vision clear, our faith confirmed, and our spirits strengthened to be Thy loyal and loving children. So we would open our hearts to Thy transforming presence.

> "O Spirit of the Living God,
> Thou Light and Fire Divine;
> Descend upon our land once more
> And make it truly Thine!
> Fill it with love and joy and power,
> With righteousness and peace,
> Till Christ shall dwell in human hearts,
> And sin and sorrow cease."

Amen.

TUESDAY, MAY 10, 1966

God is not far from each one of us, for in Him we live and move and have our being.—Acts 17: 28.

O Thou in whom we live and move and have our being, without whom no one is strong, no one is good, we pause in Thy presence once again to lift our hearts to Thee in prayer. We need Thee, our Father, we need Thee as we confront the problems of this day, as we endeavor to meet the challenges of this hour and as we seek to make wise use of the opportunities of this moment. Grant us wisdom, grant us courage for the living of these days that we fail not man nor Thee; through Jesus Christ our Lord. Amen.

WEDNESDAY, MAY 11, 1966

I am the vine, ye are the branches. He that abideth in me, and I in him, the same bringeth forth much fruit.—John 15: 5.

We thank Thee, our Father, for Thy spirit which follows us all our days, for Thy love which will not let us go, and for the strength of Thy presence which never lets us down. Help us to open wide the door of our hearts that we may receive Thy spirit, welcome Thy love, claim the strength of Thy presence and thus be made ready for the experiences and responsibilities of this day.

By Thy grace may we put goodness before evil, truth before falsehood, high principle before low prejudice, the rights of the weak before the wrongs of the strong, and may we put Thee above all else, in the name of Jesus Christ our Lord we pray. Amen.

TUESDAY, MAY 17, 1966

God is love: and he that dwelleth in love dwelleth in God, and God in him.—I John 4: 16.

O GOD, WHO ART THE FATHER OF ALL, we thank Thee for every expression of Thy love to us, and for the experience of love we enjoy in the home, in our circle of friends, and here in the Halls of Congress. Strengthen Thou the ties that bind us together. Give us courtesy and consideration in our attitude toward one another. May we not allow our disagreements to make us disagreeable, or our differences to make a difference in our relationships, but now and always may the spirit of good will abide in our hearts. Keep us ever mindful of Thy presence, eager to do Thy will and loyal to the royal within ourselves as did Jesus Christ our Lord. Amen.

WEDNESDAY, MAY 18, 1966

They that wait upon the Lord shall renew their strength; they shall mount up with wings as eagles; they shall run and not weary; and they shall walk and not faint.—Isaiah 40: 31.

QUIETLY AND SINCERELY, OUR FATHER, do we wait upon Thee. Without the strength which Thou alone can give we faint and falter and walk not in faith and love. With the strength Thou dost cause to arise within us we are made ready for every responsibility, equal to any experience and adequate for all of life. Make us ready for responsibilities of this day, equal to the experiences of this hour and adequate for the actions we take this session of Congress.

Strengthen our President as he leads us; our Speaker as he presides over us; and all Members of Congress as they take action on behalf of our people. In Thy strength may we be made strong indeed, in Jesus' name we pray. Amen.

THURSDAY, MAY 19, 1966

This is life eternal, to know Thee the only true God, and Jesus Christ, whom Thou hast sent.—John 17: 3.

E TERNAL FATHER OF OUR SPIRITS, once more we humbly and reverently bow in Thy presence, offering unto Thee the devotion of our hearts. Thou art the source of light and life. Thou art the fountain of flowing love. Thou art in everything that lifts and liberates the human soul. Lift us, we pray

Thee, and liberate our spirits that we may be led from the seen to the unseen, from the unreal to the real, from things as they appear to be to the things as they truly are. May each one of us draw the things as we see it, for the God of things as they are: in the dear Redeemer's name. Amen.

TUESDAY, MAY 24, 1966

I am the vine, ye are the branches. He that abideth in me, and I in him, the same bringeth forth much fruit; for without me ye can do nothing.— John 15: 5.

O GOD, OUR FATHER, without whom our world drifts into darkness and despair, let the light of Thy spirit shine upon us as we for this moment worship Thee in spirit and in truth. Deliver us from unworthy ambitions which close our eyes to the rights of others and from a self-centeredness which grows into suspicion and ill will. Make us mindful of the needs of people in our Nation and around our world. Beneath all differences of race or creed help us to see human aspirations coming to fruition and seeking to be satisfied. Abiding in Thee, may the fruit of compassion and understanding and love be brought forth anew within us—pray in the name of Jesus Christ, Thy Son, our Lord. Amen.

FRIDAY, MAY 27, 1966

*Blessed are the dead who die in the Lord from henceforth: Yea, saith the Spirit, that they may rest from their labors; and their works do follow them.—*Revelations 14: 13.

ALMIGHTY GOD, OUR HEAVENLY FATHER, from whom we come, with whom we live, and unto whom our spirits return, grant us Thy blessing as we pray and enable us so to put our trust in Thee that we may find comfort and courage for the facing of these days.

We remember before Thee those who have given their lives for our country. Comfort the hearts and the homes that walk in sorrow and in grief. Even as they journey through the valley of the shadow of death, may they feel Thy presence near and in the assurance of Thy love find strength sufficient for every need.

May we and all our people hear the summons to a greater and nobler living which comes to us as we remember our loyal and loving dead—a summons to give our best that a government of the people, by the people, and for the people shall not perish from the earth.

We pray for one of our number who lost a little one this week. May Thy presence make them strong and truly comfort their hearts. In Jesus' name we pray. Amen.

WEDNESDAY, JUNE 1, 1966

Blessed is the man that walketh not in the counsel of the ungodly, nor standeth in the way of sinners, nor sitteth in the seat of the scornful. But his delight is in the law of the Lord; and in his law doth he meditate day and night.—Psalm 1: 1, 2.

WRITE THY LAW UPON OUR HEARTS, OUR FATHER, and Thy words upon our minds, as we lift our souls to Thee. We believe in Thee, O God, and we pray that Thy spirit may so dwell in us that Thy peace and Thy power may be ours this day. Guide us in the decisions we make, give us support in our efforts to be true to Thee, and grant us courage to do what we firmly believe to be right. Just as we are now, strong and free, to be the best that we can be for truth and righteousness and Thee, Lord of our lives, we come. Amen.

TUESDAY, JUNE 7, 1966

Beloved, let us love one another; for love is of God; and he who loves is born of God, and knows God.—I John 4: 7.

ALMIGHTY FATHER, RULER OF THE UNIVERSE AND THE REDEEMER OF MEN, we praise Thee for the life Thou hast given us, for the beauty of the world in which we live, for the truth by which men live, and for the love which binds us together. Open our eyes that we may see the beauty about us, open our ears that we may hear the appeal of truth, and open our hearts that we may receive the ministry of Thy love.

Remove from within us all bitterness, all resentment, all ill will and fill us anew with the spirit of joy and peace and love. In spite of differences may we be of one mind, possessed by one spirit, motivated by one power—to serve our country with all our hearts, to keep our faith in Thee, and to work for the good of our fellow man: In the Master's name we pray. Amen.

WEDNESDAY, JUNE 8, 1966

Create in us clean hearts, O Lord, and renew a right spirit within us.—Psalm 51: 10.

O LORD, OUR GOD, before whom all deceit fades, all pretense fails, all ill will falls, who are the way, the truth, and the life—bless us this day with Thy spirit and help us to walk in Thy way, to believe Thy truth and to live Thy life.

Forgive our foolish ways, the mistakes we make, the sins we commit, the harsh criticism we direct toward those who disagree with us, and our slowness to see the good in others and the wrong in ourselves.

Create in us clean hearts, O Lord, and renew a right spirit within us—that Thy will may be done in us, in our beloved country, and in all men; through Jesus Christ our Lord. Amen.

THURSDAY, JUNE 9, 1966

In returning and rest shall ye be saved; in quietness and in confidence shall be your strength.—Isaiah 30: 15.

O God, our Father, the light of the minds that know Thee, the life of the spirits that love Thee and the strength of the souls that live with Thee—in quietness and confidence we lift our hearts to Thee in prayer.

Deliver us from unworthy thoughts, overanxious moods, tense spirits, and may we find rest and peace and joy in Thee.

Forgive our shortcomings, our failure to give Thee right-of-way in our lives, our insistence upon our way rather than Thy way. May we never think of ourselves as sufficient for our responsibilities but may we find our sufficiency in Thee. Strengthen Thou our hands and our hearts this day and use us for Thy glory and for the good of our land. In Jesus' name we pray. Amen.

MONDAY, JUNE 13, 1966

My presence shall go with thee, and I will give thee rest.—Exodus 33: 14.

Our Father in heaven and on earth, who hast given us life and the promise of life eternal, on every hand we see evidences of Thy spirit and of Thy goodness to us. For the beauty of the earth, for the glory of the skies, for the love which from our birth over and around us lies, Lord of all to Thee we raise this our prayer of grateful praise.

We thank Thee for Thy presence in our hearts making us strong, giving us confidence, and helping us to live in good will with our fellow man. We thank Thee for our country—this land of the free and the home of the brave. May we now and always play our full part in keeping the flag of freedom forever flying over our land and ultimately over the whole world.

We thank Thee for these men and women in Congress for their devotion to our country and their dedication to Thee. May Thy presence go with them all the day long. Through Jesus Christ, our Lord. Amen.

TUESDAY, JUNE 14, 1966

Let the words of my mouth, and the meditation of my heart, be acceptable in Thy sight, O Lord, my strength and my Redeemer.—Psalm 19: 14.

OUR FATHER, who art in heaven, we come to Thee conscious of our shortcomings and our sins, yet confident that Thou art with us and that with Thee sins are forgiven, discouragement gives way to encouragement, fear changes to faith, and a new glory enters human life.

Give us the courage of our convictions—the confidence to say yes to what is right, the courage to say no to what is wrong, and the wisdom and the insight to know the difference. May this spirit enter the hearts of all our people. So shall we be children of Thine serving Thee faithfully all our days. Let the words of our mouths, and the meditations of our hearts, be acceptable in Thy sight, O Lord, our strength and our Redeemer. Amen.

TUESDAY, JUNE 21, 1966

This is the day which the Lord hath made; we will rejoice and be glad in it.—Psalm 118: 24.

OUR HEAVENLY FATHER, we bow before our altar of prayer with hearts overflowing with gratitude because Thou hast been so wonderfully good to us. We are what we are, we have what we have, not because we deserve it, not because we have earned it, but because Thy goodness has attended us, Thy strength has made us strong, Thy love has undergirded us, and Thy presence has blessed us all our days. Help us to be worthy of Thy gifts and to use each day for Thy glory, for the good of our country and for the welfare of our fellow man. Thus, may every day be a glorious adventure in great living. In Jesus' name we pray. Amen.

WEDNESDAY, JUNE 22, 1966

Where two or three are gathered together in My name, there am I in the midst of them.—Matthew 18: 20.

OUR HEAVENLY FATHER, who has given Thy word that where two or three are gathered together in Thy name, there Thou art in the midst of them—make us aware of Thy presence this moment as we assemble in Thy name, invoking Thy blessing upon us and praying that Thou would make us adequate for the tasks of this day, give us wisdom for the decisions we have to make and courage always to do what is right.

Bless, Thou, our President, our Speaker, and all the Members of this House. Support us all the day long of this troublous life, until the shadows lengthen, and the evening comes, and the busy world is hush, and the fever of life is over, and our work is done. Then, of Thy great mercy, grant us a safe lodging and a holy rest and peace at the last; through Jesus Christ our Lord. Amen.

TUESDAY, JUNE 28, 1966

Thou art my God, and I will praise Thee: Thou art my God, I will exalt Thee.—Psalm 118: 28.

OUR HEAVENLY FATHER, in whom we live and move and have our being, so fill us with Thy spirit that we may not yield to temptation but be strengthened with inward power for outward tasks. May we meet our obligations with honor, our duties with faith, and our responsibilities with a high regard for the good of all.

Stimulate us with those deep and abiding convictions which keep our country strong, which makes our churches vital, and fill our homes with love and joy and peace. May noble virtues live nobly in us and may we give them hands and feet in our day and for this hour in which we live—through Jesus Christ our Lord. Amen.

WEDNESDAY, JUNE 29, 1966

The Lord is my light and my salvation; whom shall I fear?—Psalm 27:1.

ETERNAL GOD AND FATHER OF MEN, facing responsibilities that tower above us like threatening waves beyond our power to meet adequately— we bow in Thy presence, praying for the strengthening uplift of Thy Holy Spirit. In quiet confidence we come with humble and contrite hearts, acknowledging with the Psalmist—*The Lord is the strength of my life, my light, and my salvation.*

As we face the tasks of this day help us to be conscious of Thy presence, and eager to do Thy will and to work for the good of our Nation.

We pray for those in our Armed Forces, who are fighting for freedom, and sacrificing their lives that the spirit of liberty may be kept alive in our world. In this time of tumult, through these days of danger, give us a steadiness of purpose, a devotion to duty, and a determination to complete the work we are called upon to do. We pray in the Master's name. Amen.

MONDAY, JULY 11, 1966

O give thanks unto the Lord; for He is good: for His mercy endureth forever.—Psalm 118: 29.

O GOD, OUR FATHER, who knowest us better than we know ourselves, whose mercy never lets us down and whose love never lets us go—by Thy spirit help us to take an honest look at ourselves and at our frustrations, our fears and the futility that marks our daily lives—so much of which separates us from Thee and from one another. Grant unto us the assurance of Thy forgiving spirit, the consciousness of Thy redeeming love and the confidence of Thy empowering presence that we may begin again this day to walk in Thy way, to believe Thy truth and to live Thy life revealed to us in Jesus Christ our Lord.   Amen.

TUESDAY, JULY 12, 1966

Teach me to do Thy will, for Thou art my God: Thy spirit is good; lead me into the land of uprightness.—Psalm 143: 10.

ETERNAL GOD, OUR FATHER, who art ever pouring out Thy spirit upon Thy people, we thank Thee for all those in every age who have opened their hearts to Thee, for men and women who have dreamed great dreams, seen great visions and who possessed courage to stand firm for what is right and good for all. For those who trust in truth amid lies; who stand for justice amid injustice; who walk in good ways amid evil times; who quietly work for brotherhood even when men are unbrotherly; who possess a vision of life with Thee at the center even when men deny Thy presence—we thank Thee, O God. By Thy spirit help us to be in the number of these great and good men: through Jesus Christ our Lord.   Amen.

THURSDAY, JULY 14, 1966

If any man walks in the day, he does not stumble because he sees the light of this world.—John 11: 9.

O GOD, OUR FATHER, whose mercy is from everlasting to everlasting and whose truth endureth forever, in all humility and reverence we bow in Thy presence offering unto Thee once again the devotion of our hearts. Amid all the traffic of our ways, turmoils without, within, make in our hearts a quiet place and come and dwell therein. Sure of Thy presence may we face the tasks of this day with a dauntless courage, a quiet faith and with a never failing good will.

In the struggle between light and darkness in our time may we walk in the light and live in the light that we and our Nation may continue to be the light of the world: in the Master's name we pray. Amen.

MONDAY, JULY 18, 1966

He hath showed thee, O man, what is good; and what doth the Lord require of thee, but to do justly, and to love mercy, and to walk humbly with thy God?—Micah 6: 8.

O THOU WHOSE WILL IT IS THAT WE DO JUSTLY, love mercy, and walk humbly with Thee, grant unto us as we wait upon Thee the confidence to do what we ought to do, the courage not to do what we ought not to do and the wisdom to see our way clearly. Deliver us and our Nation from discord and disunity. May we find our concord and our unity in Thee. Give to each one of us the consciousness of Thy presence, the continual strength of Thy spirit and the constant awareness of our duty to lead our people in the ways of freedom and justice and peace.

Help us to keep our faith in Thee and may this faith keep us walking in the way of Thy commandments all the days of our lives: through Jesus Christ our Lord. Amen.

TUESDAY, JULY 19, 1966

Brethren, ye have been called unto liberty; only use not liberty for an occasion to the flesh, but by love serve one another.—Galatians 5: 13.

ALMIGHTY GOD, FATHER OF ALL MEN, who art ever seeking entrance into our lives, forever knocking at the door of our hearts—we open our spirits to Thee in prayer this moment.

We pray humbly and sincerely for our country—this land where we can speak our minds without fear, where we can pray as we choose and where we can elect those who govern us. May she now and ever be the land of the free and the home of the brave.

We pray also for the captive nations of the world—the oppressed people of our planet. Grant that they may keep alive their outreach for liberation to those who sit in darkness, and those who walk through the valley of the shadow of death—may the consciousness of Thy presence bring courage to endure and strength to overcome.

During these trying days help us to think clearly, to make decisions wisely and to courageously do what is right and good for all. Above all may we put our trust in Thee and keep this faith as long as we live. In the Master's name we pray. Amen.

THURSDAY, JULY 21, 1966

God is able to provide you in abundance for every good work.—II Corinthians 9: 8.

O GOD, OUR FATHER, whom we seek to serve and to whom we look for guidance, we bow before the altar of prayer offering unto Thee the gratitude and the loyalty of our hearts. We thank Thee for this new day fresh from Thy hand with its possibilities for great and good living. By Thy spirit may we always be honest and kind and forgiving: may we be generous in our criticism of others, patient with those who criticize us and considerate with those who differ from us. As we follow Him who went about doing good, may we also stop merely going about and begin, like Him, to go about doing good to all.

Through these trying times, bless Thou our President, our beloved Speaker, Members of Congress and all who work with them. May the benediction of Thy presence rest upon us all this day and every day. Together lead us in the paths of unity and peace for Thy name's sake. Amen.

MONDAY, JULY 25, 1966

Blessed is the nation whose God is the Lord.—Psalm 33: 12.

O GOD, OUR FATHER, who are the creator and the sustainer of all mankind, without whose blessing all our labor is in vain, we pray that our lives may be built not upon the shifting sands of superficial and shallow living but upon the rock of eternal truth and enduring love—so we come to offer unto Thee once again the devotion of our hearts, the dedication of our minds, and the discipline of our lives. May this moment of devotion at the beginning of this week be the open door to an increasing fellowship with Thee and with one another.

We are mindful of the experiences and the events which bind us together as a nation. By a common devotion to a common cause—the welfare of our beloved land—may we close ranks and by understanding and sympathy and good will bring together our different classes, heal the rift between races and make us a nation united in spirit, eager to do Thy will and to keep Thy commandments.

We remember with honor and affection those who are giving their lives for our country. May their devotion become our devotion, their dedication our dedication that in an unselfish spirit we may serve our Nation well this day. Amen.

TUESDAY, JULY 26, 1966

Let Thy mercy, O Lord, be upon us, according as we hope in Thee.— Psalm 33: 22.

Eternal Father of our spirits, we pause in Thy presence with heads bowed in prayer as we begin the demanding duties of this day. Make Thy spirit real to us, for we need Thee, every hour we need Thee. Temptations lose their power when Thou art nigh.

We come disturbed by the spirit of our day, weighed down by worry, concerned by our failure to do what really needs to be done, tempted at times to give up—yet here we are. Give us the faith we need for this hour, the courage to do what is best for our country and the confidence to leave the results with Thee. In the dear Redeemer's name we pray. Amen.

WEDNESDAY, JULY 27, 1966

*They that wait upon the Lord shall renew their strength.—*Isaiah 40: 31.

Our Father God, who art from everlasting to everlasting, to Thee we come and unto Thee do we lift our hearts in prayer. Always art Thou with us, always dost Thou seek to arise anew within our minds. Help us to be aware of Thy presence and by clear thinking, clean living, and a creative faith we may find Thy spirit coming to new life deep within our own being.

We pray for greater strength—strength to resist evil, strength to overcome our temptations, strength to do what we ought to do and to live as we ought to live. O God, come into our hearts and help us do for ourselves what we cannot do by ourselves—win the battle over our own weaknesses. Thus, may we be given strength to do our full part in making the heart of our Nation good and sound and wise. In the name of Christ we pray. Amen.

FRIDAY, JULY 29, 1966

*Now, O God, strengthen Thou my hands.—*Nehemiah 6: 9.

Almighty God, our Heavenly Father, the source of all that is beautiful and good in life, again we come to Thee, restless, seeking rest in Thee; weak, seeking strength from Thee; uncertain, seeking certainty in Thy presence. Lesser things have laid their hands upon us, we have majored in minors, we have triumphed with trifles—yet Thou art always with us endeavoring to lead us along the better way to life and to a greater life together.

Strengthen us with Thy spirit and help us to deal wisely and well with the high business before us this day. May we go from this moment of prayer to be true children of Thine, serving Thee and our fellow men with all our hearts. Because we have lived this hour and thought and prayed, may the world become a better place in which men can live together in peace. In Jesus' name we pray. Amen.

TUESDAY, AUGUST 2, 1966

God is Spirit: and they that worship Him must worship Him in spirit and in truth.—John 4: 24.

O GOD OF TRUTH AND LOVE, without whom our world drifts into the valley of darkness and despair, let the light of Thy spirit glow within us as we worship Thee this moment. Deliver us from greed and bitterness, from misunderstanding and ill will—which are the seeds of contention and confusion. By the might of Thy presence and by the strength of Thy spirit in our hearts make us one in Thee. With this oneness may we launch out into an adventurous cooperation among men which shall be a pattern of life for our own Nation and for all the nations of the world.

Underneath all differences of race or color or creed help us to see human life struggling to be free and to find satisfaction on higher levels of daily life. We believe Thou art showing us the way in Thy word—help us to walk in it to the glory of Thy name and for the good of our fellow man, through Jesus Christ our Lord. Amen.

WEDNESDAY, AUGUST 3, 1966

The Lord is my helper, and I will not fear what man shall do unto me.—Hebrews 13: 6.

ETERNAL GOD, OUR FATHER, in whom we live and move and have our being, we are children of Thine—creatures of Thy hands, sustained by Thy spirit, redeemed by Thy love and guided by Thy wisdom. Steady us, we pray Thee, and give us strength to do what we ought to do. Save us from accepting too easy answers to the problems that confront us. Save us from yielding to the temptation to accept the second best when the best can be ours. By the power of an inner spiritual triumph may we conquer all pettiness, all narrowness, and all unworthy desires. May we put first that which is first, second that which is second, and last that which is last. May Thy spirit rule our hearts, and together may we serve our Nation to the limit of our faith and our ability, through Jesus Christ our Lord. Amen.

THURSDAY, AUGUST 4, 1966

For thus saith the Lord God, in returning and rest shall ye be saved; in quietness and in confidence shall be your strength.—Isaiah 30: 15.

O God our Father, eternal source of wisdom, power, and love, whose mercy is over all Thy works and whose will is ever directed to Thy children's good—in quietness and in confidence we lift our hearts unto Thee. In the assurance of Thy presence we face the responsibilities of this day. May the brightness and the glory of good will dwell in our hearts and may all ill will die. Fill us with kindness, compassion, and understanding—with all those moral qualities which make our life together a happy and enduring experience. May we lead our people away from the treacherous road of deceit, hypocricy, and pretense and along the pathway of justice, freedom, and peace. Thus, may we follow Thee all the days of our lives. In the Master's name we pray. Amen.

FRIDAY, AUGUST 5, 1966

You are the light of the world.—Matthew 5: 14.

Eternal God, our Father, spirit of light and life, in this day of distress, in this world of suffering and sorrow we would purify our own hearts as we face the high responsibilities and great demands committed to our care and to our attention this day. Let our littleness be swallowed up in Thy greatness, our pettiness in Thy pursuing presence, and our trite criticisms in Thy triumphant spirit.

Before the altar of prayer we bow, confessing our faults, asking Thy forgiveness, and praying that Thou will give us strength and wisdom that in these days we fail not man nor Thee. In the Master's name we pray. Amen.

MONDAY, AUGUST 8, 1966

Love bears all things, believes all things, hopes all things, endures all things.—I Corinthians 13: 7.

O God, fount of all that is good and true and beautiful, whose love endures forever, we thank Thee for the reverence which lifts our hearts to what is real, and for the love of home that reflects Thy gracious spirit. Bless we pray Thee, those whom Thou hast joined together. May their consecration be beautiful and everlasting.

We invoke Thy blessing upon our labors this day that we may help to build a better world in which men and women can live together in peace and good will and in which their children may grow into fuller manhood and finer womanhood. Teach us that only through love can we begin to perceive the divine mysteries of life and the true glory of man's relationship to man.

Blest be the tie that binds our hearts in steadfast love; the fellowship of kindred minds is like to that above. In the dear Redeemer's name. Amen.

WEDNESDAY, AUGUST 10, 1966

The eternal God is thy refuge, and underneath are the everlasting arms.— Deuteronomy 33: 27.

O GOD, OUR HEAVENLY FATHER, who art the refuge and strength of all who put their trust in Thee, grant unto us a real measure of Thy good spirit as we lift our hearts unto Thee in prayer. Thou art the Father of all men and we are Thy children. Help us to love Thee as children ought to love their parents. Help us to love one another as we ought to love one another in all sincerity and truth. In this free land may we learn to live together in peace and good will.

Bless our country with Thy continued presence and may our Nation be Thy servant for peace and for freedom in this world of human need.

Lift upon us all the light of Thy countenance and breathe Thou Thy peace into our hearts. In the Master's name we pray. Amen.

MONDAY, AUGUST 15, 1966

Thou wilt show me the path of life: in Thy presence is fullness of joy.— Psalm 16: 11.

O GOD, OUR FATHER, RULER OF NATIONS AND THE FATHER OF ALL MAN-KIND, Thou has surrounded us with Thy mercies, Thou hast guided us with Thy wisdom, Thou hast blest us with Thy love. Continue to breathe upon us, breath of God, fill us with life anew, that we may love what Thou dost love and do what Thou wouldst do—so may our lives be more worthy in Thy sight and our labor be in accordance with Thy holy will.

Deliver us from pride and prejudice and bless us with the glorious liberty of the open mind and the responsive heart. Clothe us with the spirit that never fails to bear the fruit of happiness and integrity and love.

Bless Thou our Speaker, every Member of Congress and all citizens of our beloved country. Together may we keep our Nation free and strong and good. In the name of Christ we pray.   Amen.

TUESDAY, AUGUST 16, 1966

The steps of a good man are ordered by the Lord: and he delighteth in his way.—Psalm 37: 23.

Eternal Father of our spirits, who has promised unto the upright in heart a light that shines in the darkness and a strength that never fails, grant unto us such good attitudes and such high purposes that shall lift us above the shadow of doubt and fear and help us to realize the power of Thy presence. Give to us the wings of faith, the lift of love, and the heart of hope as we commit ourselves anew to Thee and to Thy will for our lives.

May we walk the ever-changing roads of our daily life with confidence and courage, knowing that Thou art with us always and all the way. Give to us this day a healthy body, an understanding mind, a happy spirit, a loving heart and with it all a will ready to do good to others where we can do good and to be faithful unto Thee, through Jesus Christ, our Lord.   Amen.

WEDNESDAY, AUGUST 17, 1966

These things have I spoken unto you, that my joy may remain in you and that your joy might be full.—John 15: 11.

O Thou whose light never fades, whose love never fails, and whose life never dies—as we open the windows of our hearts to Thee in prayer may we be filled with the glory of Thy presence, with the greatness of Thy spirit, and with the grandeur of Thy grace.

Grant unto us the royalty of an inward happiness and the serenity of mind which comes from living close to Thee. Daily renew in us the sense of joy and let Thy eternal spirit dwell in our minds and bodies, filling every corner of our hearts with light and grace, so that, bearing about with us the infection of a good courage, we may be diffusers of life and may meet all ills and accidents with a gallant and highhearted happiness giving Thee thanks always for all things: through Jesus Christ our Lord.   Amen.

MONDAY, AUGUST 22, 1966

O satisfy us early with Thy mercy; so that we may rejoice and be glad all our days.—Psalm 90: 14.

O GOD AND FATHER OF US ALL, who art a tower of defense to all who put their trust in Thee—we come before Thee this moment in gratitude for Thy steadfast love and for Thy enduring faithfulness. In The alone is our hope, our strength, and our very life. Inspire us, the leaders of our people, with a clear vision and a definite mission to meet the needs of our country with clean minds, understanding hearts, and loyal spirits. We pray that Thy spirit may be so alive with us that we will be men who put truth before falsehood, good will above ill will, self-denial in place of self-interest, high principles over low prejudices—so shall we be champions of justice and peace, so shall we continue to hold a high regard for personality everywhere. May Thy will be done in us and in all men. In the Master's name we pray.

Amen.

TUESDAY, AUGUST 23, 1966

The Lord is my shepherd.—Psalm 23: 1.

O GOD, whose strength sustains us in our work, whose hand supports us in our weariness, and whose presence gives us security in the time of trouble, grant unto us the renewing power of Thy holy spirit as we wait upon Thee in prayer. Lead us into green pastures, beside still waters, and along paths of righteousness in which our souls are restored. When we walk through the valley of the shadow of death, may we feel Thy presence near and in the assurance of Thy love find deliverance in the midst of our distresses.

Fill our hearts with such a faith in Thee, that by night and by day, at all times and in all seasons we may commit ourselves and those near and dear to us to Thy never-failing compassion and to Thy never-faltering mercy. Thus, may Thy goodness and Thy mercy follow us all the days of our lives, and in spirit may we dwell in Thy house forevermore. Amen.

WEDNESDAY, AUGUST 24, 1966

Let us come before His presence with thanksgiving.—Psalm 95: 2.

LET THY PRESENCE BE REVEALED TO US, OUR FATHER, as in this quiet moment of prayer we wait upon Thee.

Strengthen us by Thy spirit that no trouble may overcome us, no difficulty may overwhelm us, and no duty may overtax us, but may we now and always be equal to every experience, ready for every responsibility, and adequate for every activity. Help us to be more positive in our thinking, to look increasingly on the bright side of life, to be awake to the good everywhere present, and to be ever grateful for Thy gifts to us and for the love which surrounds us all our lives.

This day help us to live our faith, to rejoice in Thy presence, to maintain an attitude of good will toward all Thy children, to learn to forget ourselves, and to serve our Nation and our people faithfully and well. Take Thou Thy rightful place in our hearts—for in Thee alone is peace and joy and life. Amen.

THURSDAY, AUGUST 25, 1966

I will say of the Lord, He is my refuge and my fortress: my God, in Him will I trust.—Psalm 91: 2.

ETERNAL GOD, OUR FATHER, who art the Creator of the world and the everlasting sustainer of our spirits, without whom no one is wise, no one is good—we pause in Thy presence to invoke Thy blessing upon us and to offer unto Thee the devotion of our hearts.

Bless us as we meet this day and may we be given wisdom to make sound decisions, strength to walk in the way of justice and freedom for all, and good will to motivate all we say and do.

Bless Thou our country and make us now and always a people mindful of Thy favor, eager to do Thy will, willing to obey Thy commandments, and ready to live in Thy spirit of love.

Bless our Armed Forces at home and abroad. Strengthen their families and all their loved ones—separated from one another as they are; and, as some journey through the valley of the shadow of death, let them feel Thy strengthening presence and Thy comforting spirit.

May we as the leaders of this free land match this devotion by a deep dedication of our own spirits to the welfare of our beloved country. In the Master's name we pray. Amen.

MONDAY, AUGUST 29, 1966

God is our refuge and strength, a very present help in trouble, therefore will we not fear.—Psalm 46: 1.

ETERNAL GOD, OUR FATHER, who art the refuge and strength of Thy people in every age and whose creative spirit is ever calling us to new frontiers of thought and action, we pause in Thy presence as we greet the coming of another day. In Thy strength we would be made strong, with Thy wisdom we would be made wise, and by Thy grace we would be made good.

We are grateful for this day of opportunity and challenge. By a clarity of thought, by a sincerity of spirit, by a genuineness of motive, and by a goodness of life may we show ourselves ready for the responsibilities we face this hour.

Kindle in our hearts and in the hearts of all Thy children a real love for peace and may the rule of Thy spirit increase in the minds of men until justice and good will shall be established upon this planet: in the name of Christ we pray. Amen.

TUESDAY, AUGUST 30, 1966

There is one God and Father of all, who is above all and through all and in all.—Ephesians 4: 6.

ALMIGHTY GOD, OUR HEAVENLY FATHER, we pause in the midst of pressing duties and commanding needs to open our hearts in prayer unto Thee—who art the source of goodness and love and truth—that the light of Thy spirit may shine upon our pathway and illumine the way to righteousness, to justice, and to peace.

Keep our hearts clean, our spirits courageous, and our minds clear as we face the tasks of this day. Lead us and all men to that realm where good will shall reign and truth shall rule and freedom shall regulate the actions of men.

Before this altar of prayer we dedicate ourselves anew to Thee and we pledge our loyalty to our Nation and to the well-being of men everywhere: through Christ our Lord. Amen.

THURSDAY, SEPTEMBER 1, 1966

Let us love one another: for love is of God; and everyone that loveth is born of God, and knoweth God.—I John 4: 7.

O GOD, who hast guided our fathers to build on these shores a nation of the people, by the people, and for the people and who didst give them faith to believe that they may become one in spirit with liberty and justice for all, move Thou within our hearts that we may live according to Thy holy will and that we may be open to the leading of Thy gracious spirit.

Remove from our minds all bitterness and all contempt for one another, that departing from all that divides us we may by Thy grace arrive at a new unity of spirit that being one with Thee we may be one with our fellow man.

May our spirit be the spirit of good will, may our security be the security of good will, may our strength be the strength of good will where each may live for all and all may care for each. In the Master's name we pray. Amen.

TUESDAY, SEPTEMBER 6, 1966

Trust in the Lord and do good.—Psalm 37: 3.

O GOD, OUR FATHER, eternal source of wisdom, power, and love, who art above us and within us, who dost keep the planets in their courses and yet art mindful of the faint whispers of our human hearts, before Thee we pause in reverence and awe, contemplating the grandeur of Thy being, the greatness of Thy power, and the glory of Thy love.

Keep us restless until we find our rest in Thee, keep us dissatisfied until we find our satisfaction in Thee, keep us in weakness until we find our strength in Thee.

Into our lives come appeals for causes, some of which are good and some of which are not good. We pray that by Thy spirit we may be led to make wise choices that our reactions may be good and for the good of all. Help us to keep our minds and hearts responsive to Thee, that Thy grace may find an outlet in our lives and that we and our Nation may be channels for Thy spirit to establish justice between men, good will within men, and peace in our world: through Jesus Christ our Lord. Amen.

THURSDAY, SEPTEMBER 8, 1966

My grace is sufficient for thee: for my strength is made perfect in weakness.—II Corinthians xii: 9.

ETERNAL FATHER OF OUR SPIRITS, the light of all that is true, the strength of all that is good, and the glory of all that is beautiful, at the beginning of another day we would lift our minds and hearts unto Thee in prayer, seeking strength and wisdom and love sufficient for our needs.

Help us to walk in the light, to share our strength, and to build upon love that we may be ready for all our responsibilities and equal to every experience. May we always think clearly, speak confidently, and act courageously and may the world of today be a better world than the world of yesterday because of our devotion and our work.

We pray that Thy spirit may enter the hearts of all our people, that they and we may be delivered from all malice and all hatred, and may be led to do justly, to love mercy, and to walk humbly with Thee. Upon our majority leader and upon all who are sick lay Thou Thy hand in healing and blessing. In the Master's name we pray. Amen.

MONDAY, SEPTEMBER 12, 1966

Give ear to my prayer, O God; and hide not Thyself from my supplication.—Psalm 55: 1.

O UR FATHER GOD, whose love is from everlasting to everlasting and whose truth endureth forever, we pause in Thy presence with bowed heads, lifting our spirits unto Thee—unto whom all hearts are open, all desires known, and from whom no secrets are hid. Cleanse Thou the thoughts of our hearts by the inspiration of Thy holy spirit that we may love Thee more perfectly, do Thy will more confidently, and serve Thee and our Nation more faithfully.

We come disturbed by the troubles of our time, burdened by the weight of worry, and distressed by our inability to do what we ought to do. We pray for our Nation and for our world and for ourselves that we may increase the spirit of good will and thus be a part of the solution and not a part of the problem that confronts us. Give us the courage to carry on knowing that in Thee we find strength for each task. In the name of Christ we pray. Amen.

WEDNESDAY, SEPTEMBER 14, 1966

Behold, God is my salvation, I will trust and not be afraid.—Isaiah 12: 2.

A LMIGHTY GOD, FATHER OF ALL MANKIND, whom to know is life eternal, whom to love is life glorified and whom to serve is life filled to the full, in spirit and in truth we bow before this altar of prayer offering unto Thee once again the devotion of our hearts. Some of our number are celebrating the coming of another new year—may they and we enter it in the power of Thy spirit. We acknowledge that in days past we have done what we ought not to have done and we have not done what we ought to have done. We have had opportunity to forward Thy spirit of good will among men and we have fallen by the way. Forgive us, O God, and renew a right and a good spirit within us—that this year may witness a renewed purpose to struggle for the right in church and city and country that poverty and violence and misunderstanding may disappear, and that justice and peace and understanding may appear in our Nation and in our own hearts. Amen.

THURSDAY, SEPTEMBER 15, 1966

Unto Thee O Lord, do I lift up my soul.—Psalm 25: 1.

O SPIRIT OF THE LIVING GOD, whose still, small voice still summons us to turn aside from the feverish ways of foolish men, drop Thy still dews of quietness, till our strivings cease; take from our souls the strain and stress, and let our ordered lives confess the beauty of Thy peace.

In this mood we come this day and bow our hearts at this altar of prayer. May we be led into green pastures, beside still waters, and find restoration of spirit and a renewal of our faith in Thee. Even though we walk through the valley of the shadow of death we will fear no evil for Thou art with us, strengthening us and supporting us.

Bless Thou the Members of this House that they may have wisdom and faith and courage for the experiences of this day, and may they never fail man nor Thee. So may we and other nations together find the way to peace. In the Master's name we pray. Amen.

TUESDAY, SEPTEMBER 20, 1966

Great is our Lord and of great power: His understanding is infinite.— Psalm 147: 5.

O GOD, OUR FATHER, who dost reveal Thyself in numberless ways, deepen within us this day the sense of Thy presence as we wait upon Thee in prayer. Strengthen us by Thy spirit that no danger may overwhelm us, no difficulty may overcome us, no distress may overburden us, and no discouragement may cause us to turn aside from walking with Thee. May Thy grace sustain us in our labor, Thy hand uphold us when we fall, Thy joy make our hearts glad, and Thy presence give us courage to face the experiences of this hour unashamed and unafraid. Help us to grow in strength, in understanding, in never-ending good will; and may we ever commit our lives to goals great enough for free men. In the Master's name we pray. Amen.

WEDNESDAY, SEPTEMBER 21, 1966

O give thanks unto the Lord, for He is good: for His mercy endureth forever.—Psalm 107: 1.

ETERNAL GOD, OUR FATHER, who are the source of wisdom and beauty and goodness, whose spirit ever seeks to arise within our hearts and in the hearts of men everywhere—make Thyself known to us as we bow in prayer before Thee. We thank Thee that Thou art everywhere—that no condition and no distance can ever separate us from Thee and from Thy love. We thank Thee that Thy mercies never fail and Thy loving kindness never ceases. We are grateful for our lives which are in Thy hands and for Thy continuous goodness which blesses us all our days. Help us to be worthy of Thy gifts and to use them for Thy glory and for the welfare of our Nation and of our world. Grant that each one of us may do our part to bring about, on these shores, an order of society in which there will be no injustice, no bitterness of spirit, and one in which each person may come to the fullness of life for which he was made, through Jesus Christ, our Lord.   Amen.

THURSDAY, SEPTEMBER 22, 1966

Open Thou mine eyes, that I may behold wondrous things out of Thy law.—Psalm 119: 18.

ETERNAL GOD, OUR FATHER, who didst lead our fathers through the wilderness into the promised land, we thank Thee for Thy providential care from that day to this. Thou didst guide them with a pillow of cloud by day and a pillow of fire by night, and cause them to dwell in the secret place of the most high. As Thou didst bestow upon them the blessing of Thy law, as Thou didst pour out upon them the gifts of Thy spirit, as Thou didst lead them in the way of Thy commandments—so teach us to follow in their footsteps that we, like them, may seek after truth, strive to deal justly, to love mercy and to walk humbly and reverently with Thee.

Grant, O Lord, that we may love Thy law and live Thy life that the benediction of Thy peace and the blessing of Thy presence may rest upon us and upon our Nation now and always.   Amen.

MONDAY, SEPTEMBER 26, 1966

David encouraged himself in the Lord his God.—I Samuel 30: 6.

ALMIGHTY FATHER, whose spirit is within all Thy creation, whose love faileth never, and whose presence is with us all our days, make us more aware of Thee, more responsive to Thy call, more obedient to Thy will, and more ready to help our fellow man.

Grant unto us a greater honesty of purpose, a more generous attitude toward others, and a most genuine faith in Thee—which will help us live unashamed before Thee and those who love us. When we are tempted, give us strength to overcome our temptations; when we begin to give way to discouragement, help us to find our encouragement in Thee; when we fail and would give up, grant us courage to try again.

May the light of truth illumine our way, may the love of life illumine our hearts, and may the life of love illumine our relationships with one another.

> "Spirit of life, in this new dawn
> Give us the faith that follows on,
> Letting Thine all pervading power
> Fulfill the dream of this high hour."

Amen.

TUESDAY, SEPTEMBER 27, 1966

Thou wilt keep him in perfect peace, whose mind is stayed on Thee: because he trusteth in Thee.—Isaiah 26: 3.

O GOD, OUR FATHER, who art the creator of the world, the sustainer of life everywhere, and the companion of our way—touch Thou our lives with spirit-hand as we come to Thee in this our morning prayer. Facing the tasks of this new day we pray for wisdom to make wise choices, for strength to stand firm for what is good and just for all, and for courage to walk confidently in the way of Thy commandments.

We do not pray for release from burdens, but for renewed strength to carry them; not for an escape from problems, but for an increased power to meet them and to solve them; not for less work, but for greater faith to do our work without worry.

We pray for all who are working in the cause of justice and peace in our Nation and in our world. May the peace of Thy presence abide in all our hearts. Amen.

THURSDAY, SEPTEMBER 29, 1966

Be strong and of a good courage; be not afraid, neither be thou dismayed; for the Lord thy God is with thee whithersoever thou goest.—Joshua 1: 9.

O GOD OF ALL GOODNESS AND GRACE, bless us as we lift our spirits unto Thee in prayer. Make us increasingly aware of Thy presence as in this moment we close our eyes and open our hearts unto Thee. Help us to meet our experiences this day with a singing faith, a strong courage, and a steadfast love.

When disappointments come, when discouragements would shut us in and threaten to shut us out, when the clouds of distress hover over us, give us strength to launch out into the duties of each day—not understanding all that is happening—but in the midst of it all remaining steady and serene, masters of ourselves and servants of Thine. Give us such a confidence in Thy sustaining grace that no weakness of our own may cause us to lose faith and no shortcoming may make us give way to undue anxiety. In all things, by all ways, through all experiences keep us faithful that our consciences may be clear, our hearts clean, and our spirits confident. In Jesus' name we pray. Amen.

FRIDAY, SEPTEMBER 30, 1966

He that loveth not, knoweth not God; for God is love.—I John 4: 8.

God of our fathers and our God, to Thee do we come in prayer, lifting our minds and hearts into Thy holy presence. Assure us that Thou art with us and that we have a real place in Thy heart and in Thy endeavors to bring righteousness and peace and good will to our world. We know that we are all too imperfect and that we have offended Thee time after time— yet we believe that Thou art with us, loving us with a love that never lets us go and never lets us down. In Thy love we would live, by Thy love we would learn, and through Thy love we would find light for our day.

May we be our loving best as we face the tasks of this day. In the Master's name we pray. Amen.

MONDAY, OCTOBER 3, 1966

I will lift up mine eyes unto the hills, from whence cometh my help.— Psalm 121: 1.

O God, the Eternal Father of us all, who art ever near and ever ready to help those who put their trust in Thee, clear our vision and strengthen our hearts as we wait upon Thee. Deliver us from doubt, free us from fretfulness, and save us from the spirit that promotes confusion and disunity. Help us to turn away from all movements which would stifle the liberties of free men and lead us into the fresh air of freedom, justice, and good will. By Thy grace may we and our Nation live in this high moral climate all our days—so shall we be true children of Thine and so shall we serve well the citizens of our beloved land. In the name of Christ we pray. Amen.

WEDNESDAY, OCTOBER 5, 1966

My help cometh from the Lord, who made heaven and earth.—
Psalm 121: 2.

ALMIGHTY GOD, who hast given us this good land for our heritage, we humbly pray that we may always be a people mindful of Thy favor, eager to do Thy will, and glad to be of service to our fellow man.

Save us from discord and discrimination, from pride and prejudice, from vindictiveness and violence, and lead us into the glorious liberty of those who put their trust in Thee, and who walk in the way of Thy commandments.

Give us wisdom to know Thy will, and the strength to do it. Fill us all with the love of truth and righteousness and good will, that we may be a blessing to our Nation and in turn our Nation be a blessing to our world. In the dear Redeemer's name we pray. Amen.

THURSDAY, OCTOBER 6, 1966

In Him we live and move and have our being.—Acts 17: 28.

ETERNAL FATHER, who art the life of our spirits, the law of our minds, and the love in our hearts, with simple trust we draw near to Thee, opening our lives to Thy renewing presence. Strengthened with might by Thy spirit in the inner man, may we launch out into this new day sustained by an unfaltering faith which holds us up and supported by an unfailing fortitude which will carry us through with honor to ourselves, to our country, and to Thee.

Into Thy keeping we commit our loved ones, our Armed Forces throughout the world—especially in Vietnam—our Nation, and the cause of freedom.

During this time of danger and trouble keep us steady, make us confident, and give us the courage to face each day with a firm trust in Thee: through Jesus Christ, our Lord. Amen.

FRIDAY, OCTOBER 7, 1966

The Lord taketh pleasure in them that fear Him, in those that hope in His mercy.—Psalm 147: 11.

GOD OF LIFE AND LIGHT, by whose love we have the gift of a new day, we thank Thee for this moment of prayer when we may draw nigh unto Thee and let Thee draw nigh unto us—as we face the demanding duties of these hours.

From the noise of the outer world we would turn to the quiet of the inner world where in quietness and in confidence we may find strength in Thee for this day.

Help us to accept our privileges with thanksgiving, to carry our responsibilities with honor, to meet our difficulties with courage, and to discharge our duties with fidelity. Whatever good we do this day—may we do it with cheerfulness and with all sincerity of mind and heart, and to Thee shall be the praise world without end. Amen.

TUESDAY, OCTOBER 11, 1966

God has not given us the spirit of fear; but of power, and of love, and of a sound mind.—II Timothy 1: 7.

ETERNAL GOD, OUR FATHER, who art the refuge of Thy people in every age and our strength in this present hour—make Thyself real to us as we bow humbly in Thy presence. Help us to recognize our dependence upon Thee, our constant need of Thy strength, Thy guidance, and Thy love. Give us to know that Thou art always with us and that with Thee we can be made ready for every responsibility and equal to every experience.

We pray for peace in our world, for good will among our people and for a faith in Thee which makes us strong, gives us courage and helps us on our upward way.

May Thy spirit touch each one of us with healing power. Kindle our faith, make sensitive our consciences, dedicate our strength, fortify us in our difficulties and send us out strong in Thee and in the power of Thy might. In the name of Christ we pray. Amen.

THURSDAY, OCTOBER 13, 1966

Be still and know that God is.—Psalm 46: 10.

ETERNAL GOD, OUR FATHER, so high above us that we cannot comprehend Thee and yet so deep within us that we cannot escape Thee, make Thyself real to us as we pray today.

Tired are we of our littleness and we pray that Thou wilt lift us into the fellowship of great minds. Tired are we of our thoughts of discouragement and pray that Thou wilt lift us into the companionship of great hearts— that in these relationships our faith may be renewed, our hope strengthened, and our courage confirmed.

Bless these Congressmen as they wait upon Thee. May they be wise with Thy wisdom, strong with Thy power, and faithful in Thy faithfulness to them. According to our needs, may the riches of Thy grace enter the hearts of everyone of us. In Jesus' name we pray. Amen.

FRIDAY, OCTOBER 14, 1966

Why are thou cast down, O my soul? and why art thou disquieted in me—hope thou in God.—Psalm 42: 5.

Eternal God, our Father, from whom our spirits come, with whom they live and unto whom they return when life on earth is over—in the quiet of this moment we humbly lift our hearts unto Thee in prayer. We believe in Thee with all our minds—do Thou make Thyself real to us in our hearts. Grant unto us a song on our lips in the morning, strength for the day, good will for one another, a steadfast loyalty to our country, courage to maintain high ideals in our political life, and a faith that gives us confidence and helps us to overcome the evil in the world.

Give to us an inner spirit of hospitality to that which is high in life and send us forth masters of ourselves because we are mastered by Thee. By Thy spirit of truth alive within us may we be among that company of Thy children who lift the world and do not lean upon it, and who leave it a better place in which to live. In the Master's name we pray.   Amen.

WEDNESDAY, OCTOBER 19, 1966

I will extol Thee, my God, O King; and I will bless Thy name for ever and ever.—Psalm 145: 1.

Eternal God, who committest to us the swift and solmen trust of life; since we know not what a day may bring forth, but only that the hour for serving Thee is always present, may we wake to the instant claims of Thy holy will, not waiting for tomorrow, but yielding today. Consecrate with Thy presence the way our feet may go that the humblest work may shine and the roughest places be made smooth. Lift us above fear and doubt by a simple and steadfast reliance on Thy holy will.

May the light of faith burn brightly within us, may the life of hope ever glow in our hearts, and may the love of truth always lead us in the way of Thy peace. In Thy name we pray.   Amen.

THURSDAY, OCTOBER 20, 1966

Peace I leave with you, My peace I give unto you. Let not your heart be troubled.—John 14: 27.

Eternal God, our Father, from the shifting scenes of our mortal life we pause to lift our hearts in prayer unto Thee—who are from everlasting to everlasting.

From daily duties which consume our strength, from meetings and schedules which take up so much of our time, we would for this fleeting moment put our hands upon the windowsill of heaven and gaze upon Thy face.

In all our anxious moments grant unto us the assurance that Thou art with us; that behind every shadow stands Thy presence; within every situation abides Thy spirit and beneath every experience are Thine everlasting arms.

Breathe Thou Thy peace upon us, upon our Nation and upon our world—in the spirit of the Prince of Peace we pray. Amen.

FRIDAY, OCTOBER 21, 1966

Blessed is everyone that feareth the Lord; that walketh in His ways.— Psalm 128: 1.

O GOD, who art the Creator and the Sustainer of all mankind, without whose benediction all our labor is in vain and with whose blessing we walk the way to life and light—we pause before Thee this moment seeking strength and peace and guidance from Thee.

Strengthen us when we are weak. May the peace of Thy presence still the turmoil in our hearts and when we would go astray or stumble on the way make straight our paths before us and give us courage to walk with Thee.

For our loved ones, for our Nation and for the whole world of persons we pray. Together may we be led from war to peace, from fear to faith, from ill will to good will, from the depths of shallow living to the heights of a noble and sincere devotion.

So may a new world be born, even in our day. Amen.

SATURDAY, OCTOBER 22, 1966

The Lord will give strength unto His people; the Lord will bless His people with peace.— Psalm 29: 11.

O UR FATHER GOD, grant us Thy peace as we begin to tread our homeward way—peace in our own hearts, peace in our homes, peace in our Nation and in our world. Bless Thou our President as he visits countries in Asia seeking this peace. Grant unto him, and all who meet with him, the sense of Thy presence and the power of Thy spirit. Out of these endeavors may there come a greater peace to our planet and an increasing desire and determination to live together in greater harmony and finer accord.

May we meet the pressures of this present period with courage and faith through the presence of Thy spirit living in our hearts. In the Master's name we pray. Amen.

NINETIETH CONGRESS

First Session

TUESDAY, JANUARY 10, 1967

My presence shall go with Thee.—Exodus 33: 14.

ALMIGHTY GOD, OUR HEAVENLY FATHER, who art from everlasting to everlasting, whose truth endureth forever and whose love never faileth, we pause before Thee this moment as we turn another page in the history of our beloved country and in the story of our lives together as the leaders of this great Republic. Awaken within us the realization that Thou hast a purpose for each one of us, that Thou art not only the sustainer of the rolling spheres but also the supporter of our own human spirits. As we launch upon the new year, may Thy presence strengthen us, Thy spirit guide us and Thy wisdom make us wise.

Bless our President, our Speaker, and the newly elected Representatives of this Congress, together may they strive for peace in our world and for the well-being of mankind everywhere.

Before Thee we remember one who suddenly has left our midst and we are sad indeed. May the blessing of Thy comfort rest upon his family. Strengthen them with Thy spirit and give them courage and faith for the days that lie ahead.

Hear us as we unite in offering unto Thee the Lord's Prayer: *Our Father who art in heaven, hallowed be Thy name. Thy kingdom come. Thy will be done on earth, as it is in heaven. Give us this day our daily bread. And forgive us our trespasses as we forgive those who trespass against us. And lead us not into temptation, but deliver us from evil. For Thine is the kingdom, and the power, and the glory, forever.* Amen.

WEDNESDAY, JANUARY 11, 1967

Look unto Me, and be ye saved, all the ends of the earth: for I am God, and there is no other.—Isaiah 45: 22.

SPIRIT OF GOD, arise within our hearts and make us ready for the tasks of this day. Help us to turn our thoughts unto Thee and to open our hearts to Thy spirit that we may always be honest in our dealings, understanding in our endeavors, and loving in our relationships.

From this moment of prayer may there come a power which will carry us through every experience with courage and with faith.

Bless our people with Thy favor, that being mindful of Thy spirit we may live together in peace and good will, and all of us work for the good of all.

May those who walk through the valley of the shadow of death find comfort and strength in Thee. In the name of Christ we pray. Amen.

THURSDAY, JANUARY 12, 1967

Let the words of my mouth, and the meditation of my heart, be acceptable in Thy sight, O Lord, my strength, and my Redeemer.—Psalm 19: 14.

Our FATHER WHO ART IN HEAVEN AND ON EARTH, we pause in Thy presence once again to acknowledge our dependence upon Thee, and to offer unto Thee the devotion of our hearts. Make plain to us what we should do this day and give us courage to walk in that way. In all our thinking, in all our speaking, in all our doing, may Thy love motivate us, Thy strength support us, and Thy spirit guide us for the good of our country and for the well-being of all mankind. In the Master's name we pray. Amen.

TUESDAY, JANUARY 17, 1967

He that dwelleth in the secret place of the Most High shall abide under the shadow of the Almighty.—Psalm 91: 1.

O GOD, who art a tower of strength to all who put their trust in Thee, help us to turn from the noise and clamor of the world, and to find peace in the assurance of Thy presence. Keep us sensitive to the needs of others, understanding amid our differences, and determined to live in the spirit of good will. May we ever be mindful of the fact that we are one family in Thee, and in this oneness may we do our work and live our lives.

Our minds and hearts reach out in prayer for those in the Armed Forces of our country. Keep them strong in temptation, resolute in duty, and faithful to Thee, who art ever with them and with us. Lord God of Hosts, be with us all—lest we forget, lest we forget Thee. Amen.

WEDNESDAY, JANUARY 18, 1967

Commit thy works unto the Lord, and thy thoughts shall be established.—
Proverbs 16: 3.

ETERNAL FATHER OF OUR SPIRITS, as we bow before the altar of prayer, grant unto us a realization of Thy presence and the assurance that as we face the demanding duties of these days Thou art with us. As we turn to Thee, may we find wisdom to make wise decisions, strength to stand for what is good for all, and good will to motivate all our endeavors.

May we think of Thee—not only this moment—but throughout this day, and from these moments may there come a confidence and a courage which will enable us to lead our Nation to better days, to a greater spirit between our people and to a finer relationship between the nations of the world.

We pause to thank Thee for our companion who has fallen along the way. Receive him into Thy everlasting glory and may the comfort of Thy presence and the strength of Thy spirit abide in the hearts of his beloved family. In the Master's name we pray. Amen.

THURSDAY, JANUARY 19, 1967

*In God we live, and move, and have our being.—*Acts 17: 28.

O GOD, who art the source of light and life, and whose glory is in all the world, without whom no one can live—make us one with Thee as we move through the experiences of this day. By ourselves we are not adequate for our daily tasks, but with Thee we are made ready for every responsibility and equal to every experience. This day, help us to think, and to think clearly; help us to speak, and to speak wisely; help us to live, and to live faithfully. May we always do our very best and then leave the results with Thee. In the Master's name we pray. Amen.

MONDAY, JANUARY 23, 1967

*I remind you to rekindle the gift of God that is within you, for God did not give us the spirit of fear, but of power, and of love and of a sound mind.—*II Timothy 1: 6-7.

O GOD, OUR FATHER, beyond whose love and care we cannot drift, in the glory of a new day we come lifting our hearts unto Thee, praying that Thy spirit may guide us, Thy strength support us, and Thy peace pervade our minds and hearts.

Within the noise and commotion of this day may we hear Thy still small voice and responding find our weakness changed to strength, our fear to faith, and our ill will to good will.

We are disturbed by the dangers in our world, weighed down by many burdens, and tempted to be critical if not cynical, because of human error and human evil. Give us the spirit to carry on with courage and faith, believing that Thou art with us, and believing that together we can do what needs to be done. In the name of Christ we pray. Amen.

TUESDAY, JANUARY 24, 1967

Rest in the Lord and wait patiently for Him; fret not thyself.—Psalm 37: 7.

ETERNAL GOD, OUR FATHER, who hast made us for Thyself so that our hearts are restless until they find rest in Thee, we pause in silence before Thee as we begin the duties of another day. We would quiet our spirits in Thy presence and find rest in the support of Thy sustaining strength.

Forgive our folly and our excuses, our coldness to human suffering, our indifference to those treasures of the spirit which are light and life, and our neglect of Thy wise and gracious laws. So change our minds and turn our thoughts unto Thee that we may walk in the way of Thy commandments and with courage serve our Nation, with compassion help our brethren, and with confidence keep our lives committed to Thee.

In the name of Christ we pray. Amen.

MONDAY, JANUARY 30, 1967

Peace I leave with you, My peace I give unto you: not as the world giveth, give I unto you. Let not your heart be troubled, neither let it be afraid.— John 14: 27.

ETERNAL GOD, OUR FATHER, our refuge and strength in every generation and whose creative spirit does ever call us to new frontiers of thought and action, we bow before Thee this moment as we enter another week together. With Thy wisdom we would be made wise, by Thy strength we would be made strong, inspired by Thy spirit we would be made ready for our responsibilities.

May no danger overwhelm us, no difficulty overcome us, no discouragement overburden us, no duty overtax us, but may we now and ever keep our faith in Thee and in the leading of Thy wise and gracious spirit.

Bless our Nation and the nations of the world—together may we seek peace, patiently pursue it and persevere in our pursuit until peace reigns in the hearts of men and in the heart of our world. In the name of the Prince of Peace we pray. Amen.

TUESDAY, JANUARY 31, 1967

Trust in the Lord with all thine heart; and lean not unto thine own understanding.—Proverbs 3: 5.

DEAR LORD AND FATHER OF MANKIND, our spirit's unseen friend, make Thy way known to us as we bow in Thy presence. May this moment of prayer be an open door to the reality of Thy spirit and as we look up to Thee may we find our strength renewed, our souls restored and be given courage and wisdom for the living of these days.

Endow us with one mind to do justly, to love mercy, and to walk humbly with Thee, and in so doing to promote the welfare of all our people. Give to us and to all our citizens a love for truth, a passion for doing our duty, and a dedication to Thee which will hold us steady amid difficult times. In the name of Christ, we pray. Amen.

WEDNESDAY, FEBRUARY 1, 1967

I will lift up mine eyes unto the hills, from whence cometh my help.— Psalm 121: 1.

ALMIGHTY GOD, OUR HEAVENLY FATHER, who are ever present in our world and with us always all our lives, grant unto us Thy spirit which will enable us to live this day with dignity, do our work with patience, and serve our country with complete devotion. Lift up before our eyes the standards of truth and love. May they lighten our path and may we be given courage to walk in that way for the good of our spirits, for the well-being of our country, and for the welfare of all mankind.

We commend to Thy wise and loving care those who walk in sorrow, those who have given their lives for our country. May we match their devotion with our dedication, their willingness to sacrifice with our readiness to serve our great Republic. In the Master's name we pray. Amen.

MONDAY, FEBRUARY 6, 1967

The Lord is good unto them that wait for Him, to the soul that seeketh Him.—Lamentations 3: 25.

ALMIGHTY AND ETERNAL GOD, whose love is eternal and whose patience never ends, in all quietness of mind and sincerity of heart we wait upon Thee.

Fill us with Thy holy spirit that this day may be a good day and this week a great week. Purify our hearts from every vain and sinful thought and prepare our spirits to live with Thee and to work for the welfare our beloved Nation.

Strong in Thee, may we receive power to think good thoughts, strength to triumph over temptation, a heart to love our fellow man, and a mind to do our duty to ourselves, to others, and to Thee.

Grant unto us the confidence to say "yes" to what is good; the courage to say "no" to what is evil and the insight to know the difference. So may Thy will be done in us and in all men—through Jesus Christ our Lord.

Amen.

WEDNESDAY, FEBRUARY 8, 1967

The Lord is just in all His ways, and kind in all His doings.—Psalm 145: 17.

O GOD, OUR FATHER, unto whom all hearts are open, all desires known and from whom no secrets are hid, cleanse our hearts as we this moment wait upon Thee in prayer. And as we prepare ourselves for the period of Lent, give us grace to recognize the awakening of Thy spirit within us and to listen to all Thou hast to say to us. Let us not yield to the temptations of the world, but strong in Thee may we face our experiences with courage and faith.

In all sincerity do we pray for each other and for all those with whom we associate this day. In our minds may we think of our friends with love, our enemies with forgiveness, and our fellow man with abounding good will. Unto Thee do we commend ourselves and our Nation. Together may we walk in the way of Thy commandments, speak Thy word of love, and obey Thy will to serve our fellow man. In the Master's name we pray.   Amen.

MONDAY, FEBRUARY 13, 1967

Blessed is the nation whose God is the Lord.—Psalm 33: 12.

A LMIGHTY AND ETERNAL GOD, who didst lead our forefathers into this good land, and who gave them guidance to produce on these shores a great nation, give us grace that we in this day may prove ourselves a people mindful of Thy favor, eager to do Thy will, and ready to preserve the democratic spirit of our Republic.

We thank Thee for those who, in times past, have led us in right and good paths. Particularly do we thank Thee for Abraham Lincoln—for the spirit of his great life, for the example he set before our people, and for his dedication to freedom and justice for all. May his spirit be born anew in us. In our hearts and in all our endeavors may there live forever his words:

"With malice toward none; with charity for all; with firmness in the right, as God gives us to see the right, let us strive on to finish the work we are in; to bind up the Nation's wounds; to care for him who shall have borne the battle, and for his widow, and his orphan—to all which may achieve and cherish a just and lasting peace among ourselves and with all nations."

In the Master's name we pray. Amen.

WEDNESDAY, FEBRUARY 15, 1967

Blessed are the poor in spirit: for theirs is the kingdom of heaven.— Matthew 5: 3.

O GOD, the Creator and Sustainer of mankind, the strength of those who labor and the supporter of all who put their trust in Thee, in reverence we bow before Thee this moment. Thou art ever with us and we pray that we may always be aware of Thy presence and keep our lives open to the guidance to Thy word.

By Thy spirit may we become conscious of our own sins and shortcomings, our own limitations and liabilities. May we not mistake prejudice for principle nor conceit for confidence, but in all humility depend upon Thee for guidance and grace for daily living.

Cleanse our hearts of selfishness, pettiness, and narrowness of mind. Create in us a new spirit—a new faith in Thee, a new joy in living, a new courage for life, and a new enthusiasm for good will among all our people.

In the dear Redeemer's name we pray. Amen.

MONDAY, FEBRUARY 20, 1967

Blessed are they that mourn: for they shall be comforted.—Matthew 5: 4.

O THOU ETERNAL FATHER OF OUR SPIRITS, who art the light of the minds that know Thee, the life of the souls that love Thee, and the strength of the hearts that serve Thee, help us so to know Thee that we may come to love Thee, so to love Thee that we may be able to serve Thee with all our hearts.

We face tasks that are beyond our power to meet adequately; we have responsibilities that are more than we can manage acceptably; we are confronted by duties that are greater than our ability to master competently— so we pray for the sustaining power of Thy presence in our lives. Even in distress and sorrow may we feel the comfort of Thy holy spirit.

Lead, Kindly Light, amid the encircling gloom, lead Thou on us—that with clean hearts, clear minds, and courageous spirits we may usher in the day when peace shall reign and good will rule the hearts of men. So may Thy kingdom come and Thy will be done on earth. In the Master's name we pray. Amen.

WEDNESDAY, FEBRUARY 22, 1967

Preserve me, O God; for in Thee do I put my trust.—Psalm 16: 1.

ALMIGHTY GOD, OUR HEAVENLY FATHER, on this day—ever to be remembered by our people—we think again of our first President, whose name shines as a star in the firmament of our Nation and whose personality still towers above us, calling us to new courage in adversity, new loyalty in hours of distress, and a new faith in prayer that we may walk humbly with Thee.

As we listen to his immortal words, may the record of his undying devotion to our country cross our minds, and may the memory of his great life stir our hearts, strengthen our spirits, and send us forth to work more faithfully for the good of our Nation and for the benefit of all mankind. In the Master's name we pray. Amen.

THURSDAY, FEBRUARY 23, 1967

Blessed are the meek: for they shall inherit the earth.—Matthew 5: 5.

O GOD AND FATHER OF US ALL, in these anxious moments and uncertain hours, we come to Thee with needs and longings only Thou canst help us meet. As we live through these troubled days, grant unto us beliefs big enough, hearts honest enough and spirits strong enough to make us more than a match for the mood of this modern time.

By Thy spirit help us to rise above all that is narrow and petty and selfish, and with increased devotion may we work together for the well-being of our Nation and for the welfare of all mankind.

To this end guide us in our thinking, direct us in our speaking, and govern us in our living, that at the end of the day we may hear Thy voice say, "Well done, good and faithful servant." In Jesus' name we pray.

Amen.

WEDNESDAY, MARCH 1, 1967

Blessed are they who hunger and thirst after righteousness, for they shall be filled.—Matthew 5: 6.

ETERNAL GOD AND FATHER OF US ALL, amid the maddening maze of daily duties and the fever and fret of trying times, we would dwell for a moment in the secret place of the Most High and abide under the shadow of the Almighty.

In this quiet moment of prayer we would make ourselves receptive to Thee. Help us to hear Thy voice and to be obedient to the call of Thy spirit. May our hunger for truth and our thirst for life find their fulfillment in Thy presence. As we live through this day may we keep our hearts open to Thee, who art the source of strength for the faithful soul.

To Thee we bring the Members of this body and for them we pray. Give them clarity of insight to see what is right, confidence to do what is right, and the courage to keep on the right path now and always. In the Master's name we pray. Amen.

THURSDAY, MARCH 2, 1967

Blessed are the merciful, for they shall obtain mercy.—Matthew 5: 7.

ALMIGHTY GOD, HEAVENLY FATHER, the creator of all things, the sustainer of all life, and the giver of every good gift—again we bow in Thy presence and in spirit kneel before the Throne of Mercy. We acknowledge our selfishness, our shortcomings, and our sins. We have done that which we ought not to have done, and we have left undone that which we ought to have done. We do earnestly repent and are heartily sorry for these our misdoings. Have mercy upon us, most merciful Father, we humbly beseech Thee. Forgive us, and receiving Thy forgiveness, may we in turn, forgive one another; as we have received mercy may we also be merciful; as love has come to us may love also go out from us to others.

As we bow before Thee in prayer give to us the assurance, that with Thee, all good things are possible. So may we do good, speak good, live good, because in Thee, we are good. In the Master's name we pray. Amen.

TUESDAY, MARCH 7, 1967

Blessed are the pure in heart; for they shall see God.—Matthew 5: 8.

GOD OF OUR FATHERS AND OUR FATHER, from the busy traffic of daily living we would pause in Thy presence and wait upon Thee seeking strength for the day, wisdom to make wise decisions, courage to carry our responsibilities with honor, and love to motivate all our endeavors.

Should we fail in achieving some of our objectives, let not the spirit of defeat dampen our devotion to the highest we know; should others criticize, let not criticism get us down, but seeing the good in it may we let it lift us up; if others misunderstand, let not bitterness blight our best judgment; and if we can win, help us to be humble in victory.

In this moment of prayer we recharge our lives that we may face this day with high principles, real integrity, abounding good will, and with a pure heart that sees Thee. In the spirit of Christ we pray.   Amen.

WEDNESDAY, MARCH 8, 1967

Blessed are the peacemakers: for they shall be called the children of God.— Matthew 5: 9.

OUR FATHER, we know that by ourselves we are not adequate for this day, nor are we ready for our responsibilities, nor are we equal to our experiences. By Thy grace we can become adequate, by Thy spirit we can be made ready, and by Thy presence we can be equal to every experience.

As we wait upon Thee in prayer, reveal Thyself anew to us, and come Thou into our hearts. Then with new peace, greater power, and with better perspective may we serve our Nation well this day and all days. Help us, the Representatives of our people, to see clearly, to choose wisely, and to act courageously, that we may be among the true peacemakers of our time. In the name and spirit of the Prince of Peace we pray.   Amen.

MONDAY, MARCH 13, 1967

*Blessed are those who are persecuted for righteousness sake: for theirs is the kingdom of heaven.—*Matthew 5: 10.

O GOD AND FATHER OF US ALL, who art in heaven and in earth, we acknowledge our dependence upon Thee and offer unto Thee the devotion of our hearts. We come because we need Thee, every hour we need Thee. Temptations lose their power when Thou art near, bitterness fades away in Thy presence, resentments lose their weight, and we are given courage to stand for what we believe to be right.

Grant unto us Thy spirit as we in quietness lift our hearts in prayer unto Thee. If we are criticized because of the stand we take, if we are misunderstood in our decisions, may we not let the disagreements of others make us disagreeable, nor may we allow a difference of opinion to make a difference in relationships, but through it all help us to keep our faith in Thee and in righteousness, justice, and good will. Thus may Thy kingdom come in us and through us begin to come in all men. Through Jesus Christ our Lord. Amen.

TUESDAY, MARCH 14, 1967

Rejoice, and be exceeding glad: for you are the salt of the earth.— Matthew 5: 12, 13.

O GOD AND FATHER OF MANKIND, who art above us yet within us, far off yet very near—nearer than breathing and closer than hands and feet— we bow in Thy presence with hearts filled with gratitude because Thou hast been so wonderfully good to us.

We are what we are and we have what we have not because we deserve them, but because Thy goodness hast blessed our days, and Thy spirit hast led us along the way.

We thank Thee for these men and women who are giving themselves in real and deep devotion to our country, who are seeking to put justice above injustice, good will above ill will, principle above prejudice and liberty above license. May they continue to have the courage of their convictions and in these crucial days fail not man nor Thee.

Bless our Nation with Thy favor and these leaders with Thy spirit. Together may we be channels for peace and for prosperity in our world. In the Master's name we pray. Amen.

MONDAY, MARCH 20, 1967

*You are the light of the world.—*Matthew 5: 14.

ETERNAL GOD, OUR FATHER, whose truth endureth forever, whose love never faileth, and whose mercy is from everlasting to everlasting, we come to Thee with minds aglow with Thy presence and with hearts aflame with the desire to serve Thee, our country, and our fellow man.

> "Lord of all we ask Thine aid, keep us ever unafraid;
> Hold us loyal, keep us true to the task we have to do;
> Lead us on to victory, we shall triumph praising Thee."

In the quiet of this moment, help us to hear Thy still small voice, which alone can change our attitude from fear to faith, from caution to courage and from darkness to light. Together may we abide in the confidence of Thy sustaining strength and in the peace of Thy supporting presence. In the name of Christ we pray. Amen.

WEDNESDAY, MARCH 22, 1967

Let your light so shine before men, that they may see your good works, and glorify your Father who is in heaven.—Matthew 5: 16.

ETERNAL FATHER OF OUR SPIRITS, in this sacred moment of quiet prayer, we turn our thoughts to Thee and open our hearts to Thy spirit that we may be wise in our decisions, understanding in our relationships, and faithful in our devotion to Thee and to our country.

Let not this period of prayer be the only time we think of Thee this day, but as the hours pass may we continue to be mindful of Thy presence and ready to do Thy will.

Bless the people of our Nation with Thy continued favor. May we be great enough in spirit and good enough in heart to be the channel for peace and justice in our world and among men everywhere. To this end, help us this day, and lead us in Thy way—through Jesus Christ our Lord. Amen.

THURSDAY, MARCH 23, 1967

This is my commandment, that ye love one another, even as I have loved you.—John 15: 12.

O THOU, who art the source of every noble impulse and the goal of every worthy aspiration, we bow in Thy presence this holy day of sacred meaning, praying that humbly and sincerely we may receive Thy spirit anew into our all-too-human hearts. Grant that in the midst of troubled times and demanding duties we may be sustained by Thy presence, supported by Thy grace, and strengthened by Thy spirit.

Lead us into the fellowship of those, who in an upper room, heard Thy voice speaking to them and responding found in Thee new life, new light, and new love.

Inspire us with the assurance that Thou art with us, and may our faith in Thee give us confidence to face this day with courage and to live through these holy days with good will. May we be forgiven as we forgive and may we love as we ought to love. In us and in all men may Thy name be glorified.

Amen.

MONDAY, APRIL 3, 1967

I am the vine, ye are the branches. He that abideth in Me, and I in Him, the same bringeth forth much fruit; for without Me ye can do nothing.— John 15: 5.

O LORD, who art the source of light and life, and the fountain of peace and power, let Thy spirit arise within us as we worship Thee this moment. Open our hearts that we may receive the good seeds of Thy Word and let Thy spirit ripen them into the fruits of righteousness and love.

Prosper our Nation in all its life and work that there may be no want anywhere and favor us with Thy presence that good will may reign in the hearts of all our people.

Bless our President, our Speaker, and all these Representatives of our Nation—may they be filled with Thy spirit, the spirit of wisdom and understanding, of faith, and of love. Undergird us in our freedom that we may be forever the land of the free and the home of the brave.

Be Thou with us and may we be with Thee. In the name of Christ we pray. Amen.

TUESDAY, APRIL 4, 1967

We know that in everything God works for good with those who love Him.—Romans 8: 28.

ALMIGHTY GOD, OUR HEAVENLY FATHER, from whom we come, with whom we live, and unto whom our spirits return, may we feel the tap of Thy finger upon our shoulders and the touch of Thy spirit upon our hearts as we this moment lift ourselves unto Thee in prayer.

Always are Thou with us—always. Help us to become more aware of Thy presence renewing our faith in the goodness of life, restoring our spirits to the comfort of Thy love, and reinvigorating our minds with fresh and positive thoughts.

We do not pray for relief from heavy responsibilities but for a release of Thy power which will help us to meet them with honor; not for fewer burdens but for greater strength to manage them with patience; not for less trouble but for more trust in Thee which will help us to master trouble with confidence. In all of life may we be more than conquerors through Him who loves us. In the Master's name we pray. Amen.

THURSDAY, APRIL 6, 1967

"Fear not," saith the Lord, "for I am with you."—Isaiah 43: 5.

Our Father, we give Thee thanks for the rest of the night and for the gift of a new day with its opportunities of serving Thee and our fellow man, and leading our Nation into right and good paths.

By the might of Thy presence in our hearts help us to master the spirit of pride and prejudice which separates men and causes them to strive against each other. Lead us and our people into the paths of mutual helpfulness and mutual concern, that in all good will and as free men we may live together in peace.

Guide the nations of the world into the ways of justice and truth and establish among them that peace which is the fruit of righteousness, through Jesus Christ our Lord. Amen.

MONDAY, APRIL 10, 1967

The Lord is my shepherd.—Psalm 23: 1.

O Thou Seeking Shepherd of our seething spirits, in days of doubt and in times of trouble, we realize anew our need of Thee. We need Thy grace to cleanse us, Thy love to strengthen us, Thy power to heal us, and Thy spirit to keep us free. Truly Thou art our shepherd, Thy rod and Thy staff are our sure support. Strengthen Thou our assurance that Thy hand is upon us leading us in Thy way and giving us the courage to walk in that way with Thee.

Guide our President as he journeys to South America. Out of this Conference may there come good news for all the countries of our hemisphere.

Bless Thou our men and women in the Armed Forces of our country facing constant danger and death. Comfort the bereaved, sustain those who are wounded, strengthen those who face the ordeal of battle, and by Thy spirit make us worthy of victory and ready to seek an enduring peace. In the name of the Prince of Peace we pray. Amen.

WEDNESDAY, APRIL 12, 1967

My presence shall go with thee, and I will give thee rest.—Exodus 33: 14.

O God and Father of us all, beyond whose enduring love we cannot drift, in the glory of a new day we lift our hearts unto Thee ere we devote ourselves to the duties that demand our attention. We would be still in Thy presence and rest in the assurance of Thy sustaining strength.

Bless Thou these Representatives of our people as they think together, plan together, and work together for the good of our country. Help them to take the tensions and the trials of their tasks, the stress and strain of modern iife in their stride, and to overcome them by learning to relax both body and mind; by continuing to think wise and wholesome thoughts and by taking time to keep Thy spirit real in their hearts.

Thus may they and we discover the secret of power; thus may we be led in right paths and thus may our days be filled with faith and hope and love. In Thy name we pray. Amen.

MONDAY, APRIL 17, 1967

He that doeth the will of God abideth forever.—John 2: 17.

G OD OF GRACE AND GOD OF GLORY, pour Thy power upon us as we wait upon Thee in prayer. In days of darkness we have no light but Thine, in times of trouble no refuge but in Thee, in periods of perplexity no strength but the strength Thou dost bestow upon the believing heart. To Thee do we commit ourselves and our Nation praying that in weakness we may be made strong; restless may we find rest in Thee, and when confused may we be aware of Thy presence.

Grant unto us the courage to walk in the way of Thy commandments, the confidence to do Thy will and the consciousness that Thou art with us every moment of every day. So may we live as we pray and as we pray so may we live. In the Masters name we offer this our morning prayer. Amen.

THURSDAY, APRIL 20, 1967

Lord, who shall abide in Thy tabernacle? who shall dwell in Thy holy hill? He that walketh uprightly and worketh righteousness, and speaketh the truth in his heart.—Psalm 15: 1–2.

O GOD, OUR FATHER, who art never far from any one of us, for in Thee we live and move and have our being, help us to be aware of Thy presence, to walk in the way of our faith and to receive Thy love which daily is offered to us. Give to us such a regard for truth, such a desire for guidance, and such a readiness to love that we may go beyond all doubt and discouragement and center our minds on Thee for Thou wilt keep him in perfect peace whose mind is stayed on Thee.

There are times when we do not know what to do, yet something must be done. Help us to pray—not will it help me only but will it be a benefit to others and to our country; not is it for my good but is it for the good of everyone; not is it expedient but is it right. O God, help us to do what is right. Amen.

MONDAY, APRIL 24, 1967

He leadeth me in the paths of righteousness for His name's sake.—Psalm 23: 3.

Eternal God, our Father, whose love never lets us go, whose patience never lets us down, and whose justice never lets us off, hear us again as we offer unto Thee our morning prayer. We come out of a sense of need, out of a conviction that Thou art with us, and we would find our confidence and our courage in the support of Thy sustaining strength.

We pray for light upon our way, love along our path, and life amid the daily duties of our demanding day. Center our lives and the lives of our people around faith rather than fear, around justice rather than injustice, and around high principles rather than low prejudices. Strengthen us where we are weak, hold us firm when we would fall, steady us when we start to slip, and lift us up when down we go.

Remind us of the integrity which has undergirded our Nation, the freedom which is our rich heritage, and of our faith in Thee which has made and still makes our Nation great and strong. Lead us in the paths of righteousness for Thy name's sake. Amen.

THURSDAY, APRIL 27, 1967

It is more blessed to give than to receive—Acts 20: 35.

O God and Father of us all, who hast created man in Thine own image and made him a living soul that he might live in fellowship with Thee, grant unto us Thy blessing as we wait upon Thee in prayer. Make us good in thought, gentle in word, and generous in deed.

Call to our minds again that it is better to give than to receive, better to minister unto others than to be ministered unto ourselves, better to be governed by Thy spirit than to be goaded by our own selfish desires.

Bless our President, our Speaker, and these Representatives of our people. May the benediction of Thy spirit abide in their hearts and lead them in the paths of righteousness, truth, and good will that the lamp of freedom may burn more brightly in our day and the banner of a just good will may fly forever at the masthead of our Nation. In the name of Christ we pray. Amen.

FRIDAY, APRIL 28, 1967

For the kingdom is the Lord's: and He is the governor among the nations.—Psalm 22: 28.

ETERNAL FATHER OF OUR SPIRITS, we pause in Thy presence once again to listen to Thy voice and to receive the ministry of Thy grace. Thou art ever calling us to work with Thee to keep justice and freedom and good will alive in our world. May Thy spirit be so real to us that we shall continue to erect in this land a temple of understanding and love to which all nations may turn for healing and for a helping hand.

We pray that all the peoples of this planet may be open to the leadership of Thy spirit. We pray for the President of our United States, for our Speaker, and for these Members of Congress who represent our people on Capitol Hill. Guide them, sustain them and bless them with courage and faith.

We pray for our men and women in Vietnam. For their loyalty to duty, for their response to the call of our country, for their courage in the midst of danger and for their willingness to give themselves we thank Thee. We pray that the offering of their lives may not be in vain. Out of their suffering and sacrifice may there come a better nation and a better world for all mankind. Through Jesus Christ our Lord. Amen.

TUESDAY, MAY 2, 1967

The fear of the Lord is the beginning of wisdom: a good understanding have all they that do His commandments.—Psalm 111: 10.

O GOD OUR FATHER, the Creator and Sustainer of all mankind, without whose benediction all our labor is in vain, we pray that we may build our lives not upon the shifting sands of a sacrilegious spirit but upon the eternal rock of truth and love—so we would dedicate ourselves anew to Thee. Keep us restless until we find our rest in Thee; keep us dissatisfied until we find our satisfaction in the doing of Thy will; keep us ever searching until we find the end of our seeking in our devotion to Thee and to the coming of Thy kingdom on earth.

Throughout the deliberations of this day may we be mindful of the altar within our hearts where a constant reminder of Thy presence may save us from cynicism and may lead us to a more creative life in Thee. In the Master's name we pray. Amen.

THURSDAY, MAY 4, 1967

Cleanse Thou me from secret faults.—Psalm 19: 12.

O GOD, OUR FATHER, facing the demanding duties of this day and conscious of our pressing problems we feel our need of Thee—so we come lifting our hearts unto Thee in prayer. Make us ready for every responsibility, equal to every experience and adequate for every activity. May we be more than a match for the mood of this moving moment.

Remove from us any resentment which may be ruining our disposition, any bitterness that may be blighting our lives, and any animosity which may activate ill will in us. Cleanse the thoughts of our hearts by the inspiration of Thy Holy Spirit, that we may perfectly love Thee, worthily magnify Thy holy name, and truly serve our Nation well this day, through Jesus Christ our Lord. Amen.

MONDAY, MAY 8, 1967

A faithful man shall abound with blessings.—Proverbs 28: 20.

E TERNAL FATHER OF OUR SPIRITS, we rejoice in the glory of a new day and in the beginning of another week. During this time when the foundations of the world seem to be shaken and the bite of bitterness would blight the best of men, we would use this hallowed moment of prayer to be assured of Thy presence and to tap the spiritual resources we need as we face the pressing duties of these hours.

May we feel Thy spirit leading us as we make our decisions, may we possess Thy power which holds us steady amid the constant pressures of daily life, and may our trust in Thee deliver us from those tensions which would tear us to pieces, and from those worries which would wear us out. All through this day may we think our best, do our best, and be our best, and thus be worthy of our calling to this high office.

Hasten the day when justice and love shall rule the hearts of men and reign in the lives of all people. In the spirit of Christ we pray. Amen.

TUESDAY, MAY 9, 1967

Why art thou cast down, O my soul? Hope thou in God.—Psalm 42: 5.

O UR FATHER IN HEAVEN AND ON EARTH, who dost love all the children of men, teach us to trust Thee and to live in good will with all our people.

Forgive those moments when we find it difficult to believe in Thee, discouraging to trust one another, and disheartening to have faith in ourselves. We are weighed down by the problems we face as a nation and by the burdens we carry day by day. So often we want to change conditions and circumstances without any thought of changing ourselves or of letting Thy spirit change us.

So we pause in Thy presence, praying that Thou wilt change us, restoring our faith in Thee, retrieving our belief in one another, and renewing our respect for ourselves.

Thus, may we live this day keeping our lives and the life of our Nation in Thy strong hands. In the Master's name we pray. Amen.

WEDNESDAY, MAY 10, 1967

O give thanks unto the Lord; for He is good: for His mercy endureth forever.—Psalm 106: 1.

O GOD OF TRUTH AND LOVE, who art worthy of a nobler praise than our lips can utter, and worthy of a greater love than our hearts can offer, in Thy presence we bow this moment as into Thy hands we commit our lives.

May the thoughts in our minds become channels for Thy goodness, may the noble dreams in our hearts find their fulfillment in Thee and may the work of our hands be honest and true. Together may we build a greater Nation and a better world upon the foundations of the faith of our fathers and our faith in the possibility of a new day.

Open our eyes to the manifestations of Thy spirit in our world. Give us courage in weakness, steady us when we would fall, enlarge our sympathies that we may become brothers to all the sons of men. Make us a people grateful for our privileges, faithful in our stewardship, and sensitive to the need of our countrymen. In the Master's name we pray. Amen.

MONDAY, MAY 15, 1967

The fear of the Lord is the beginning of wisdom: a good understanding have all they that do His commandments: His praise endureth forever.—Psalm 111: 10.

GOD OF GLORY AND LORD OF LIFE, in these days throbbing with the beauty of spring, we bow in Thy presence grateful to be alive in a day like this. Before this altar of our daily devotions we open our hearts unto Thee and endeavor to make them channels for Thy power in our Nation and in our world. Keep our thinking clear and clean, our emotions in complete control, and give us the mind to keep our bodies healthy and fit for finer service to Thee and for greater service to our country.

Give to these Members of Congress faith, hope and love that they may lead our people into the right paths of enduring peace and abounding goodwill. In the name of Him who summons us to higher fields of endeavor—we pray.

Amen.

TUESDAY, MAY 16, 1967

Have no anxiety about anything; but in everything by prayer and supplication with thanksgiving let your requests be made known unto God.— Philippians 4: 6.

ETERNAL FATHER OF OUR SPIRITS, whose mercy is from everlasting to everlasting and whose truth endureth forever—in this moment of prayer may we hear Thy voice speaking to us and with receptive minds may we respond. Always and in all ways Thou art very, very near. Help us to be aware of Thy presence and to keep ourselves open to the leading of Thy spirit. Strengthen us when we fail; support us when we fall and sustain us when we falter.

Open our eyes that we may see the higher virtues, open our ears that we may hear the greater voices as they speak to us, open our hands that we may deal wisely and justly the cards that life hands to us—not that we may always win but that we may play the game fairly and honorably.

By Thy spirit help us to live together in this dear land of our birth and preserve us, O God, for in Thee do we put our trust.   Amen.

WEDNESDAY, MAY 17, 1967

*The Lord is the strength of my life.—*Psalm 27: 1.

O GOD, OUR FATHER, whose still small voice calls us to turn aside for a moment from the weary ways of a worried world to wait upon Thee and to find our strength in Thee—make us aware of Thy Spirit, as we bow before the altar of Thy presence. Amid the haste of daily duties and the pressure of persistent problems may we find in Thee strength for the day, wisdom to make sound decisions, and the spirit of good will to motivate all our endeavors on behalf of our beloved country.

With a consciousness of Thy presence alive within us and tapping the unfailing resources of our faith may our souls be restored, our minds refreshed, our bodies renewed and together may we be made ready for the tasks and the responsibilities we face these hours.

> "Lead us, O Father, in the paths of right:
> Blindly we stumble when we walk alone,
> Involved in shadows of a darksome night;
> Only with Thee we journey safely on."

Amen.

MONDAY, MAY 22, 1967

Trust in the Lord with all thine heart; and lean not unto thine own understanding. In all thy ways acknowledge Him, and He shall direct thy paths.— Proverbs 3: 5, 6.

OUR FATHER GOD, Thou hast given us the morning light, give us also the morning blessing as we lift our hearts unto Thee in prayer.

Grant unto us the blessing of wisdom—not only to make wise choices, but also to find the right paths we ought to take. Lift high our vision that we may see clearly and be given courage to walk in Thy way.

Grant unto us the blessing of love. Deepen our understanding, expand our sympathy, enlarge our capacity for good will. Give us grace to rise above the low prejudices that separate man from man and help us to enter the realm of high principles where men are brought together in spirit and in love.

Grant unto us the blessing of faith—in these difficult and trying times may we keep our faith with Thee and in Thee, and may this faith keep us strong and pure and good.

As statesmen grant us wisdom, grant us love, grant us faith that in these days we fail not man nor Thee, through Christ, our Lord.   Amen.

WEDNESDAY, MAY 24, 1967

The Lord will give strength unto His people; the Lord will bless His people with peace.—Psalm 29: 11.

O MERCIFUL GOD, from whom no secrets are hid, help us in this opening moment of prayer to draw near unto Thee with sincere and humble hearts. With Thy presence alive within us may we face the tasks of this day with courage and faith and in all honesty of mind and heart. May no deceit dim our vision, no hatred mar our relationship with others, and no pretense affect our attitude toward ourselves.

Into this land which we love with all our hearts may there come a new and greater unity of spirit as sinister powers without conscience and without morals seek to destroy our freedom and to belittle our reverence for personality. As we live through these days of destiny which call aloud for wisdom and good will, make us worthy of our positions and give us courage and strength to preserve liberty, to defeat tyranny, and to establish a just and enduring peace in our world. Not easy, O Lord, not easy, but with Thee we can do it and by Thy grace we will. In the Master's name we pray. Amen.

WEDNESDAY, MAY 31, 1967

For their sake I consecrate myself, that they also may be consecrated in truth.—John 17: 19.

ETERNAL GOD, OUR FATHER, who hast guided us in ages past and who art our hope for years to come, in Thee do we put our trust for today. We recall once again our Nation's day of remembrance when we call to mind those who have given their lives for our country. For the ministry of memory, for the heritage of sacrificial deeds and for the hallowed thoughts which go through our minds as we think of those who gave themselves for freedom—we pause in gratitude before Thee.

Inspired by their devotion and challenged by their dedication may we now give ourselves afresh to the cause for which they gave the last full measure of devotion that a government of the people, by the people, and for the people may not perish from the earth. In the name of Him who died that men might live, we pray. Amen.

MONDAY, JUNE 5, 1967

Be of good courage, and He shall strengthen your heart, all ye that hope in the Lord.—Psalm 31: 24.

O GOD, OUR FATHER, whose law is truth and whose life is love, as we enter the gates of a new week we would pause in reverence before Thee to acknowledge our dependence upon Thee and to pray for strength as we face the demanding responsibilities of this day.

Give us courage and faith for the tasks before us. May we now and always do our best to preserve liberty, to prevent tyranny from spreading, to promote peace in our world, and to proclaim the good news of freedom to all mankind.

May we live worthily as Thy children and be faithful and true in every experience. Help us to rise above fear and hatred and to maintain our integrity in this free land of our birth. We do not pray for easy tasks but for power to meet them; not for easy burdens but for strength to carry them;

not for less dangerous times in which to live but to keep loyal to our ideals in an all too unideal world.

So may we go forward conscious of Thy presence, eager to do Thy will and to live in good will with all Thy children. In the Master's name we pray. Amen.

WEDNESDAY, JUNE 7, 1967

That He would grant you, according to the riches of His glory, to be strengthened with might by His spirit in the inner man.—Ephesians 3: 16.

OUR FATHER GOD, who art the light of life and the glory of every noble endeavor, we thank Thee for this quiet moment when facing important issues and carrying heavy responsibilities we can turn our hearts to Thee who alone can renew our strength and hold us steady amid the troubles of this time. In the secret place of the Most High may we find the resources we need for this high hour.

In all the perplexities of this period may we not lose our perspective and certainly not our poise. May the principles of freedom and justice upon which this Nation was founded still be our support as we face the challenge of this day. Grant that our faith may be triumphant over our fears, our courage surmount every discouragement and our loyalty to truth and good will be the solid ground upon which we walk together.

Strengthened by Thy spirit may we think clearly, plan creatively and act courageously. In the name of Christ we pray. Amen.

MONDAY, JUNE 12, 1967

They looked unto Him, and were lightened; and their faces were not ashamed.—Psalm 34: 5.

O GOD, OUR FATHER, source of all life and the ever-flowing fountain of love, we open the gates of a new week with prayer and bow before Thee reverently and in all humility of mind and heart. In this time of trouble we need to renew our strength, to restore our courage, and to receive Thy spirit which makes us equal to every emergency. So we pray that now and all through these days Thou wilt help us to be conscious of Thy presence and by Thy grace may we do Thy will.

Save us from recounting our resentments, from harboring any hatred, and from remembering the slights that dim the lights of our day. May we accept the duties of this week with confidence, carry our responsibilities with faith, and enjoy the work we are doing building a better and a stronger nation. Always and in all ways may we follow the way that leads beyond the dark to the dawn and Thee. In the name of Him who is the Light of the World we pray. Amen.

WEDNESDAY, JUNE 14, 1967

Thou hast given a banner to them that fear Thee, that it may be displayed because of the truth.—Psalm 60: 4.

GOD OF OUR FATHERS, whose almighty hand hast made us a nation and preserved us as a people, we thank Thee for days like these when we lift up before our eyes the flag of our beloved country. Grant, O Lord, that this day may kindle in our minds a greater love for our United States and a deeper loyalty to the princely principles which are the foundation stones of our American way of life. Make us aware of our duties as citizens of this free land and help us to accept our responsibilities to keep this land strong and good.

Together may we endeavor to strengthen the moral and spiritual life of our people and do all we can to protect our free institutions, to preserve our liberty and to proclaim freedom to all the world.

Bless Thou this flag of our national life. May it now and always be the symbol of hope to the world and may it wave in glory and majesty over free people for all times.

So we pledge allegiance to the flag of the United States of America, and to the Republic for which it stands one nation, under God, indivisible, with liberty and justice for all. Amen.

MONDAY, JUNE 19, 1967

Bear ye one another's burdens and so fulfill the law of Christ.—Galatians 6: 2.

ETERNAL GOD, OUR FATHER, before the work of a new day begins we would be still in Thy presence and receive the benediction of Thy spirit. May the words of our mouths and the meditations of our hearts be acceptable in Thy sight O Lord—our strength and our Redeemer. Cleansed by Thy forgiving love, made stronger by Thy spirit, and becoming wise with Thy wisdom we would face the unfinished tasks committed to our care this day.

These are times which call for greater courage, higher wisdom, broader sympathy, and deeper faith. May they increasingly become ours as we wait upon Thee. In all our decisions and in all our doing may we keep our hearts confident, our spirits courageous, our minds clear, and our hands clean.

Together may we move forward to a greater day when men shall live together in good will and each one be ready to bear another's burden. Amen.

TUESDAY, JUNE 20, 1967

And they that know Thy name will put their trust in Thee: for Thou, Lord, has not forsaken them that seek Thee.—Psalm 9: 10.

O THOU IN WHOSE PRESENCE OUR SPIRITS FIND STRENGTH, our minds are given fresh insights and our hearts feel the warmth of Thy love—at the gateway of another day we pause in silence before Thee. Incline our souls to seek wisdom and truth and mercy at Thy hands. Reveal to us the way we should go, the decisions we should make, the plans we should follow and may all our work be based upon intelligent conviction and dynamic faith.

Hear us as we pray for those who bear the burden of war and are ready to give their lives that we may continue to live as free men. May we not be heedless of their courage but be ready to bear with them and to support them that out of this turmoil there may come an enduring peace.

Cleanse our national life from discord and violence and suspicion. Keep us from hating one another lest in our ill will we destroy ourselves. Lead us, O Lord, in the ways of unity and peace and good will for Thy name's sake.

Amen.

TUESDAY, JUNE 27, 1967

Restore unto me the joy of Thy salvation; and uphold me with Thy free spirit.—Psalm 51: 12.

ETERNAL GOD, OUR FATHER, our refuge and strength in every hour of need, we come to Thee in this moment of prayer opening our hearts to Thy love, our minds to Thy truth, and our spirits to Thy redeeming grace. Help us to accept our privileges with gratitude, to face our difficulties with courage, and to carry our responsibilities with fidelity.

Deliver us from petty annoyances and pernicious antagonism which corrode the souls of men and pull us down. Help us so to live with the lift of good will in our hearts that life may be better and brighter for us and for all men. Bind us together in one great effort to keep democracy and freedom and faith alive and growing in our day.

God bless America and these leaders of a free people. Give wisdom to these in authority that they may use their power for the welfare of our people and for the well-being of all mankind.

Having done our work faithfully and sincerely may we come to the end of the day unashamed and unafraid and with the peace of a quiet heart. In the Master's name we pray. Amen.

THURSDAY, JUNE 29, 1967

Let not mercy and truth forsake Thee; bind them about Thy neck; write them upon the table of Thine heart.—Proverbs 3: 3.

O God, our Father, the source of all that is good in life, once again we come to Thee: weak—seeking greater strength; tired—needing more rest; worried—desiring a deeper peace. We have sought satisfaction in the minor details of daily life that do not matter much and have left undone the major duties that matter most. Forgive us, our Father, and strengthen us by Thy spirit that the business of this day may be done with Thy cause in our hearts.

Awaken within us the spirit of friendliness and kindliness and good cheer. Keep us from allowing disagreements to make us disagreeable and from permitting differences in us to make differences between us. Kindle in our hearts and in the hearts of all people the spirit of good will. Let tolerance and understanding and compassion rule our spirits and possess our souls.

Send us out into this day to do our work with all our might and at eventide may this world be a better place because we have lived and worked and prayed.

In the spirit of Christ, we pray.   Amen.

MONDAY, JULY 10, 1967

Thou shalt rejoice in every good thing which the Lord thy God hath given unto thee.—Deuteronomy 26: 11.

Almighty God, our Father, again we come to Thee with gratitude for the rest and change of our recess and for the opportunity of serving Thee and our country this present hour provides. We pray that Thou wilt help these Representatives of our people to face the challenge of these times with courage: to accept their responsibilities with confidence and to solve their ever-present problems with creative wisdom.

May they learn anew the lesson that the secret of finding life and happiness is not to do what you like to do but to learn to like what you have to do. In this spirit we pray and in this spirit may we do our work this day.

Our Father, we pray for him whose companion has entered into the life immortal. May the comfort of Thy spirit abide in his heart and in the heart of his family. Help them and us to trust Thee more fully, to remember that love and life are everlasting and that Thy mercy endures forever. May our sympathy draw us closer to him and to each other and make Thy presence more real in all our lives. Through Jesus Christ our Lord. Amen.

WEDNESDAY, JULY 12, 1967

Behold, the Lord our God has shown us His glory and His greatness, and we have heard His voice out of the midst of the fire; we have seen this day that God does talk with man and that He lives.—Deuteronomy 5: 24.

O GOD, OUR FATHER, we thank Thee for the gift of a new day fresh from Thy hand. Help us to use these hours to live cleanly, to labor industriously, to love wisely, and to keep our spirits elevated to high levels of thought. May we have the strength to overcome our difficulties and the courage to carry our responsibilities with honor and with uplifted hearts.

Sustain us in every effort to make a better world and to bring good will to all the children of men. In the midst of this day's work assure us of Thy presence and let the light of Thy wisdom fall upon our pathway. In Jesus' name we pray. Amen.

MONDAY, JULY 17, 1967

Finally, my brethren, be strong in the Lord, and in the power of His might.—Ephesians 5:10.

O THOU WHOSE SPIRIT IS TRUTH AND WHOSE HEART IS LOVE, we would bring our little lives to Thy greatness, our weakness to Thy strength, and our ill will to Thy never failing good will. As flowers open to the sun, as children turn to their parents in moments of need, so we come lifting our seeking souls unto Thee praying that we may feel about us the power of Thy life and the peace of Thy love.

We pray for our President, our Speaker, and all the Members of this body. With pressures which tax their resources to the utmost, with duties which demand their attention and absorb their time, with criticisms which come from minds that do not understand, may our people begin to think of these men and women more and more with sympathetic hearts, understanding minds, and supporting spirits; and less and less with provincial prejudices, fruitless fault finding, and carping criticisms.

So we, the leaders of our people, bow before the altar of Thy presence and pray for a greatness of spirit, a purity of heart, and a will to serve Thee and our country with all our being. In the Master's name. Amen.

WEDNESDAY, JULY 19, 1967

For you were called to freedom, brethren; only do not use your freedom as an opportunity for the flesh, but through love be servants of one another.—Galatians 5:13.

ALMIGHTY AND EVERLASTING GOD, FATHER OF ALL MEN, in our hearts we kneel before Thee in all reverence and humility, confessing our need of Thy forgiving grace and our desire for Thy directing guidance. Help us to lift our spirits to Thee in prayer and praise and give us grace to dedicate our lives anew to Thee, to our country, and to the welfare of all mankind.

We pray for the captive nations of the world—for the oppressed, the downtrodden, the persecuted—those who live in the darkness of fear and death. Grant that they may keep aglow in their hearts the desire for freedom. May they have the courage to endure their trials with faith, the strength to resist temptation with honor, and the spirit that continues to dream of a day when justice and mercy shall rule the hearts of men.

During these days that test men's souls may the awareness of Thy presence give us steady faith and steadfast love enabling us to minister to those in need. In the spirit of Christ we pray. Amen.

MONDAY, JULY 24, 1967

In Thee, O Lord, do I put my trust: let me never be put to confusion.—Psalm 71: 1.

LORD OF OUR LIVES, we know of no finer way to begin this week than by pausing before Thee in prayer and in praying renew our faith, restore our spirits, and rededicate our lives to Thee and to the welfare of our beloved land. In these days that call for wisdom, understanding, and good will may we possess Thy spirit or better still may Thy spirit possess us that we may plan with faith, work with courage, and live with love in our hearts.

Grant unto us and unto all our people the grace to fearlessly contend against evil, to make no peace with oppression, to be on guard against violence, and may we use our freedom to maintain justice and good will between men and women to the glory of Thy holy name. Amen.

WEDNESDAY, JULY 26, 1967

Let love be genuine; hate what is evil, hold fast to what is good.—Romans 12: 9.

ETERNAL FATHER OF OUR SPIRITS, we pray that in this sacred minute of prayer we may receive guidance for the day, wisdom for each hour, and good will for every moment. Help us to think more and talk less; to pray more and procrastinate less; to live more by high principles and less by low prejudices. Make us so dissatisfied with ourselves that we may turn away from loud professions to quiet practice, from friendly looks to friendly lives, and from speaking excellent words to speeding excellent works.

So we pray this morning that Thou wilt renew a right spirit within us and send us out into this day with gracious thoughts, good words, and a great spirit. In the Master's name we pray.   Amen.

THURSDAY, JULY 27, 1967

I sought the Lord, and He heard me and delivered me from all my fears.— Psalm 34: 4.

Eternal God and Father of mankind, whose creative spirit summons us to walk in the way of justice and peace and good will, in all reverence of mind and heart we bow before Thee at the altar of prayer. Lest we lose our way in the tragedy of these trying times we would turn from the noise of the seen world to the quiet of the unseen world in Thy presence where we can be still and know that Thou art God.

In the tense wilderness of our human relationships reveal to us Thy will. In the dense darkness of our day let Thy light shine upon our path. In the confusion of conflicting counsels give us wisdom to see clearly the signs of the times and the courage to walk worthily in the way of Thy word to us.

This day may we depart from evil and do good; may we seek peace and pursue it; may we do justly, love mercy, and walk humbly with Thee. In the Master's name we pray.   Amen.

TUESDAY, AUGUST 1, 1967

*Therefore I tell you, whatever you ask in prayer, believe that you receive it, and you will.—*Mark 11: 24.

In response to the call of our President that we unite in prayer for our country—we pause in Thy presence this moment praying that Thy spirit may come anew into our hearts and into the hearts of all our people. May we not only hear the cry of humanity for justice and freedom but may we heed it. May violence cease, may understanding between the races increase, may intelligent good will prevail, may the needs of the needy be met that there be no cause for bitterness and hatred.

We pray that everyone may have his chance to grow and to work and to live that our Nation may be in deed and in truth the home of the brave, **the land of the** free, **and the** one country which has liberty and justice for all. In the Master's name we offer our prayer. Amen.

THURSDAY, AUGUST 3, 1967

Prove all things; hold fast that which is good.—Thessalonians 5: 21.

ETERNAL GOD, OUR FATHER, our refuge in ages past, our strength for the present hour and our hope for future days, we come up to Thee conscious of our own failures and faults but with faith and fortitude because our trust is in Thee.

Deliver us from feverishly following foolish fashions and from walking the weary ways of a worried world. Remove from us all bitterness which blights our lives, all resentment which ruins our dispositions, all pride which makes us intolerant and closes the door to the needs of others.

Grant that in the adventure of building a better world we may saturate our good ideas with great idealism; we may combine commonsense with an uncommon spirit and we may be confident that light will triumph over darkness, right will win over wrong and love will outlast hatred. To this end keep us devoted to the light, to the right, and to love. In the Redeemer's **name we pray.** Amen.

MONDAY, AUGUST 7, 1967

"Obey My voice," saith the Lord "and I will be your God and you shall be My people; and walk in all the ways that I command you, that it may be well with you."—Jeremiah 7: 23.

O GOD, OUR FATHER, who art the spirit of truth and the life of love, as we set out upon another week of work may Thy presence within give us courage and strength and fidelity. Cleansed by Thy forgiving grace we would make our bodies temples of Thy spirit, our hearts the dwellingplace of Thy love and our minds the center of Thy wisdom.

We bring to this altar of prayer ourselves, cluttered up with a lot of little things and confused at times about what is right and wrong. May the splendor of Thy spirit and the glory of Thy greatness shame our little thoughts, our petty prejudices, and our unworthy ways. May the vision of what we ought to be, and by Thy grace can be, spur us on to do our best for our country and for the people we represent.

Grant unto each one of us an inner greatness of spirit, an inner purity of heart, and an inner nobility of mind.

> "God who touches earth with beauty
> Make us lovely, too,
> Keep us ever, by Thy spirit,
> Pure and strong and true."

Amen.

WEDNESDAY, AUGUST 9, 1967

Do not be overcome by evil, but overcome evil with good.—Romans 12: 21.

FATHER OF OUR SPIRITS, open to us the gates of the morning and reveal to us the glory of a new day as we pause a minute at the altar of prayer. We are facing difficult days and living through troubled times. For this we need courage and strength and an inner stability of spirit. Grant unto us now the grace of a quiet mind, a steady faith, and a strong will which will make us more than a match for the mood of this moving moment.

Help us to stand up for the rights of man, for obedience to the laws of our land, and for the principles of good government believing that Thy spirit will guide us, Thy power will strengthen us, Thy presence will bless us as we do what we firmly believe to be right. We pray also that the people of our country may seek to do what is right and good for all that we may learn to live together in peace and good will. In the Master's name we pray.

Amen.

THURSDAY, AUGUST 10, 1967

Be strong and of a good courage; be not afraid, neither be thou dismayed: for the Lord thy God is with thee whithersoever thou goest.—Joshua 1: 9.

OUR FATHER GOD, in a changing world filled with fear and ferment we turn to Thee in whose unchanging presence is hope and strength and peace. In this quiet moment of prayer may we be lifted above our lower selves into a higher realm where Thy spirit is real and we can receive anew the ministry of Thy grace.

Forgive our surrender to unworthy compromises and our succumbing to unwarranted concessions. Deliver us from majoring in minors and trifling with trivia in this period of peril. May we give our highest thought and best efforts to what is truly important that out of our creative endeavors may come that which is worthwhile for all.

Give to these Representatives the will to work together for the well-being of our country. Amid the persistent pressures of daily duty may they hear Thy voice speaking to them and, responding, to be given the faith to trust Thee for guidance in the decisions which have to be made and in the work which must be done. In the Master's name we pray.   Amen.

MONDAY, AUGUST 14, 1967

Let us not be weary in welldoing; for in due season we shall reap, if we faint not.—Ephesians 6: 9.

Almighty and Everlasting God, Creator of the world and the Comforter of the human spirit, we commend unto Thy gracious care the citizens of our beloved country. Especially do we pray for our President—that health and strength and wisdow may be his as he endeavors to lead our people in these troubled and trying times.

Upon our Speaker may there rest the rich blessing of Thy grace and the wise guidance of Thy spirit. To these Representatives, their staffs, and co-workers, may there come anew a realization of Thy presence as they bow at the altar of prayer and dedicate themselves to Thee and to the welfare of our people. Increase their faith, deepen their devotion, and enlarge their vision that they may continue to labor for the greater good of our country. May they never grow weary in well-doing. In the Master's name we pray.

Amen.

WEDNESDAY, AUGUST 16, 1967

He looked for a city which hath foundations, whose builder and maker is God.—Hebrews 11: 10.

O God, our Father, may the spirit of wisdom and compassion move our hearts and our hands as we wait upon Thee at the altar of prayer. Day after day we pray, night after night we lift our hearts unto Thee—knowing that often our words are without wings and that at times we say what we do not mean—yet in the midst of the pressure of persistent problems may we feel the touch of Thy healing hand, receive the guidance of Thy wise providence, and become one with Thee in the adventure of making the world a better place in which to live.

Purge our minds of all prejudice, cleanse our hearts of all cynicism, re-move far from us all ill will, and make us builders of the bridges of understanding and good will which span the differences between men and unite them in the shining endeavor to create a world in which righteousness reigns and peace prevails and the welfare of all is the desire of every heart. In the name of Christ we pray. Amen.

THURSDAY, AUGUST 17, 1967

Trust ye in the Lord forever; for in the Lord God is everlasting strength.— Isaiah 26: 4.

O GOD WHO HAST GIVEN US THIS GOOD LAND FOR OUR HERITAGE, we humbly beseech Thee that we may always prove ourselves a people mindful of Thy favor and glad to do Thy will. Bless our land, our people and our leaders that under the guidance of Thy wise and good spirit we may not grow weary in working nor wavering in worship.

Save us from violence, discord and confusion; from pride and prejudice and from every evil way. Fashion us into one people, united in purpose and spirit, faithful to Thee and fruitful in all good works as we seek the welfare of all. Endow with wisdom and charity these leaders of our Nation that there may be justice at home and peace in our world. In the time of prosperity fill our hearts with gratitude and in the day of trouble let not our trust in them fail; through Jesus Christ our Lord. Amen.

MONDAY, AUGUST 21, 1967

*Blessed is the man where strength is in thee.—*Psalm 84: 5.

O GOD, OUR FATHER, grant unto us the spirit of understanding and good will as we face the glory of a new day by waiting upon Thee in this moment of prayer. We would be still in thy presence and receive the strength which sustains us, the wisdom which makes us wise and the peace which holds us steady through troubled times.

Forgive our impatience revealed in discouragements, outbursts of temper and hasty words we so often regret. Forgive our impetuosity made known in worried attitudes, careless conversation and hurried actions for which we are so repeatedly sorry. Strengthen us to do our best in this hour of our Nation's need—to think constructively, to speak courageously and to act confidently that here in this place men may see democracy in action and democracy at its very best. In the spirit of Christ we pray. Amen.

TUESDAY, AUGUST 22, 1967

The Lord is nigh unto all them that call upon Him, to all that call upon Him in truth.—Psalm 145: 18.

WITH REVERENT AND THANKFUL SPIRITS, OUR FATHER, we bow before Thee in the quiet peace of this moment. Our hearts are filled with gratitude for all the privileges and opportunities which are ours. Knowing that we can show our thankfulness through lives of usefulness to Thee, we pray that Thou wilt give us courage in the face of temptation, confidence when confronted by difficulties and calmness amid danger. As Thou hast made this world fair for our use, grant that the trials of life may not, through our grumbling ingratitude be turned into occasions of unhappiness and misery, but that we may accept with cheerfulness whatever Thou dost send.

Make us true and just in all our dealings and straightforward in all our ways. Give us, we pray Thee, such quiet strength as will enable us to prevail without loud speaking and such gentleness of spirit as will enable us to use our strength with due regard for the rights of others. Reveal to us the path we should take, tune our ears to hear Thy call, keep us ever in Thy way, and be with us as we go. Through Jesus Christ our Lord. Amen.

MONDAY, AUGUST 28, 1967

The Lord shall preserve thy going out and thy coming in from this time forth and even forever more.—Psalm 121: 8.

ETERNAL FATHER OF OUR SPIRITS, at the beginning of another week, we pause a moment in Thy presence seeking guidance at Thy hand, strength for the day and wisdom for the decisions we have to make.

May Thy blessing rest upon these Representatives of our people and may Thy spirit move in their hearts as they seek to promote justice in our land, good will between our people and cooperation among the nations of the world. As a result of their endeavors may obedience to law, the rights of the individual and loyalty to our country be firmly established among us. God bless America, keep her true to Thee, and do Thou keep her free now and forever. In the Master's name we pray. Amen.

WEDNESDAY, AUGUST 30, 1967

He that loveth not knoweth not God; for God is love.—I John 4: 8.

GOD OF LOVE AND LORD OF MERCY, lay Thy hand upon us and hold us steady amid the troubles of this time. The days come and go so fast that we lose our grip on life. We hurry here and there and wonder why we are weary and worn out. We are slaves rather than masters. In fact our work controls us rather than in faith we control our work.

Halt Thou our haste, heal our ailing spirits, direct us in the doing of our duty, stay Thou with us and we with Thee until we come to ourselves. Then let us arise with a strength born of Thy spirit to face the tasks of this day with courage and to keep our faith even against the fury and violence of a world which has lost its true purpose and real destiny.

Abide Thou with us and encourage us to do Thy will that we may be open channels through which Thy redeeming love may flow to heal the differences between men and nations. In the Master's name, we pray. Amen.

MONDAY, SEPTEMBER 11, 1967

Teach me Thy way, O Lord, that I may walk in Thy truth.—Psalm 86: 11.

ETERNAL GOD, OUR FATHER, who art the refuge and strength of Thy people in every age and our refuge and strength in this present hour, come Thou anew into our hearts as we bow humbly in Thy presence. Help us to realize our dependence upon Thee, our constant need of Thy strength, Thy guidance, and Thy love. Give us to know that Thou art always with us and that with Thee we can be made ready for every responsibility and equal to every experience.

We pray for peace in our world, for good will among our people, and for a faith in Thee which makes us strong, gives us courage, and helps us on our upward way.

May Thy spirit touch each one of us with healing power. Kindle our faith, make sensitive our consciences, dedicate our strength, fortify us in our troubles, and send us out into this day strong in Thee and in the power of Thy might. In the name of Christ we pray. Amen.

WEDNESDAY, SEPTEMBER 13, 1967

Let not your heart be troubled; believe in God.—John 14: 1.

O GOD, OUR FATHER, who are ever seeking to strengthen Thy children, make us strong as we face the arduous tasks of this day and as we carry the heavy responsibilities placed upon us—keeping freedom alive in our world and promoting justice and good will among our people. Give to us the faith which will enable us to meet fearlessly the forces of tyranny which threaten to engulf us.

Bless the Members of this body. Lead them in their labors, direct them in their decisions, fortify their faith, strengthen their spirits, elevate their endeavors that they may lead our Nation into wider areas of truth and righteousness and good will.

Bless our men and women in the service of our country—many exposed to danger and death. Heal the wounded, strengthen the prisoners, relieve the suffering, and comfort the sorrowing. Hasten the day when nations will learn to live together in peace and good will.

In the name of the Prince of Peace we pray. Amen.

THURSDAY, SEPTEMBER 14, 1967

Blessed are they that hear the word of God and keep it.—Luke 11: 28.

Eternal God, our Father, so high above us that we cannot comprehend Thee and yet so deep within us that we cannot escape Thee, make Thyself real to us as we pray today.

Tired are we of our littleness and pray that Thou wilt lift us into the fellowship of great minds. Tired are we of our thoughts of discouragement and pray that Thou wilt lift us into the companionship of great hearts. In this fellowship and from this companionship may our faith be renewed, our hope strengthened, and our courage confirmed.

Bless these Representatives of our people. During these days may they be wise with Thy wisdom, strong in Thy power, and faithful through Thy faithfulness to them. According to our needs may the riches of Thy grace enter the heart of every one of us. In Jesus' name we pray. Amen.

MONDAY, SEPTEMBER 18, 1967

I will say of the Lord, He is my refuge and my fortress: my God; in Him will I trust.—Psalm 91: 2.

O God and Father of us all, at the beginning of another week we draw near to Thee humbly and reverently realizing our need of Thy spirit and praying for guidance, strength, and wisdom at Thy hands. For this moment may we enter the secret place of the Most High and continuing so to do learn to dwell under the shadow of Thine almighty presence.

Thou art the source of all our being. Thou art the fountain of every noble aspiration. Thou art in everything that lifts and liberates our souls. Therefore we pray that Thou wilt lead us from the unreality we find about us to the reality in our own hearts. May our faith in Thee be real. May our love toward our fellow man be real. May the spirit of good will forever be real within us.

Grant us Thy spiritual resources for this day and may we ever be receptive to Thy inner voice. In the name of Christ we pray. Amen.

THURSDAY, SEPTEMBER 21, 1967

Speak, Lord, for Thy servant heareth.—I Samuel 3: 10.

Eternal God, our Father, we stand at attention before Thee this moment to listen to Thy voice and to hear Thy word for us this day. Guide us as we work, give us patience when we must wait, grant unto us to be genuine in faith, gentle in love, and great in spirit.

Help us to take time to pray, time to open our hearts to Thee, time to discover Thy way for us and for our Nation. Then give us the commonsense to become aware of Thy will and the uncommon spirit to obey it for the good of our country and the glory of Thy holy name. Amen.

MONDAY, SEPTEMBER 25, 1967

Thou shalt rejoice in every good thing which the Lord, thy God, hath given unto thee.—Deuteronomy 26: 11.

Almighty God, grant that through the ministry of this moment of meditation we may draw near to Thee and receive from Thy hand wisdom to make wise decisions, good will to relate ourselves affirmatively to others, and faith to hold us steady amid the troubles of this time. May we be with Thee and through all our discussions we pray that Thou wilt keep us mindful of Thy presence.

We pray for our country that in this day our Nation may be Thy channel for peace in our world and Thy servant for good will among the people on this planet. As leaders and as a people may we grow in spirit, and as mature persons assume our position of responsible leadership among the nations of the world. In Jesus' name we pray. Amen.

WEDNESDAY, SEPTEMBER 27, 1967

Trust in Him at all times ye people; pour out your heart before Him; God is a refuge for us.—Psalm 62: 8.

O God, who art the Creator and Preserver of all mankind, without whose blessing all our labor is in vain, we pray that our lives may be built not upon the sands which shift with the tide but upon the rock of eternal truth and love. As we worship Thee reveal to us Thy presence; give us wisdom; awaken within us a greater desire for goodness and truth and love. To Thee we bring our affections to be purified, our ambitions to be refined, our minds to be cleansed, and our hearts to be responsive to Thy spirit.

We ask Thy blessing upon our President, our Speaker, and all Members of this body. May the fires of Thy spirit burn brightly within them. May they ever be friendly in spirit, clear in purpose, strong in integrity—men and women of high principles, great faith, and never failing good will. Protect them from all evil and may public office be to them a public trust which will issue in a public service unexcelled in the history of our beloved land. In the Master's name we pray. Amen.

THURSDAY, SEPTEMBER 28, 1967

Thou shalt worship the Lord thy God and Him only shalt thou serve.— Matthew 4: 10.

ETERNAL GOD, OUR FATHER, from whom our spirits come, with whom they live and unto whom they go when life on earth is over—in the quiet of this moment we humbly lift our hearts unto Thee in prayer. We believe in Thee with all our minds—do Thou make Thyself real to us in all our hearts. Grant unto us a song on our lips in the morning, strength for the day, good will for one another, a steadfast loyalty to our country, courage to maintain high ideals in our national life, and a faith in Thee that gives us confidence and helps us overcome the evil in the world.

Give to us an inner spirit of hospitality to that which is high in life and send us forth masters of ourselves because we are mastered by Thee. By Thy spirit of truth alive within us may we be among that company of Thy children who lift the world and do not lean upon it, and who leave it a better place in which to live. In the Redeemer's name we pray. Amen.

FRIDAY, SEPTEMBER 29, 1967

*They that wait upon the Lord shall renew their strength.—*Isaiah 40: 31.

OUR FATHER IN HEAVEN AND ON EARTH, we, the Representatives of the people of our land, bow before Thee humbly praying for strength, for guidance, and for good will from Thee. Make this a sacred moment in which we become aware of Thy presence, a moment when strength is given, guidance provided, and good will arises anew within us.

We need Thee, every hour we need Thee. We hurry too much, we eat too fast, we sleep too little, and then wonder why we are weary and worried and worn out. As we wait upon Thee renew our strength, restore our spirits, reinvigorate our minds, that this day we may think good thoughts, make wise decisions, and do it all free from tension and filled with faith. Trusting in Thee, may we sing even in the rain. In the Master's name we pray.   Amen.

MONDAY, OCTOBER 2, 1967

In God is my salvation and my glory; the rock of my strength and my refuge is in God.—Psalm 62: 7.

O GOD AND FATHER OF US ALL, we know of no better way to begin the week than by lifting our hearts unto Thee in prayer and by pledging unto Thee the desire of our hearts to serve Thee by devoting ourselves to the welfare of our country and to the well-being of our fellow man.

In these stirring days which search our souls, try our faith, and often dampen our spirits, we pray for guidance that we may know Thy will, for courage to walk in Thy way, and for uplifting strength to keep on without faltering and without fainting.

We pray for peace and as we seek it may we be determined to protect our freedom against any aggressor. Both militarily and morally may we stand strong, and filled with Thy spirit continue to labor for liberty and justice for all. In the Master's name we pray.   Amen.

WEDNESDAY, OCTOBER 4, 1967

Hear, O Israel, the Lord our God is one Lord; and thou shalt love the Lord thy God with all thine heart, and with all thy soul, and with all thy might.—Deuteronomy 6: 4, 5.

O LORD, OUR GOD, and God of our fathers, who hast been the dwelling place of Thy people in all generations and who in Thy gracious mercy hast brought us to the close of another year—we thank Thee for the way by which Thou hast led us and we pray that as we look forward we may continue to grow in grace and in the knowledge of Thy law. Lead us step by step, and from strength to strength, that we may serve Thee more perfectly and love our fellow man more sincerely.

Increase our faith as Thou dost increase our years and the longer we live on earth the better may our service be, the more willing our obedience, the more consistent our daily lives, the more loving our hearts, and the more complete our devotion to Thee.

Be Thou with us, O God, and receive us in Thy boundless love, for Thou art our hope and our support.   Amen.

THURSDAY, OCTOBER 5, 1967

He giveth power to the faint; and to them that have no might He increaseth strength.—Isaiah 40: 29.

O GOD, OUR FATHER, who art always the same, whose saving truth never lets us down and whose patient love never lets us go, make us conscious of Thy presence as in spirit we kneel before Thee in this morning moment of meditation. Speak Thou Thy word to us and give us ears to hear, minds to heed, and hands and feet to do Thy will in Thy way for Thy work.

Humble us in our pride, strengthen us in our weakness, and make us great in heart when we would be little in spirit that we may have joy in our endeavors and peace in our hearts.

Bless Thou our country and every institution, every person, every effort made which helps men to love one another and to live together in peace. May Thy kingdom come and Thy will be done in us now.   Amen.

MONDAY, OCTOBER 9, 1967

The Lord is my strength and my song, and He has become my salvation; this is my God, and I will praise Him, my Father's God and I will exalt Him.—Exodus 15: 2.

ALMIGHTY AND ETERNAL GOD, before whom a thousand years pass as a watch in the night, rekindle within us Thy spirit and replenish us with Thy grace as we face the tasks of another week. Be Thou a pillar of fire to us by night and a pillar of cloud by day. Lead us into green pastures, beside still waters, along right paths, that our spirits may be restored, that we may find comfort in hours of need, and that goodness and mercy may follow us all the days of our lives.

In these trying times help us to rise above that which is mean and small and enable us to work together in glad good will for the honor and security of our Nation, for the good of our people and for the welfare of all mankind. In Thy most holy name we pray.   Amen.

TUESDAY, OCTOBER 10, 1967

Search me, O God, and know my heart: try me and know my thoughts: and see if there be any wicked way in me and lead me in the way everlasting.—Psalm 139: 23, 24.

O GOD AND FATHER OF US ALL, let Thy spirit arise within us as we—the Representatives of our people—wait upon Thee in prayer. With unfailing wisdom and unfaltering good will enable us to meet the demanding duties of this day and manage the moods that move in our minds. Strengthen us as we sincerely strive to step along straight paths and as we endeavor to do what is right for our country and for our world.

Inspire us with greater faith to climb the heights of national honor and security realizing that the closer we are to the summit of Thy presence the nearer we are together. In periods of strained relations touch Thou our hearts with spirit hand and make us souls that understand. Through Jesus Christ our Lord. Amen.

WEDNESDAY, OCTOBER 11, 1967

And I say unto you, ask and it shall be given you; seek and ye shall find; knock and it shall be opened unto you.—Luke 11: 9.

O Lord, our God, infinite in wisdom, power, and love, we come to Thee conscious of our needs and with the confidence that Thou art with us to lead us in Thy way, to strengthen us to do Thy will, and to be our inspiration as we do our duty and make ourselves ready for the responsibilities of this day.

May the blessings of health, courage, and moral strength be ours and may our lives show their gratitude by good conduct motivated by genuine motives.

Bless our country and all the institutions of our beloved land. Increase the faith of our people in our Government and may we the leaders prove ourselves worthy of their trust. Forgive our shortcomings, save us from hypocrisy and from forever justifying ourselves. Simply let us do our best and leave the rest to Thee. In the Master's name we pray. Amen.

MONDAY, OCTOBER 16, 1967

Blessed be the Lord, who daily bears us up; He is our salvation.—Psalm 68: 19.

Dear Lord and Father of mankind, disturbed by the demanding duties of this disruptive day and pursued by the persistent problems of this present period we would pause again at the altar of prayer to remember that Thou art God, that this is our Father's world, and to remind ourselves that though the wrong seems oft so strong Thou art the ruler yet. In Thy strength we would be made strong, with Thy wisdom we would become wise, and by Thy grace we would face the tasks of this week with confidence.

We pray for our country—for our President, our Speaker, and all the leaders of our people. Rule their hearts and direct their endeavors that law and order, justice and peace may prevail everywhere in our land. Make us mighty in moving along right paths that we may be worthy of Thy blessing and in turn become a blessing to all nations, to the glory of Thy name, through Jesus Christ our Lord. Amen.

WEDNESDAY, OCTOBER 18, 1967

When you pray, say, Our Father.—Luke 11: 2.

Eternal God, our Father, who has set eternity in our souls, the spirit of love in our hearts, and a song of praise on our lips, in the quiet hush of this moment we bow at the altar of prayer.

We come at the call of our President to pray and to pray for the people of our land. Pour out Thy spirit upon us and join us together in greater loyalty to our Nation, in greater justice to our fellow man, and in greater faith in Thee. Keep us faithful in the defense of freedom, and with courage and confidence may we preserve and promote the blessings of liberty everywhere.

Enlighten the minds of our people that we may work together to remove inequalities, to reduce friction, to renounce prejudice, and by the strength of Thy spirit may we foster an increasing good will in the hearts of all. Help us to take the law into our hearts and not into our hands and to respect the rights of all men. In the Master's name we pray. Amen.

THURSDAY, OCTOBER 19, 1967

You have need of patience, so that you may do the will of God and receive the promise.—Hebrews 10: 36.

O God and Father of us all in this quiet moment of prayer we come with humble and contrite hearts acknowledging our dependence upon Thee and praying that with Thee we may live through these critical days with courage and with faith. Give to us an inner greatness of spirit, an inner graciousness of heart, and an inner gentleness of mind that we may be more than a match for the challenge of this hour. Make us patient with each other and understanding, for we do not know the battles others are fighting nor the experiences they are facing.

We pray for the men and women defending our freedom with their lives. Grant unto them strength in need, help in danger, healing in body, and courage of mind and heart. May their sacrifice not be in vain. With them may we unite in proclaiming the life of liberty and the fruits of freedom now and forever. Amen.

MONDAY, OCTOBER 23, 1967

Jesus said, "I am the light of the world: he that followeth Me shall not walk in darkness, but shall have the light of life."—John 8: 12.

OUR FATHER GOD, in the darkness of our day we turn to Thee who art the light of the world and the light our world needs this present hour. Amid the discontent and dissatisfaction of this age we come to Thee for guidance and direction.

Lead, kindly light, amid the encircling gloom, lead Thou us on. Keep Thou our feet; we do not ask to see the distant scene; one step enough for us. Help us to see it and to have the courage to take it—that step by step we may move in the direction of more harmonious relationships among our people, greater cooperation among the nations of the world, and an ever increasing good will in the hearts of all men. In the name of Him who is the light of the world we pray. Amen.

WEDNESDAY, OCTOBER 25, 1967

Trust in the Lord with all thine heart; and lean not unto thine own understanding.—Proverbs 3: 5.

ETERNAL GOD, OUR FATHER, unfailing source of light and life, we thank Thee for Thy presence which gives power to Thy people and courage to Thy children. With Thee may we find strength in the time of trouble, deliverance in the hour of temptation, and serenity in the moment when we wrestle with worry.

Save us from false ambitions and feverish activities, from plans and policies which are contrary to Thy will, and from a foolish trust in our own powers. Turn us to Thee in all humility that Thou canst forgive us and heal us and lead us in paths of righteousness for Thy name's sake.

Teach us to love Thee with all our hearts and our fellow man as ourselves. Give us such a measure of Thy spirit that we may be used by Thee to usher in a greater day for our country and a better day for all mankind. In the Master's name we pray. Amen.

FRIDAY, OCTOBER 27, 1967

Hear my prayer, O Lord, give ear to my supplications: in Thy faithfulness answer me and in Thy righteousness.—Psalm 143: 1.

BREATHE ON US, BREATH OF GOD, as in this moment we bow at the altar of prayer and offer unto Thee the devotion of our hearts. Thou hast bound us together with our neighbors in a struggle for liberty and a striving for peace. Grant unto us the insight and the inspiration that we may continue on the path of freedom and together maintain peace, promote justice, and increase our fellowship with each other.

So rule our hearts and prosper our endeavors that law and order, faith and good will may prevail between us forever. Thus may we be one in spirit as we face the events and the experiences of this day. In the name of Christ we pray. Amen.

MONDAY, OCTOBER 30, 1967

Our soul waiteth for the Lord: He is our help and our shield.—Psalm 33: 20.

ETERNAL GOD, the sustainer of life and the Father of all men, in Thy presence we pause in silence knowing that with Thee all our labor is worthwhile. We pray that our lives and the life of our Nation may be built upon the rock of eternal truth and invincible good will. So we dedicate ourselves anew to Thee who are the way, the truth, and the life.

We thank Thee for our country, for our glorious heritage, for this challenging hour, and for the faith with which we can meet the days that lie ahead. Bless Thou our President—give him wisdom as he leads our people through these troubled times. Bless these Representatives and help them ever to look to Thee who art the fountain of wisdom and the source of all good. Bless our men and women in Vietnam, strengthen them in every noble endeavor and hasten the day when war shall cease and peace rule in the hearts of men and of nations.

May Thy mighty spirit surging through us and our people translate our principles into practices and our dedication to Thee into a greater devotion to truth and freedom. In the Master's name. Amen.

WEDNESDAY, NOVEMBER 1, 1967

As many as are led by the spirit of God, they are the sons of God.—Romans 8: 14.

O THOU WHO ART THE SOURCE OF ALL OUR STRENGTH AND THE REFUGE OF THOSE WHO PUT THEIR TRUST IN THEE, steady us with Thy spirit lest the disagreements of this day hide Thy presence from us. Within the shadow of our concern stands Thy love waiting to cross the threshold of our need. As we pray may we receive Thy love and thus led step by step be strengthened for the journey of this day.

We pray for those we love, whose faithfulness warms our hearts and brings joy to our spirits. We commend them to Thy loving care which shepherds their days with a wisdom and love greater than our own.

We pray for our country. Cleanse our hearts of all harsh misunderstandings and hostile ill will which are the seeds of strife. Make us quick to welcome every adventure in cooperation and every effort to strengthen our relationships with each other. Open the door of opportunity and give us courage to walk through it to a greater life together under the banner of free men. In the Master's name we pray.   Amen.

THURSDAY, NOVEMBER 2, 1967

By this shall all men know that you are my disciples, if you have love for one another.—John 13: 35.

O GOD, OUR FATHER, who hast revealed Thyself in the history of mankind, who dost reveal Thyself to the open mind and heart of man today, make us responsive to Thee and grant us faith and fidelity as we live through the maddening maze of modern movements.

We rejoice when we realize that Thou art never far from anyone of us, and our hearts take courage when we think again that we can never drift beyond Thy love and care.

Grant that the spirit of love and concern may permeate our hearts and the good seed we sow this day bear fruit in an abundant harvest of justice and liberty for all. In the spirit of the Master we pray.   Amen.

FRIDAY, NOVEMBER 3, 1967

Blessed are they that hear the word of God and keep it.—Luke 11: 28.

E TERNAL GOD, OUR FATHER, we thank Thee for the coming of another day and for the opportunity it provides to work with Thee in the service of our

country. May the hours glow with the glory of Thy presence and in everything we do may we be mindful of Thy good spirit.

We come to Thee with real regrets and high hopes, each one of us with a
prayer of our own. If we are weary, strengthen us; if we are worried, grant
us a peace that calms anxiety; if we are wayward in thought and deed,
steady us; if we are wavering in our allegiance to high ideals, be Thou our
rock and our fortress; if we are forever seeking our own way, help us to see
that there may be other ways and above all to see Thy way.

Enable us to meet the tasks of this day with unwavering strength and
unwearying endurance. May we continue our work with an integrity of
spirit and a steadfastness of purpose to Thy glory and for the good of our
Nation. In the name of Christ, we pray.   Amen.

MONDAY, NOVEMBER 6, 1967

My meat is to do the will of Him that sent me and to finish His work.—
John 4: 34.

G OD OF OUR FATHERS AND OUR GOD, we would begin the day conscious
of Thy presence and committing our lives anew to Thee. Sustain us with
Thy spirit and make us ready for our responsibilities, equal to our experiences, and adequate for every task. In the midst of the heat of daily duties
let not our strength fail, nor our steps falter, nor our vision fade.

Make us patient with each other and understanding, remembering that
each one of us walks a lonely road and each one has struggles no one else
knows.

Give to us a real reverence for personality, a deep desire to speak the
truth, and an unending enthusiasm for the reign of liberty and justice in
our Nation and in our world. In the Master's name we pray.   Amen.

WEDNESDAY, NOVEMBER 8, 1967

*I am ready for anything through the strength of the One who lives within
me.*—Philippians 4: 13.

O GOD, OUR FATHER, who gives us the day for work and the night for
rest, grant us health of body, cleanness of mind, and courage of spirit that
we may do our work this day with all our might. Deliver us from the
bitterness that blights our lives, from the fears that frustrate our faith,
and from the ill will which dampens our upward struggle.

Make us one in Thee that we may be hospitable to the highest in life
and thus be ready with new strength for a new day.

May we walk in straight paths until Thy glory shall be revealed in our
efforts to make the world a better place in which men can learn to live

together and to work together and to pray together. To this end may Thy will be done in us and in all men, through Christ our Lord. Amen.

MONDAY, NOVEMBER 13, 1967

O man greatly beloved, fear not, peace be with you; be strong and of good courage.—Daniel 10: 19.

GOD OF OUR FATHERS, who has called forth a great nation in these United States and has bound us together in the struggle for liberty and justice for all, keep us one in spirit as we endeavor to provide order, to promote good will, and to produce an enduring peace in our world.

We are mindful of those who are giving their lives for our country and for free men everywhere. For them we pray with all our hearts. Grant that we may so live our lives, so use our influence, so conduct ourselves that their dedication shall not be in vain. By Thy spirit make us worthy of their devotion.

O Lord, as I go my uncaring way,
Help me to remember that somewhere out there a man died for me today.
So long as there be war
I must ask and I must answer,
Am I worth dying for?

Amen.

WEDNESDAY, NOVEMBER 15, 1967

In all these things we are more than conquerors through Him who loves us.—Romans 8: 37.

ALMIGHTY AND EVERLASTING GOD, who art always more ready to hear than we are to pray, and art wont to give more than we desire or deserve, we humbly beseech Thee to take our lives into Thy loving hands and to hold us steady in the midst of these troubled times that we may feel Thy power underneath us, Thy love about us, Thy truth above us, and Thy spirit within us.

Help us to cast out every fear, strengthen us to walk in all good ways, set our affections upon things above, and give the joy that humble service bestows and the peace of heart that comes to those committed to Thee and to the coming of Thy kingdom.

Bless Thou our President, our Speaker, and all these Representatives of our people. Grant unto them the spirit of wisdom, goodness, and truth; and so rule their hearts and bless their endeavors, that law and order, justice and peace may everywhere prevail to the honor of our Nation and glory of Thy Name, through Jesus Christ our Lord. Amen.

THURSDAY, NOVEMBER 16, 1967

Watch and pray, that ye enter not into temptation.—Matthew 26: 41.

SLOW US DOWN, LORD, slow us down until in our inmost being we kneel quietly and reverently before Thee. For this moment deliver us from coldness of heart and wanderings of mind, that with steadfast thoughts and kindled affections we may worship Thee in spirit and in truth. Save us from the anxieties and confusion of the world and strengthen the tie that binds us together and to Thee.

Grant us in all doubts and uncertainties the spirit to seek what Thou wouldst have us do, that the spirit of wisdom may save us from false choices and lead us into all truth.

Guide, we beseech Thee, our Nation and the nations of the world into the ways of justice and good will, and establish among us the peace which is the fruit of righteousness. In Thy light may we see light and in Thy straight path may we not stumble. In the Master's name we pray. Amen.

FRIDAY, NOVEMBER 17, 1967

I will hear what God the Lord will speak: for He will speak peace unto His people.—Psalm 85: 8.

O LORD, OUR GOD, we are beginning to discover that without Thee we are never at our best. It has taken some of us a long time to realize it. We have been too proud, too stubborn, too determined to have our own way. Somehow Thou hast caught up with us and we know that with Thee alone is life and love. May Thy spirit so come to life in us that we may truly live and triumphantly love.

We pray for the people of our beloved land that they, too, may grow in spirit and by Thy grace be made more than a match for the mood of this day.

Help us to work together for peace in our world, for justice among our citizens, and for good will in the hearts of all.

In the Master's name we pray. Amen.

MONDAY, NOVEMBER 20, 1967

The Lord is nigh unto all them that call upon Him, to all that call upon Him in truth.—Psalm 145: 18.

WE PAUSE IN THIS MOMENT OF PRAYER, OUR FATHER, to lift our hearts unto Thee. Speak Thou Thy word to us and to our Nation, and help us not only to hear it but to heed it; not only to receive it but to respond to it; not only to listen to it but to live by it.

May we be gentle with each other and generous; may we be masters of ourselves and in so doing manage our relationships with good will; may we so live our lives that we can respect ourselves and thereby be worthy of the respect of others.

Minister to us in our prayers that we may be able to change what we can change, accept what we must accept, and do it all with grateful hearts and genuine faith. In the Master's name we pray.   Amen.

WEDNESDAY, NOVEMBER 22, 1967

O give thanks unto the Lord; for He is good: for His mercy endureth forever.—Psalm 106: 1.

ETERNAL GOD, OUR FATHER, creator of the world and the ruler of men, on this Thanksgiving Eve we come to Thee with humble and grateful hearts. Thou hast been wonderfully good to us, Thy presence has guided us, Thy power has made us strong, and Thy providence has surrounded us all our days. We pray that Thou wouldst make us ever mindful of Thy spirit, ever eager to do Thy will, and ever grateful for Thy goodness.

We thank Thee for our country—for the freedom we enjoy, for the rights which are ours, and for the future which beckons us to higher aspirations. We thank Thee for those who fight that the flag of freedom may fly gloriously in this day. Bless them with courage and strength and give them to know that we are with them and that they do not struggle alone.

We thank Thee for our homes and for the love and understanding they provide for us. Keep us from being impatient, impersonal, and impertinent. Make our hearts happy, our words good, and our hands ready to help. By Thy spirit may we be kind to those we love.

Accept our gratitude and make us worthy of Thy blessings; through Jesus Christ our Lord.   Amen.

MONDAY, NOVEMBER 27, 1967

If ye fulfill the royal law according to the scripture, thou shalt love thy neighbor as thyself, ye do well.—James 2: 8.

O GOD, OUR FATHER, whose light is above us, whose love is about us, and whose life is within us, grant unto us a joy of spirit and a courage of heart as we enter upon the tasks of another week. Give us to feel that we can meet every demand made upon us and manage every duty which comes our way because Thy spirit lives in our hearts. With Thee may we face our work in the high mood of integrity and the upward moving spirit of good will.

In this land we love with all our hearts may there be a greater unity of purpose as we seek to remove discrimination and poverty and as we endeavor to promote liberty and justice for all. In the Master's name we offer this our morning prayer.   Amen.

TUESDAY, NOVEMBER 28, 1967

Teach me Thy way, O Lord, and lead me in a plain path.—Psalm 27: 11.

O GOD, who art our refuge and strength, our help in trouble, we pray that Thou wilt lead us to a higher plane of courage and faith and patience that the influence of our lives and the example of our spirits may always be for Thy glory and for the good of our country.

Renew in us a deeper devotion to Thee, a greater love for our fellow man, and a stronger faith that right is right and will ultimately prevail even in uncertain times.

To Thee we commend our Nation. Be Thou the source of her strength and make her ever mindful of Thy providence. Bless Thou our Speaker, every Member of this body, every officer, every clerk, every secretary, every reporter, every page. As men and women selected for service to our Nation may we keep our record true.

> To think without confusion clearly;
> To love our fellowmen sincerely;
> To act from honest motives purely;
> To trust in God and heaven securely.

Amen.

WEDNESDAY, NOVEMBER 29, 1967

Let Thy mercy, O Lord, be upon us, according as we hope in Thee.—Psalm 33: 22.

ETERNAL GOD, OUR FATHER, in this time of trouble and this day of demanding duties and persistent problems we bow in Thy presence praying that we may be calm and confident in the discharge of the responsibilities placed upon us. We would be true, for there are those who trust us; we would be pure, for there are those who care; we would be strong, for there is much to suffer; we would be brave, for there is much to dare.

Keep us ever faithful in the great office to which we have been elected and ever loyal in the grand adventure which seeks the high road of freedom and justice for all.

Cleanse the thoughts of our hearts that we may live in good will with our fellow man and in good faith with Thee. Amen.

MONDAY, DECEMBER 4, 1967

Beloved, if God so loved us, we ought also to love one another.—I John 4: 11.

O Thou who art from everlasting to everlasting, in whose will is our peace, at the beginning of another week we pause before Thee with reverent hearts and humble spirits. Make us realize that Thou art God, that this is Thy world and that though the wrong seems oft so strong Thou art the ruler yet.

Grant unto us the grace to repent, the courage to turn from our evil ways and to look to Thee who alone can forgive us and cleanse us and heal us. Bring us into fellowship with Thee that we may have good will in our hearts and through us may good will flow into the heart of our Nation and into the life of our world. May love which is the light of life become the law of our lives. So may we grow in spirit and so may our people increase in faith, in fortitude and in fellowship with Thee and with one another. In the Master's name we pray. Amen.

TUESDAY, DECEMBER 5, 1967

He that doeth the will of God abideth forever.—I John 2: 17.

Out of a deep sense of need, Our Father, we come to Thee, praying that Thou wilt help us to be aware of Thy presence as we kneel at the altar of prayer and offer ourselves to Thee at the beginning of another day.

At times we seem to talk too much and think too little, we are heard professing loudly but practicing in such small ways, we worry often but worship so seldom. Forgive us, O Lord, and help us to think more, to practice more, and to pray more that Thy spirit may come to new life in us and through us come to new life in our Nation.

Grant unto us, the Representatives of our people, wisdom and faith as we meet in this troubled hour. Help us to accept our responsibilities with courage, make our decisions with confidence, and plan for the future with creative hope.

We pray that Thou wilt awaken the faith of Americans in America that our laws may be obeyed, order made to prevail and good will move in the hearts of all our countrymen. In the spirit of Christ, we pray. Amen.

WEDNESDAY, DECEMBER 6, 1967

If any man will come after Me, let him deny himself and take up his cross daily and follow Me.—Luke 9: 23.

O GOD OF GRACE AND GOODNESS, we acknowledge our dependence upon Thee, our need of Thy mercy and our desire for Thy guidance. We beseech Thee to make us more and more aware of Thy presence, give us to know that Thou art ever with us and that with Thee we can face the day with confidence, do our work with fidelity, and be calm in the midst of trying experiences.

We do not pray for freedom from disappointment or defeat but we do pray that Thou wouldst give us the faith and fortitude we need for these hours and such strength as will enable us to do the work we are called upon to do and to do it honorably and well.

Renewing our strength, reinvigorating our minds, and restoring our souls, send us out into this day to do what we can for others, to keep our Nation great, and to make the world a better place where men can learn to live together in peace. In the Master's name we pray.   Amen.

THURSDAY, DECEMBER 7, 1967

The people who walked in darkness have seen a great light.—Isaiah 9: 2.

O GOD, most mighty and merciful, we come to Thee for insight and inspiration which Thou alone canst give to the human mind and heart. In this moment of prayer do Thou plant our feet on the higher ground of Thy spirit that we may find deliverance from thoughts that weaken us, from desires that worry us, and from a selfishness that closes the door to the needs of others.

Thou who didst cause light to shine out of darkness, shine Thou upon our way, that we may see the road we should take, and by Thy spirit be given strength to walk on it—fulfilling Thy will for us and for our Nation. Send us out into this day with the assurance that Thou art with us and by Thy grace may we be made adequate for every activity, equal to every experience, and more than a match for every mood.

Kindle in the hearts of our people a love for justice, an enthusiasm for good will and a joy in living that our Nation may turn from the low road of poverty and prejudice and take the high road that leads to the plains of peace and prosperity for all. In the Master's name we pray.   Amen.

MONDAY, DECEMBER 11, 1967

Let the peace of God rule in your hearts.—Colossians 3: 15.

O GOD, OUR FATHER, who art above us and yet within us, afar off yet very near, we pause in silence before Thee knowing that with Thee all of life glows with meaning and grows with purpose. Quiet the turmoil in our spirits: soothe the irritations in our hearts and in quietness and confidence may we open the inner doors of our being to Thee.

Speak to us through our consciences and help us to be more honest with ourselves and more friendly with others.

Speak to us through our wills and help us to choose the right way that the decisions made this day may make the days to come useful and joyful for all.

Speak to us through the needs of the world and help us to live in the confidence that justice can conquer injustice, peace can overcome war, and that love is stronger than hate.

So speak to us and to all our people that this advent season may bear witness to a new birth of Thy spirit in the hearts of men. In the name of Christ we pray. Amen.

TUESDAY, DECEMBER 12, 1967

With God all things are possible.—Mark 10: 27.

O GOD, OUR FATHER, the light of the true-hearted and the life of the wholehearted, strong in Thy strength we greet the coming of another day. May the hours be radiant with Thy presence and the minutes reflect the glory of Thy love. In everything we do and say may we be mindful of Thy spirit, eager to do Thy will, and ready to serve our country with all our hearts.

Make us great enough to face these hours with courage, good enough to live through these days with confidence, and generous enough to share our faith that in these trying times we fail not man nor Thee.

> Not for ourselves alone may our prayer be;
> Lift Thou Thy world, O God, closer to Thee.
> Cleanse it from guilt and wrong; teach it salvation's song,
> 'Till earth, as heaven, fulfill Thy holy will.

Amen.

THURSDAY, DECEMBER 14, 1967

God is spirit; and they that worship Him must worship Him in spirit and in truth.—John 4: 24.

FATHER OF MERCY, who hast spoken to Thy people in the past and who art speaking to us in the present, help us to hear Thy word this day. Each time we come to Thee we bring the same discouragements and the same desires. We ask for help without any honest endeavor on our part to discipline ourselves to receive it.

Forgive us, O Lord, forgive our petitions made without any promise of performance on our part, our requests spoken without any renewal of spirit in our hearts, our words uttered without any serious intention in our minds. Grant us light by which to see, love by which to live, and faith by which to act that we may be redeemed from the error of our ways and be delivered from the evil that infests the world.

Help us now to make a new beginning, to remove the spirit of bitterness and resentment, to reduce our anxieties and our prejudices, and to work together in true Christmas spirit for the good of our country, the welfare of mankind, and the peace of the world. In the Master's name we pray. Amen.

FRIDAY, DECEMBER 15, 1967

Glory to God in the highest and on earth peace, good will among men.— Luke 2: 14.

O GOD, OUR FATHER, who has taught us in Thy word that we should always pray and never lose heart—we come to Thee for help which Thou alone canst give.

Some of us are weary—may we find rest in Thee. Some of us are anxious and troubled about many things—may we find Thy grace sufficient for every need. Some of us are tempted, sorely tempted—may we find in Thee strength not only to resist but to overcome.

Give us grace to put our trust in Thee and to go forth in the direction of Christmas with the assurance that Thou art with us and amid the troubles and trials of daily living may we find strength for the day, rest for the night, and peace in our hearts.

Grant unto us and unto all men this Christmastide the blessings of Thy grace and the benediction of Thy spirit. May good will live in all our hearts and in the heart of all our people. In the name of Him whose birthday we celebrate we pray.

May the Lord bless us and keep us; the Lord make His face to shine upon us; the Lord lift the light of His countenance upon us and give us peace. Amen.

NINETIETH CONGRESS

Second Session

MONDAY, JANUARY 15, 1968

Be strong and of good courage; be not afraid, neither be thou dismayed; for the Lord your God is with you wherever you go.—Joshua 1: 9.

O GOD, OUR FATHER, our help in ages past and our hope for years to come, our help and our hope in this present hour—in all reverence of mind and with true humility of spirit we lift our hearts unto Thee seeking strength and wisdom from Thy never-failing and ever-faithful presence.

In this hour, as we turn another page in the glorious history of our growing country, may we be strengthened with might by Thy spirit that we may meet these demanding days with creative courage and become more than a match for the mood of these troubled times.

Bless Thou our President, our Speaker, our Representatives, those employed by our Government, and all those in the Armed Forces of our country. Grant that together we may enter this new year with deeper faith, broader sympathy, higher vision, and with greater love.

Keep ever before us the endless splendor of a world cleared of poverty, cleansed of prejudice, and concerned with peace between men and nations. May we so live our lives, so lead our people, so guide our Nation that we may build on earth a better and a brighter brotherhood, in the spirit of Him who taught us to pray:

Our Father who art in heaven, hallowed be Thy name; Thy kingdom come, Thy will be done on earth as it is in heaven. Give us this day our daily bread. And forgive us our trespasses as we forgive those who trespass against us. And lead us not into temptation, but deliver us from evil. For Thine is the kingdom, and the power, and the glory, forever. Amen.

TUESDAY, JANUARY 16, 1968

Restore to me the joy of Thy salvation; and uphold me with Thy glorious spirit.—Psalm 51: 12.

O GOD AND FATHER OF US ALL, whose goodness never fails and whose love never fades, as we bow before Thee in this quiet moment, we pray that Thou wilt fill us with Thy spirit that we may be made ready with steady faith and steadfast love to face the shifting scenes of our modern day. In the discharge of our duties, enable us to be confident and courageous, keeping our trust in Thee, our concern for the welfare of our country, and our belief in good will among the children of men.

Make us ever loyal to the royal in life everywhere and send us out along the high road of creative adventure and constructive activity which will open the way for men and nations to live together in peace. In the Master's name we pray. Amen.

WEDNESDAY, JANUARY 17, 1968

Depart from evil and do good; seek peace and pursue it.—Psalm 34: 14.

O THOU ETERNAL FATHER OF OUR SPIRITS, whose creative spirit is ever summoning us to new frontiers of thought and action—we pause in Thy presence to offer unto Thee the devotion of our hearts as we seek for peace in our world and for good will within our Nation.

We pray that we with all the people of our land may be open to the leadership of Thy spirit. As man by his scientific inventions has made the world a neighborhood, grant that by his spiritual cooperation he may make the world a brotherhood.

May fear, suspicion, and ill will pass away from the hearts of men. May strife between Thy children cease, may social justice and international friendship be established, the oppressed be liberated, the downtrodden be uplifted, and upon those who sit in darkness may Thy light shine.

Give us grace to keep Thy commandments. Make us gentle and honest, men and women of sound understanding and genuine sympathy, and may we be ready to make sacrifices for peace as readily as we make sacrifices for war. So may Thy kingdom come and Thy will be done in us and in all men, through Jesus Christ our Lord. Amen.

THURSDAY, JANUARY 18, 1968

Rejoice always, pray without ceasing, in everything give thanks for this is the will of God for you.—I Thessalonians 5: 16, 17, 18.

ETERNAL GOD, OUR FATHER, in the quiet of this moment we would climb the stairway of prayer that leads to the Upper Room where we may realize anew Thy divine presence. Thou art our refuge and strength and in every hour of trouble Thou art our ever-present help.

As we pray, do Thou light the lamps of faith and hope and love in our hearts that we may see our way more clearly through the tangled trails and maddening maze of our modern day. Guide our feet in the way we should go that we may walk uprightly without anxious fear and with abiding faith. Keep our minds clear, our hearts clean, and our hands clever that our service to the Nation may be constructive and our leadership creative.

By the power of Thy spirit alive within us may we exercise our faith, expand our sympathy, and extend our horizons. Through all of life make us mindful of Thy presence which goes with us always and all the way. In Thy name we pray. Amen.

MONDAY, JANUARY 22, 1968

Let the word of God dwell in you richly with all wisdom.—Colossians 3: 16.

A LMIGHTY GOD, in whose presence our anxious spirits are quieted, our tense minds become rested, and our worried souls find peace, we wait upon Thee in this moment of prayer, seeking a renewal of our strength, a restoration of our patience, and a reawakening of our faith.

In this time of trial and trouble, during these days of distress and disappointment, through these periods of stress and strain, we need the guidance of Thy spirit and the power of Thy presence. Give them to us as we pray that we may lead our people and our Nation into the paths of peace with liberty and justice for all.

Bless all the men and women who work under the dome of this Capitol. May Thy spirit dwell richly in their hearts as they carry their responsibilities, do their duties, and direct the affairs of our beloved land. With the faith of our Founding Fathers may we fly the flag of freedom forever and forever and forever. Amen.

THURSDAY, JANUARY 25, 1968

Thou shalt keep the commandments of the Lord, thy God, to walk in His ways and to fear Him.—Deuteronomy 8: 6.

O LORD, OUR GOD, Ruler of nations and the Father of men, we come together in this opening moment to unite our hearts in prayer unto Thee.

Continue to look with Thy favor upon us and upon our Republic. We have become great among the nations of the world and we pray that Thou wilt keep us great—in faith, in fellowship, and in the fruits of our democratic life. Help us to remember that this greatness comes from Thee and that we are to use it in Thy service and for the good of our fellow man.

Save us from pride and prejudice, from superficiality and superciliousness. Make us ever mindful of the needs of others and keep us resolute in our determination to promote good will among all, to produce justice for all, and to proclaim freedom to all in our world. In the Master's name we pray. Amen.

MONDAY, JANUARY 29, 1968

You shall know the truth, and the truth shall make you free.—John 8: 32.

ALMIGHTY GOD, we pause in Thy presence in the midst of these trying times, lifting our spirits unto Thee unto whom all hearts are open, all desires known, and from whom no secrets are hid. Teach us to pray that Thy spirit may increasingly be a reality in our hearts and, becoming real, hold us steady and keep us steadfast that we may not act hastily without facts but hopefully with faith.

We are distressed by the difficulties we are facing, weighed down by worry, burdened by bitterness, and disturbed by doubt. Help us to be creatively concerned and with confident certainty to make decisions wisely for our good and for the good of all.

Give us the strength to carry on, believing that every experience that comes our way and every event that takes place in our world we can meet and meet with honor to ourselves, to our Nation, and to Thee. In the Master's name we pray. Amen.

TUESDAY, JANUARY 30, 1968

Now the God of peace be with you all.—Romans 15: 33.

MOST MERCIFUL AND GRACIOUS GOD, beyond whose love and care we cannot drift, in the glory of a new day we come lifting our hearts to Thee as we prepare ourselves for the tasks before us. We would be still in Thy presence and receive from Thy hand strength for the day, wisdom for these hours, and faith for every moment to carry us through with high honor and creative courage.

Amid the crises of these days may we hear Thy voice calling us to be faithful and true, strong and steady and hearing may we respond with all our hearts.

We pray for our divided world going separate ways to different ends. May we not increase division by our dissension but may we seek to enlarge the circle of intelligent good will whereby the people of our land and the nations of the world can learn the fine art of living together in peace.

Give to us peace in our time, O Lord. Amen.

THURSDAY, FEBRUARY 1, 1968

With God all things are possible.—Matthew 19: 26.

ETERNAL FATHER, amid the encircling gloom of our anxious days enter Thou our hearts, lift us up, lead us on, light the way, and give us courage to go forward with Thee. In this high hour, preserve us, O God, for in Thee do we put our trust.

Hear us as we pray for all those in positions of influence in our Government that they may make wise decisions and choose right paths for our Nation. Guide our President, our Speaker, these Representatives of our people, and all who work beneath this dome of our national life that in Thy strength they may be made strong, with Thy wisdom may they be made wise, and by Thy good spirit may they, too, be good.

Give us the assurance that with Thee all good things are possible, even in the tough troubles of these trying times. Help us, O God, help us this day and forevermore.

In the name of the Master of all good workmen we pray. Amen.

MONDAY, FEBRUARY 5, 1968

The Lord is gracious and full of compassion; slow to anger and of great mercy.—Psalm 145: 8.

O LORD, OUR HEAVENLY FATHER, by whose mercy we have come to the beginning of another week, grant that we may enter it with humble and contrite hearts. Confirm our purpose to walk more sincerely in Thy way and to work more surely in Thy service.

Let not the mistakes of the past master us but forgive and set us free. Lead us into a closer companionship with Thee that we may continue to walk in the ways of honesty, truth, and good will. Give us the confidence that strengthens, the faith that breeds courage, and the integrity of mind that holds us steady amid the pressures of this time.

Lay Thy hand in blessing upon each one of us. Make us worthy of this day, adequate for our tasks, and ready to lead our Nation into the paths of peace. In the Master's name we pray. Amen.

TUESDAY, FEBRUARY 6, 1968

Cast thy burden upon the Lord and He shall sustain thee.—Psalm 55: 22.

ALMIGHTY AND EVERLIVING GOD, source of all true wisdom and the fountain of flowing love, in the quiet of this moment we pledge our lives anew to Thee and to the cause of freedom in our world.

Help us to overcome the tyrannical spirit which oppresses free men, opposes free nations, and would enslave the world.

Grant unto us and to free men everywhere the common faith that promotes justice by all, produces understanding among all, provides equality of opportunity for all, and proclaims the fruits of freedom to all.

Strengthen us that with humble spirit and honorable service we may keep our Nation strong in her devotion to Thee, wise in her relationship with other nations, and great in her desire for peace.

In the spirit of the Master we offer this our morning prayer. Amen.

THURSDAY, FEBRUARY 8, 1968

Be of good comfort, be of one mind, live in peace; and the God of love and peace shall be with you.—II Corinthians 13: 11.

ETERNAL FATHER, strong to save and eager to help, who art always speaking to man and revealing Thy way to him, speak Thou to us this moment and make known Thy will as we pray that Thy spirit may live in our hearts.

Make us great in our devotion to truth, gallant in our desire for honor, gentle in our dedication to good will, and genuine in our decision to seek peace and to pursue it until we possess it.

Bless these leaders of our Nation that they may walk with Thee as they make decisions looking forward to a better day. Strengthen our people that with genuine faith, humble spirit, and patriotic fervor they may find themselves by doing Thy will, and by living together in peace, usher in a new day of peace for our world. In the Master's name we pray. Amen.

THURSDAY, FEBRUARY 15, 1968

They that seek the Lord shall not want any good thing.—Psalm 34: 10.

O THOU IN WHOSE PRESENCE OUR HEADS BOW AND OUR HEARTS ARE OPEN, we thank Thee for our country—for her glorious past, her glowing present, and her growing future. Help us to see that the greatness of our Nation does not depend on wealth or fame or success but upon character rooted in honesty, faith, and good will between men and nations.

In this sacred moment we remember again our beloved Emancipator. May his words ring out anew in our day—"with malice toward none, with charity for all; with firmness in the right, as God gives us to see the right, let us strive on to finish the work we are in; to bind up the Nation's wounds; to care for him who shall have borne the battle and for his widow and his children—to do all which may achieve and cherish a just and a lasting peace among ourselves and with all nations." Amen.

WEDNESDAY, FEBRUARY 21, 1968

I will lift up mine eyes unto the hills, from whence cometh my help.—
Psalm 121: 1.

O HEAVENLY FATHER, who are the source of truth and the giver of all good, lead us to the hills from whence cometh our help and where in steadiness of thought and stability of feeling we may be secure in mind and heart.

In these moments of prayer help us to receive Thy spirit that the life of this day may be different and this difference make a difference in the day for us.

Strengthen Thou our faith, increase our courage, and stimulate our high endeavors that we may never lose heart in the struggle for the reign of democracy and the right of people to determine their own destiny. In the spirit of Him who never lost faith we pray. Amen.

THURSDAY, FEBRUARY 22, 1968

Preserve me, O God, for in Thee do I put my trust.—Psalm 16: 1.

GOD OF OUR FATHERS WHOSE ALMIGHTY HAND HAS LED US IN THE PAST AND WHOSE CREATIVE SPIRIT IS SEEKING TO LEAD US IN THE PRESENT, be Thou our guardian and our guide in this hour of our national need.

Give to these leaders of our Nation and to the citizens of our land the faith, the hope, and the love which seeks to give rather than to get and standing up persists in doing something for our country rather than sitting down insists upon our country doing something for them.

We remember with humble pride the devotion of our first President whose name shines like a star in the firmament of freedom. May his courage in times of crises, his fidelity in periods of adversity, and his faith which sent him to his knees in prayer be ours as we face the hard facts of this hectic day. May the memory of his life and the consciousness of Thy presence strengthen our people and enable them to live in the spirit of good will and to labor for the good of these United States of America. In the Master's name, we pray. Amen.

MONDAY, FEBRUARY 26, 1968

The hand of our God is upon all of them for good that seek Him.—Ezra 7: 22.

ETERNAL GOD, OUR FATHER, we, Thy humble servants, bow before Thee at the altar of prayer. As we remember Thine unfailing goodness which has attended us all our days, we pray for Thy good spirit to move within our hearts as we start our deliberations this day.

We acknowledge our shortcomings, our selfishness and our sins. Forgive us, we pray Thee, when we fall short of Thy will for us and Thy way for our Nation. Cleanse the thoughts of our hearts by the inspiration of Thy holy spirit that we may think better, speak better, and do better than ever before.

We pray for those in positions of influence in our Nation that they may lead our people in right and just paths. Lay Thy hand in blessing upon our President, our Speaker, the Members of this body, and all who labor with them. Give them the assurance that with Thee great things are possible. Thus may our faith be renewed, our hope restored, and good will revived in all our hearts. In the name of Him who went about doing good we pray. Amen.

WEDNESDAY, FEBRUARY 28, 1968

Lord, teach us to pray.—Luke 11: 1.

LORD, what a change within us one short hour
Spent in Thy presence will avail to make!
What heavy burdens from our bosoms take,
What parched grounds refresh, as with a shower!
We kneel, and all around us seems to lower;
We rise, and all the distant and the near
Stands forth in sunny outline, brave and clear!
We kneel, how weak! We rise, how full of power!
Why, therefore, should we do ourselves this wrong,
Or others, that we are not always strong;
That we are ever overborne with care;
That we should ever weak or heartless be,
Anxious or troubled when with us is prayer,
And joy and strength and courage are with Thee.

Amen.

—ARCHBISHOP TRENCH.

THURSDAY, FEBRUARY 29, 1968

Be strong in the Lord and in the power of His might.—Ephesians 6: 10.

GOD OF GRACE AND GOD OF GLORY, on Thy people pour Thy power and as we wait upon Thee at this noontide moment of prayer may the power of Thy presence permeate our hearts.

When doubts disturb us, and worries weaken us, and frustrations follow us be Thou our guiding light that we may see that the way of truth is the way of wisdom, the path of honesty is the path of honor, and the road of faithfulness is the road of faith.

Call us to commanding convictions, refresh us with Thy renewing spirit, strengthen us with Thy steadfast presence so essential to worthy tasks worthily accepted. By Thy spirit make us courteous in our conversations, friendly in our relationships, ready to serve our country with all our hearts, and to truly represent those who have sent us here.

Bless our Nation with Thy favor, make wars to cease and cause peace to come to our world. In the Master's name we pray. Amen.

MONDAY, MARCH 4, 1968

Happy is the man that findeth wisdom and the man that getteth understanding.—Proverbs 3: 13.

ALMIGHTY GOD, OUR FATHER, who hast made us for Thyself so that our hearts are restless until they find rest in Thee, lead us into the green pastures of Thy presence and beside the still waters of Thy patience, that our strength may be renewed, our spirit restored, and refreshment for daily tasks be given us.

Grant unto us wisdom for the facing of this hour and courage for the living of these days. Make us equal to the challenge of this time and more than a match for the modern mood which would motivate our movements.

Keep our faith steady, our hope stable, and our good will strong that we may be the instruments of Thy will in leading our Nation to a higher plane of unity with liberty and justice for all.

In the name of Him whose truth sets man free we pray. Amen.

TUESDAY, MARCH 5, 1968

He who is slow to anger is better than the mighty, and he who rules his spirit than he who takes a city.—Proverbs 16: 32 .

ALMIGHTY GOD, OUR HEAVENLY FATHER, before whom we bow in adoration and unto whom we lift our hearts in prayer, help us to improve our self-mastery that we may do our duties and respond to our responsibilities with a confident courage and a high-hearted happiness.

May we feel Thy guiding hand through all the scattered details of our daily life and in the trouble of this hour may we hear Thy still small voice and feel underneath us Thine everlasting arms holding us steady, keeping us strong, and leading us in the way we should go.

Bless all efforts to remove violence and to reduce discord and prosper all endeavor to redouble our good will and to reaffirm our faith in Thee and in our country.

In the name of Him who is the way, the truth, and the life we pray. Amen.

THURSDAY, MARCH 7, 1968

Watch ye, stand fast in the faith, quit you like men, be strong.—I Corinthians 16: 13.

God of the Ages, everywhere present, everywhere available, and everywhere seeking to enter the heart of man to strengthen him and to sustain him, be Thou with us this day and reveal Thy way to our waiting hearts. Make us so conscious of Thy presence and so receptive to the leading of Thy spirit that we shall be directed into right paths, make wise decisions, and formulate great plans for the welfare of all our people and the well-being of our world.

With patience and perseverance may we meet the problems that confront us and the conflicts that rage about us. Together may we stand firm in our faith, be strong, and do all things in love.

We remember before Thee one of our leaders who has entered his eternal home. We thank Thee for him and for the contribution he made to our country and to our lives. Receive him into the glory of Thy presence, comfort his family, and make us all aware of the fact that in life and in death Thou art with us. In the Master's name we pray. Amen.

MONDAY, MARCH 11, 1968

What is impossible with men is possible with God.—Luke 18: 27.

O God of life and love, by whose creative spirit we have the gift of a new day and in whose sustaining presence we are given strength for these hectic hours, we pause in silence before Thee ere the pressure of persistent duties lays its demanding hands upon us.

We would yield our lives to Thee and go forth into the day strengthened with Thine unfailing spirit in our hearts and sustained by an unfaltering trust in the wisdom of Thy way. In these troubled and trying times give us the courage that never fails, the faith that never falters, and the hope that never fades.

Upon our President, our Speaker, the Members of this body, the leaders of our Armed Forces, upon all who make decisions which determine our destiny grant wisdom that they may be wise, strength that they may be made strong, and love that they may be filled with good will. Together may we meet the issues of these days with honor to ourselves, to our Nation, and to Thee.

In the name of Him who went about doing good we pray. Amen.

TUESDAY, MARCH, 12, 1968

The Lord is good to all; and His tender mercies are over all His works.— Psalm 145: 9.

Almighty God, Maker and Ruler of the World, Father of men and the source of all goodness and beauty, all truth and love, to Thee we turn for quiet from the noise of the world and for peace from the turmoil that rages about us.

Help us this day to accept our privileges with gratitude, our troubles with fortitude, and our responsibilities with fidelity. Deliver us from petty annoyances which disturb us and from petulant irritations which upset us.

Make us gloriously equal to our experiences and truly adequate for the task at hand to keep freedom for all, justice for all, and good will for all alive in our Nation and in our world.

In the name of Him who keeps men free and just and good, we pray. Amen.

MONDAY, MARCH, 18, 1968

Let us search and try our ways, and turn again unto the Lord.—Lamentations 3: 40.

O God, Our Father, as we seek to find our way through these distressing days make us mindful of Thy presence, eager to do Thy will, and ready to carry our responsibilities with honor to ourselves, to our country, and to Thee.

Give us clarity of vision to see what we ought to do, the courage to do it, and the faith to keep us firm amid the frustrations of these fateful days.

Bless our President, our Speaker, the Members of this body, and all who work for them and with them. May they be strengthened with lofty principles and sustained by living purposes as they seek to do their duties and to discharge their obligations with fidelity. Together may we commit ourselves to Thee and to the building of a stronger nation and a better world.

In the Master's name we pray. Amen.

WEDNESDAY, MARCH 20, 1968

In the day when I cried to Thee, Thou didst answer me and didst increase the strength of my soul.—Psalm 138: 3.

ETERNAL GOD, OUR FATHER, who art the God and Father of us all, grant that by the tides of Thy spirit we may be lifted into the blessed assurance that Thou art with us, that Thy grace is sufficient for every need and that by Thy living presence in our hearts we may meet our responsibilities with patience, manage our moods with creative faith, and master our temptations with confident strength.

Make us ever sensitive to the needs of our people and ready to dedicate ourselves to worthy endeavors that minister to the welfare of our Nation.

Bless those who struggle for freedom across our world. Crown their efforts with resounding success that all men everywhere may ultimately be free.

In the spirit of Him who sets men free we pray.   Amen.

THURSDAY, MARCH 21, 1968

He giveth power to the faint; and to them that have no might He increaseth strength.—Isaiah 40: 29.

ETERNAL GOD, OUR FATHER, in whose presence our restless spirits are stilled and our hungry hearts find the food that nourishes and quickens our understanding, increase our faith and stimulate our high resolves to walk in the way of Thy commandments, to abide in Thy love, and to serve our country with all our might.

Grant unto us an inner greatness of spirit that we may meet the challenge of this day unashamed and unafraid. Though the earth be moved, the waters roar, and the mountains shake may we find our refuge and our strength in Thee.

In the name of Him who was forever faithful to Thee we pray.   Amen.

TUESDAY, MARCH 26, 1968

I will say of the Lord, He is my refuge and my fortress: my God; in Him will I trust.—Psalm 91: 2.

O GOD, OUR FATHER, we come to Thee with joyful hearts and reverent minds realizing that this is a great time in which to be alive. By Thy spirit do Thou help us to live with high hopes, fruitful faith, and glorious goals that we may move onward and forward to a greater nation and a better world.

Strengthen our faith in Thee that when differences come we shall not fail, when difficulties burst upon us we shall not falter, and when diffidences roll over us we shall not allow ourselves to give way to frustration or give up to futility. Let us say and believe Thou art our refuge and strength, in Thee will we trust.

Help us to have the courage to stand up for the rights of all men, for the freedom of all men, and for the good of all men. May we so think and speak and act that Thy blessing may be upon us this day and all our days.

In the name of Christ we pray.   Amen.

WEDNESDAY, MARCH 27, 1968

Man shall not live by bread alone, but by every word that proceedeth out of the mouth of God.—Matthew 4: 4.

ALMIGHTY GOD, our Heavenly Father, make us conscious of Thy presence as we enter upon the work of another day that we, the Members of this body, shall be led in the ways of righteousness and justice and good will. May what we do be in accordance with Thy holy will and for the welfare of our Nation.

We pray that the dignity of the laws of our land may be respected by all our people, upheld by all our citizens, and obeyed by every individual. Only so can life and liberty and the pursuit of happiness be secure in these United States of America.

Above the din of discordant voices may we take time to listen to Thy voice, and hearing, give heed to it, remembering that man does not live by bread alone but by every word that proceedeth out of Thy mouth.

In the Master's name we pray.   Amen.

TUESDAY, APRIL 2, 1968

Unto Thee, O Lord, do I lift up my soul.—Psalm 25: 1.

O GOD, OUR FATHER, to whom we belong and with whom we live, we come to Thee in this our morning prayer seeking a fresh consciousness of the reality of Thy presence. Help us to know that Thou art with us and that Thou art always with us seeking to guide us along the ways of righteousness, justice, and peace. If some of us have been disturbed by doubt, hurt by hate, or maligned by malice until life has been drained of its worth—restore to us such a vision of Thee and of the truth about life that we may believe triumphantly once again.

For our Nation we pray that it may not miss the true and right path amid the world's confusion. Bless all efforts to create and maintain an ordered and a peaceful human family on this planet. Particularly do Thou bless the effort now put forth to bring peace in Vietnam. We pray for our

President, our Speaker, and the Members of this House of Representatives. In all truth and in all good will steady Thou their faith that life for them may not be a drifting raft but a ship with a course.

In the Master's name we pray.   Amen.

WEDNESDAY, APRIL 3, 1968

All the paths of the Lord are mercy and truth unto such as keep His covenant and His testimonies.—Psalm 25: 10.

Eternal God, Our Father, who art the creator and the sustainer of life, without whose benediction all our labor is in vain, we pray that our lives and the life of our Nation may be built upon the rock of eternal truth and everlasting love so we would dedicate ourselves anew to Thee in body, in mind, and in spirit. Satisfy us with nothing but the best in thought and life and keep us restless until we find our rest in Thee.

We thank Thee for our country, for our glorious heritage, for this challenging hour, and for the faith with which we greet the coming day. Lay Thou Thy hand in blessing upon all our leaders and all our people. Teach us to look unto Thee as the fountain of all wisdom and the source of all strength. May Thy mighty spirit surge through us and our people translating our lofty principles into living practices and our good words into good works.

All this we ask in the name of Him whose words were life and whose life was altogether worthy.   Amen.

MONDAY, APRIL 8, 1968

Yea, though I walk through the valley of the shadow of death, I will fear no evil: for Thou art with me.—Psalm 23: 4.

Almighty God, Father of all men, stunned by the suddenness of tragedy and shocked by the fury of violence, we turn to Thee for help in this hour of our national need. May the spirit of wisdom guide us, the grace of understanding lead us, and the love of compassion direct us that we may find our way to the promised land of freedom for all, justice for all, peace for all, and finding the way give us courage to walk in it.

We pray that the comfort of Thy spirit may abide in the hearts of those who walk through the valley of the shadow of death. May Thy presence make them strong, give them courage, and hold them steadfast to good will even in the midst of ill will.

"Cure Thy children's warring madness,
Bend our pride to Thy control;
Shame our wanton, selfish gladness,
Rich in things and poor in soul,
Grant us wisdom, grant us courage
That we fail not man nor Thee."

Amen.

TUESDAY, APRIL 9, 1968

The Lord is my strength and my shield; my heart trusteth in Him and I am helped.—Psalm 28: 7.

ETERNAL FATHER OF OUR SPIRITS, whose still small voice calls us to turn away from the foolish and feverish ways of a wayward and a worried world, help us to draw near to Thee in all humility of mind and with all reverence of heart. With the power of Thy spirit alive within us may we face the duties of this day with clear minds and clean hearts, without pretense and prejudice, in the assurance that the best service we can render our country in these trying times is based on understanding, truth, and love.

Standing in the tradition of our Nation with our faith in freedom for all, may be become united in purpose and strong in spirit as we face this day when plots are made to destroy our birthright by a revolt against the laws of our land and by a rebellion against the kingly virtue of nonviolence.

May we lay aside partisan allegiances that with a deeper loyalty to our country, a broader love for our fellow man, and a greater faith in Thee we may go forth to battle for the good of all Thy children.

In the name of Him who made goodness His aim in life we pray. Amen.

MONDAY, APRIL 22, 1968

Teach me to do Thy will; for Thou art my God: Thy spirit is good; lead me into the land of uprightness.—Psalm 143: 10.

A LMIGHTY AND ETERNAL GOD, we thank Thee for the lovely evidences of spring, for the beauty which surrounds us, for the glory which shines above us, and for the love which from our birth over and around us lies. Lord of all, to Thee we raise this our prayer of grateful praise.

Let us not set out on any endeavor this day which is not in accord with Thy will for us, for our Nation, and for our world. Take us by the hand and lead us, illumine our minds and direct our thinking, strengthen our spirits and give us the courage of creative convictions that our thoughts, our words, and our actions may be worthy of Thy blessing.

Bless our President, our Speaker, these Representatives of our people, and all who work under the dome of this beloved Capitol. God bless us everyone and help us to continue to labor earnestly and enthusiastically for the welfare of our country and the well-being of mankind. In the Master's name we pray.　Amen.

TUESDAY, APRIL 23, 1968

Thou shalt not avenge, nor bear any grudge against the children of thy people, but thou shalt love thy neighbor as thyself: I am the Lord.— Leviticus 19: 18.

O Thou whose will it is that we do justly, love mercy, and walk humbly with Thee—forgive our wayward ways, our foolish flings, and our majoring in minors while the world burns around us.

Remove from our national life the spirit of discord and suspicion and ill will. Let our criticism of other people be as kindly as our criticism of ourselves and our relationship to others be as good as our relationship to ourselves, lest bitterness blight our lives and in our hatred we destroy ourselves. Lead us in the paths of unity and peace and accord for Thy name's sake and for the welfare of our country.　Amen.

THURSDAY, APRIL 25, 1968

*If ye continue in My word, ye shall know the truth and the truth shall make you free.—*John 8: 31, 32.

O God, Our Father, and our father's God, in this land of liberty we sing and pray and live. Make us ever mindful of the cost of freedom to preceding generations and may we be ready to pay the price to keep freedom alive in our own day. Help us so to live in its spirit that all men everywhere may see it, and seeing it seek it, and seeking it secure it, for their own good and for the good of all.

Keep Thou the love of liberty glowing in our hearts and the faith in freedom growing in our homes—so shall we continue to be free and so shall the flag of freedom fly forever over the fortress of faith our forefathers founded on these shores.

In the name of Him whose truth keeps men free we pray.　Amen.

MONDAY, APRIL 29, 1968

*It is for you now to demonstrate the goodness of Him who has called you out of darkness into His wonderful light.—*I Peter 2: 9 (Phillips).

O Thou whose strength sustains us in our weakness and whose hand upholds us when we would give way to discouragement, grant unto us, who wait before Thee, confidence that in the face of trouble we may believe in the triumph of truth, in spite of our shortcomings we may have faith in Thy forgiving love, in moments when moral choices must be made we may walk the narrow way of an integrity of mind and heart, and thus be loyal to the royal within ourselves.

Make us creative enough that our actions will not burden the generations to come; make us courageous enough that we may vote for what we honestly believe, though the cost may be great; make us conservative enough that we may not squander the taxes of our people and liberal enough that we may have an active concern for the welfare of all.

Thus may we be led out of the darkness of our day into the light of a new life where men shall learn to live together in peace and good will. Amen.

TUESDAY, APRIL 30, 1968

The heavens declare the glory of God; and the firmament showeth His handiwork.—Psalm 19: 1.

ALMIGHTY GOD, OUR HEAVENLY FATHER, who declarest Thy glory in the heavens and who dost reveal Thyself in Thy word, deliver us as we draw near to Thee from coldness of heart and wanderings of mind that with steadfast thoughts and kindled affections we may worship Thee in spirit and in truth.

Bless these servants of our people as they give themselves in service to our fellow men. Grant unto them clear vision to see what is amiss in our society, creative wisdom to work at meeting the needs of our Nation, courageous spirit to do something about it, building self-respect and cultivating good will among the citizens of our country.

May Thy holy spirit move in the heart of our President, our Speaker, and all Members of Congress. Give to them wisdom to know Thy will and the strength to do it. So rule their hearts and so reign in their minds that law and order, justice and peace may prevail everywhere, to the glory of Thy name and the good of our beloved land.

In the Master's name we pray. Amen.

WEDNESDAY, MAY 1, 1968

And this commandment we have from Him, that he who loveth God love his brother also.—I John 4: 21.

O GOD, who art the creator and sustainer of mankind and the Father of all men, we pray that Thou wilt make Thy will known to us as we bow in this circle of prayer. May we be so governed by Thy good spirit and so guided by Thy gracious purpose that we may be led into the way of truth, along the path of peace, up the road of righteousness, and down the high-way of good will to men.

Remove the walls which separate our people and break down the bar-riers which partition one life from another, one group from another, one race from another. Purge our cities and towns of the causes of corruption and the vice of violence. By Thy grace help us to live in a new unity of spirit, with a new bond of peace, by a new righteousness of life, and for a new spirit of good will.

We commend to Thy fatherly care our beloved Nation, our leaders, and our people. Help us all to labor earnestly for the freedom, the rights, and the good of all our citizens.

In the name of Him who calls upon us to love one another we pray. Amen.

MONDAY, MAY 6, 1968

On the lips of him who has understanding wisdom is found.—Proverbs 10: 13.

O THOU WHOSE STRENGTH SUSTAINS US IN OUR LABOR AND WHOSE SPIRIT SUPPORTS US IN OUR LEISURE, grant unto us the consciousness of Thy pres-ence as we face this day that our work may not be a burden but a delight, our rest not be troubled by fear but filled with faith, and our lives not be haunted by the bitter acts of others but hallowed by the brighter attitudes of our own.

Give us the faith that never falters, the hope that never fails, and the love which never falls by the way as we live through these troubled times. May our concern for our country help us to lift the fallen, strengthen the weak, and sustain the weary that we may hasten the dawn of a new day for our people and for all mankind.

In the Master's name we pray.   Amen.

TUESDAY, MAY 7, 1968

The Lord is my rock, my fortress, and my deliverer; in Him will I trust.— II Samuel 22: 2, 3.

O GOD, OUR FATHER, who art in heaven, in the earth, and in all the world, we pray humbly and hopefully for ourselves and for our country that we and our people may face the tumult of these trying times with the strength of moral character and the courage of creative convictions.

We are grateful for the lives of men and women in the past who have given themselves that ours should be a free nation. Make us worthy of their devo-tion and give us the confidence that we may continue to be free under law, seeking the good of all and striving to be just to all.

Help us to think clearly, to make decisions wisely, and to have the wisdom to choose the hard right over the easy wrong and to walk along the high road of princely principles rather than travel the low road of petty prejudices. Above all may we put our trust in Thee now and evermore. Amen.

FRIDAY, MAY 10, 1968

Give to Thy servants understanding hearts to judge Thy people and to discern between good and evil.—I Kings 3: 9.

O GOD AND FATHER OF US ALL, whose love never lets us go and whose strength never lets us down, in the midst of these difficult days we pause in 'Thy presence to pray for the citizens of our country and for the people on our planet. Particularly do we pray for those who sit around the table and begin seeking and striving for an end of hostilities in Vietnam.

May they bring to this confrontation courageous spirits, may they be made wise with Thy wisdom, may they be blest with understanding minds and hearts that through negotiation they may find their way to an enduring peace with justice for all, with freedom to all, and with good will among all. Crown their efforts, we pray Thee, with real success.

Grant unto each one of us a compassion which includes all men in the circle of our concern as we continue to live for the glory of our Nation and to labor for the good of all mankind.

In the name of the Prince of Peace we pray. Amen.

MONDAY, MAY 13, 1968

If God be for us, who can be against us?—Romans 8: 31.

O GOD, OUR FATHER, we come together at this moment to unite our hearts in prayer unto Thee. Keep us aware of Thy presence and make us receptive to the leading of Thy spirit as we live through the stress and strain of these difficult days.

Since no man lives a stranger to trouble, grant that we may not give up before the hazards of life but may live with that hope which belongs to those who trust in Thee, confident that new paths will open to those who walk with faith.

In this day when people knock at the door of our hearts and call us to lead the way to a greater life together may we place the weight of our influence on the side of life and health and brotherhood—through Him who is the way, the truth, and the life. Amen.

WEDNESDAY, MAY 15, 1968

It is God who is at work within you, giving you the will and the power to achieve His purpose.—Philippians 2: 13 (Phillips).

OUR FATHER IN HEAVEN, we thank Thee for this sacred minute when we unite our hearts in prayer unto Thee, when for a moment we pause in Thy presence seeking guidance and strength from Thy hand.

Let not the beauty of the earth, nor the glory of the skies, nor the love which surrounds us daily blind us to the needs of the needy and the poverty of the poor. Make us so dissatisfied with large professions and little practices, with fine words and feeble works, with smiling faces and sour faiths that we will pray earnestly for the renewal of a right and a good spirit within us.

Speak Thou to us, O Lord, and may we hear Thy voice, and hearing it harken to it, and harkening to it heed it, for the glory of Thy name, the good of our Nation, and the greatness of this House of Representatives. In the Master's name we pray. Amen.

THURSDAY, MAY 16, 1968

We know that in everything God works for good with those who love him.—Romans 8: 28.

ETERNAL SPIRIT OF GOD, the light of the minds that seek Thee, the life of the spirits that find Thee, and the love of the souls that serve Thee, grant unto us a renewal of heart as we wait upon Thee in this our morning prayer. By Thy spirit make us ready for the responsibilities of this day, equal to every experience and adequate to serve the present age.

The world around us is full of the rumblings of discontent and disturbances which breed disorder. In these hours help us to keep our faith, that strong in Thee we may face these facts courageously and confidently, ever seeking liberty and justice and peace for all.

Bless our land with Thy favor and strengthen us to walk in the way of Thy commandments: through Jesus Christ our Lord. Amen.

TUESDAY, MAY 21, 1968

And thou shalt be called the prophet of the Most High to give light to those who sit in darkness and to guide our feet into the way of peace.—Luke 1: 76, 79.

OUR FATHER, at the gate of a new day we bow in silence before Thee, praying for a renewal of our spirits as we face these times which try our souls, cause us to lose patience with each other, and make us impatient with ourselves.

That we may be at our best and do our very best for Thee and for our country, grant unto us the courage of a humble mind, the creative faith of a high hope, and the confident peace of a heart stayed on Thee.

By the power of Thy spirit may we maintain our integrity, be motivated by justice, and move resolutely in the direction of peace on earth and good will to men. Bless Thou the peacemakers and may the peace made be just and enduring and for the good of all.

In the Master's name we pray.   Amen.

WEDNESDAY, MAY 22, 1968

Cast all your cares upon God, for He cares for you.—I Peter 5: 7.

O GOD, OUR FATHER, whose grace is sufficient for every need and whose spirit makes us adequate for every worthy endeavor, we take this time to lift the windows of faith, to open the doors of hope, and to part the curtains of love that the greatness of Thy truth and the wisdom of Thy way may be made known to us. In Thy light may we see the way clearly and by Thee be given courage to walk in it this day and all our days.

Bless our men and women over the world who live and fight and work for freedom. As free men and as good men may we make our Nation Thy channel for the light of liberty to shine upon the people on this planet.

> "Unite us in the sacred love
>   Of knowledge, truth and Thee;
> And let our hills and valleys shout
>   The songs of liberty.
>
> "Lord of the nations thus to Thee
>   Our country we commend;
> Be Thou her refuge and her trust,
>   Her everlasting friend."

Amen.

THURSDAY, MAY 23, 1968

*The God of peace be with you all.—*Romans 15: 33.

ETERNAL GOD, OUR FATHER, before whom we bow in adoration and unto whom we lift our spirits in prayer, come Thou into our hearts that motivated by Thy grace and moved by Thy love we may widen our sympathies, deepen our devotion and increase our faith in Thee and in our country.

By working together with Thee may we hasten the production of peace on our planet and the promotion of good will in the hearts of our people.

Renew a right and a good and a wise spirit within us, O Lord, that we may go forward to greater achievements under Thy leadership, supported by Thy strength and sustained by Thy spirit. May peace and good will come to reign in every heart.

In the name of the Prince of Peace we pray.   Amen.

WEDNESDAY, MAY 29, 1968

The righteous shall be held in everlasting remembrance.—Psalm 112: 6.

God of all the ages, our fathers' God and our God, we thank Thee that our forefathers founded on these shores a free nation, dedicated to life, liberty, and the pursuit of happiness for all, and we are grateful that our fathers continued this heritage that a government of the people, by the people, and for the people would not perish from the earth.

Grant, our Father, as we come to another Memorial Day, to remember that there are those who gave their lives that we may be free and there are those even now who are giving their lives that freedom can be ours.

We may weep over the graves of our beloved, but may there be no tears of bitterness, nor resentment, nor ill will, but only sorrow that so great a price has to be paid that men continue to be free.

Help us so to live and so to love our country that our flag may fly over a united nation, one flag, one faith, one folk, one fellowship of good will and to Thee be the glory now and forevermore.   Amen.

MONDAY, JUNE 3, 1968

My Father worketh hitherto and I work.—John 5: 17.

Our Heavenly Father, returning from the memorial recess we come again to face the unending struggle to preserve and promote the freedom which is the fruit of the faith of our fathers and which, we pray, will always be our faith.

As we share our lives in the creative endeavor to keep our country great in peace, great in war, and great in the hearts of our countrymen, may we labor diligently using all our hearts, all our heads, and all our hands. To this end strengthen Thou our hands, make serene our hearts, and put wise thoughts in our heads that our work may be well done and we may continue to be workers with Thee for good in Thy world.

O Thou who dost the vision send
And givest each his task,
And with the task sufficient strength;
Show us Thy will, we ask;
Give us a conscience bold and good;
Give us a purpose true,
That it may be our highest joy,
Our Father's work to do.

Amen.

TUESDAY, JUNE 4, 1968

Watch ye, stand fast in the faith, quit ye like me, be strong.—I Corinthians 16: 13.

O THOU WHOSE LIGHT FOLLOWS US ALL OUR WAYS, amid the tumult of these trying times we bow a moment at the altar of faith and freedom to listen to Thy still, small voice which speaks forever to our human hearts.

Give to us a real consciousness of Thy presence as we live through these hours that in doing Thy will, in serving our country, and in ministering to our people we may have abounding courage, abundant wisdom, and abiding faith.

Upon all Members of Congress who carry heavy burdens through these decisive and disturbing days grant a double measure of Thy strengthening spirit. As we determine our decisions and as we make our moves may we keep our minds clear and our hearts clean. By the power of Thy spirit may we meet great needs with great deeds, and match lofty professions with lively practices. Thus may we march forward to a better city, a better nation, and a better world.

In the Master's name we pray. Amen.

MONDAY, JUNE 10, 1968

Blessed be God, the God of all comfort, who comforts us in all our affliction.—II Corinthians 1: 3, 4.

O GOD, from whom we come and unto whom our spirits return, Thou hast been our dwelling place in all generations. Thou art our refuge and strength, a very present help in trouble.

Grant us Thy blessing in this hour as we remember our colleague in Congress who has gone home to be with Thee. We still stand stunned by the suddenness of it all and our hearts give way to sorrow. Yet in grief Thou art with us. Make us conscious of Thy presence and may we and our Nation find our security and our strength in Thee.

We pray for the family of our beloved Senator, for his wife and children, for his mother and father, for his sisters and brother. Comfort their hearts with thine indwelling spirit and give them the faith that sees beyond the earthly shadows the larger life in Thy living presence.

For our people we lift our spirits in prayer this sad hour. Together may we work to rid our world of war, may we toil at the task of ridding our Nation of crime, and may we labor to rid our hearts of ill will.

We pray for a nation united in purpose and principle, devoted to Thee and to Thy will for us, and dedicated to the good of all people and to Thy way among men of good will.

In the Master's name we pray.   Amen.

WEDNESDAY, JUNE 12, 1968

O Lord, be gracious unto us; we have waited for Thee; be Thou our arm every morning, our salvation also in the time of trouble.—Isaiah 33: 2.

ETERNAL FATHER OF OUR SPIRITS, who hast created us with minds to seek truth, with hearts to feel love, and with wills to choose the right, we bow at the altar of Thy presence praying for the establishment of justice and peace and good will in our Nation and in our world.

Breathe into our hearts and into the hearts of our people the generosity and the genuineness of great and good living. Save us from unwholesome relationships, break down the walls that separate us, and let pettiness pass away as the power of Thy love comes to life within us.

We commend our Nation unto Thee. Make us worthy of the sacrifices which have been built into the foundation of our Republic. Save us from our own folly and from that idolatry which puts another god on the throne of our national life. From lawlessness and anarchy and selfishness, O Lord, deliver us. May real religion, moral manners, public integrity, and private character become the blessing of our country.

Grant that we enter this day with Thee and may the benediction of Thy spirit rest upon us. In the spirit of Christ we pray.   Amen.

FRIDAY, JUNE 14, 1968

We will rejoice in Thy salvation and in the name of our God we will set up our banner.—Psalm 20: 5.

ALMIGHTY GOD, from whom all thoughts of life and love proceed, kindle in our hearts and in the hearts of our people a true love for peace, a sincere regard for the laws of our land, and a deep reverence for Thee.

Guide with Thy spirit those who lead our Nation in this decisive day. Make them wise with Thy wisdom, strong in Thy strength, diligent in duty, loving in life, and sincere in spirit. May Thy presence so live in their hearts and in the hearts of our countrymen that law and order, justice and peace, may everywhere prevail.

On this day we lift up before our eyes the flag of our beloved country with the glorious colors—red, white, and blue. Holding aloft this banner—the best hope of freedom in our day—may we go forth devoted to duty, steady in spirit, and firmly determined to keep liberty and law alive in our world.

In the Master's name we pray. Amen.

TUESDAY, JUNE 18, 1968

As for me, I will walk in mine integrity; redeem me and be merciful unto me.—Psalm 26: 11.

WE THANK THEE, OUR FATHER, for this moment when we unite our hearts in prayer and when in all reverence we wait upon Thee, seeking light upon our way and life for our day.

While we are mindful of our material resources may we never foget our moral resources without which we cannot truly lead our Nation in the path of justice and good will.

Bless these Representatives of our people with good health. Give to them the good sense to maintain it and to stop wearing themselves out by overwork and overworry. In their activities keep them from anxiety, in their devotion to our country keep them from destroying themselves. As they plan wisely for the future may they also pray worthily for the present. Help them to care for themselves as much as some of them care for their golf clubs and their automobiles.

This day may we not walk with leaden feet, but with the wings of the morning may we soar to the heights in our endeavor to do our best for Thee and for our Nation.

In the name of Him who always walked in integrity we pray. Amen.

TUESDAY, JUNE 25, 1968

In Him was life; and the life was the light of men.—John 1: 4.

O THOU WHOSE LAW IS LOVE, whose love is life, and whose life is the light of men, gather us who seek Thy face to the fold of Thy embrace for Thou art nigh. As we pray and as we work make us ever mindful of Thy presence, ever eager to do Thy will, ever enthusiastic about our love for our country.

In these hours when hatred is hurting the hearts of hordes of our people we thank Thee for men and women of good will, who with strength of character, sympathetic understanding, and an outreaching concern for the welfare of others are seeking to meet the imperative needs of this day. Give them and give us the insight that lights the way to brotherhood and with it the inspiration that leads us to become the brothers of men.

Here on this Hill may we continue to work for a time when nation shall not lift up sword against nation, when people shall learn to live together in peace, and when the spirit of good will will abide in the hearts of all.

In the name of Him whose life was the light of men, we pray.   Amen.

THURSDAY, JUNE 27, 1968

Restore unto me the joy of Thy salvation; and uphold me with Thy free spirit.—Psalm 51: 12.

ALMIGHTY AND MOST MERCIFUL FATHER, ever moving among Thy children and forever seeking entrance into the hearts of men, we pray for the world in which we live, a world in which we do not get along together in the spirit of brotherhood. Too often persons resort to procedures which produce pettiness in people, multiply the miseries of men, and add to the bitterness which blights the bright hopes of Thy children. Forgive, O Lord, forgive and restore unto us the joy of Thy salvation.

We pray for ourselves in this world that with a new spirit in our hearts, a new song on our lips, and a new strength in our hands we may work together to lift the fallen, hearten the disheartened, and give faith and hope to those whose spirits are low.

Lift up our heads, O Lord. Better still, lift up our hearts that we, the Representatives of our Nation, may lead our people to a better life for all, a higher hope for all, and a fuller faith for all.

In the name of Him who lived His faith to the very end we pray.   Amen.

TUESDAY, JULY 2, 1968

God is with you in all that you do.—Genesis 21: 22.

O THOU WHO ART THE COMPANION OF OUR WAY AND THE CREATIVE SPIRIT EVER ENDEAVORING TO LEAD US TO NEW FRONTIERS OF THOUGHT AND AC-TION, at the beginning of a new day we bow before Thee invoking Thy blessing upon us and praying that Thy wisdom may guide us, Thy strength support us, and Thy love hold us true all the day long.

In the midst of hectic hours and harassing happenings may Thy healing presence restore our souls and lead us in the paths of righteousness for Thy name's sake.

Forgive, O Lord, our impatient impulses, our petty prejudices, our discouraged dispositions. Strengthen us to make a striking contribution to the life of our day, to think clearly, to speak courageously, to act confidently, to keep our faith in Thee and our country and may this faith keep us steady in this time of trouble.

In the Master's name we pray.   Amen.

WEDNESDAY, JULY 3, 1968

I will keep Thy law continually, forever and ever; and I shall walk at liberty, for I have sought Thy precepts.—Psalm 119: 44, 45.

GOD OF OUR FATHERS, in whose name our Nation was conceived, under whose banner it was born and by whose spirit it continues to live in liberty under law, we pray that we may be worthy of the blessings so abundantly bestowed upon us.

In this difficult day and through these turbulent times may our faith in Thee and our faithfulness to our country reveal the superiority of our way of life. More than ever before may we be loyal to the truth, may we stand firm in honesty and at all times be deeply and sincerely compassionate.

May every lover of liberty, every citizen of our country, pledge his life and his honor to keep the laws of our land and to support the Constitution. May reverence for law and order be breathed into our children, be taught in our schools and universities, be proclaimed from our pulpits and be enforced by our courts of justice.

As we remember the signing of the Declaration of Independence let us again sing and pray:

> "Our fathers' God, to thee,
> Author of liberty,
>   To thee we sing;
> Long may our land be bright
> With freedom's holy light;
> Protect us by Thy might,
>   Great God, our King."

Amen.

TUESDAY, JULY 9, 1968

I will lift up mine eyes unto the hills, from whence cometh my help? cometh from the Lord, who made heaven and earth.—Psalm 121: 1, 2.

ETERNAL FATHER, who hast made us for Thyself so that our hearts are restless until they find rest in Thee, we, Thy children, come to Thee for help which Thou alone canst give.

Be Thou our fortress in the hour of temptation and give us the power to master ourselves. Be Thou our light when the way is dark and we do not know which way to turn. Be Thou our strength when the flesh is weak and the spirit is depressed. Be Thou our courage in the time of trouble and help us to walk in right paths. Be Thou our hope when our own hopes fail and but for Thee we would give way to despair.

Be Thou our help at all times and in all places and enable us to take from Thy hands the gifts of courage and strength and peace we need for this day in which we live.

Bless Thou our President, our Speaker, every Member of this body, and all who work with them. By Thy spirit lead us all into a greater allegiance to Thy purposes for mankind and may we become increasingly walking centers of good will in our world.

In the Master's name we pray.   Amen.

THURSDAY, JULY 11, 1968

Let Thy work appear unto Thy servants and Thy glory unto their children.—Psalm 90: 16.

O GOD AND FATHER OF US ALL, from the tumult of a troubled world and the demands of a disturbing day we would seek the quiet of Thy presence, not to evade our responsibilities, not to escape our duties but to turn to the tasks of this time with strong spirits, wise minds, and gentle hearts.

Dwelling in the secret place of the Most High and under the shadow of Thy spirit may we be given wisdom to make wise decisions, strength to carry heavy burdens, insight to see clearly, and courage to walk in Thy way as the wards of our wonderful country.

> "Lord of the nations, thus to Thee
> Our country we commend;
> Be Thou her refuge and her strength,
> Her everlasting friend,
> Both now and forevermore."

                                        Amen.

FRIDAY, JULY 12, 1968

Continue steadfastly in prayer.—Colossians 4: 2.

O Lord, our God, who knowest the problems that perplex us, the trials that trouble us, and the happenings that harass us, grant unto us the royalty of an inward happiness and the serenity of mind which comes from living close to Thee. Do Thou dwell in the heart of every one of us that we may have joy in living, courage for life, and enthusiasm for our country.

In our relations to others may we be persistent in patience, loyal in love, gentle in our goodness, and good in our gentleness. In our contacts with other nations may we be strong in spirit, generous in heart, and ready to help those who are willing to help themselves.

Before all the people on this planet may we have the confidence to stand for what is right and good for all. Thus may our deeds in private and our duties in public measure up to our devotion in prayer.

In the name of Him who took time to pray, we pray. Amen.

MONDAY, JULY 15, 1968

Thus saith the Lord, as I was with Moses, so I will be with you; I will not fail you or forsake you.—Joshua 1: 5.

O GOD AND FATHER OF MANKIND, whose creative spirit is ever seeking to lead us along the paths of truth and love, make us so mindful of Thy presence, so motivated by Thy spirit, so marked by Thy love that we may face this hour and live through these days with courage and strength and good will.

We pray for the captive nations of the world—for those who live in the darkness of fear and want, who cry for the flame of freedom and who pray for the life of liberty. Grant unto them confidence in every trial, courage to endure in every trouble, strength to resist every temptation to become cynical and in the depths of every depression may they hear Thy voice saying, "Be strong and of a good courage for I, the Lord thy God, am with thee."

Hasten the day when freedom shall be the faith of all, when good will shall dwell in the hearts of all and when men shall learn to live together with all.

Our Father, we come into Thy presence with sorrow in our hearts at the passing of one of our beloved colleagues. We thank Thee for him and pray that the comfort of Thy spirit may abide in the hearts of his loved ones. May their faith sustain them, their hope strengthen them, and their love support them.

In the spirit of Christ we pray. Amen.

WEDNESDAY, JULY 17, 1968

My soul waits upon God; from Him comes my salvation.—Psalm 62: 1.

O GOD OF GLORY AND LORD OF LIFE, we come to Thee in this our morning prayer and waiting upon Thee we would turn away from the clamor and clatter of the confused world about us.

Help us to greet this new day with the joy of gratitude, to overcome our difficulties with increased devotion, to carry our burdens with added strength, and to meet all ills and accidents with a gallant and high-hearted happiness, giving Thee thanks always for all things.

Deliver us from disagreements which make us disagreeable, from differences which make a difference in our associations, and from resentments which ruin our relationships.

Make us adequate for every adjustment we have to make, ready for every responsibility we have to carry, and equal to every emergency which comes our way. In the midst of busy days may we not forget Thee or be unmindful that we are here to serve our people and to keep our country physically strong, mentally awake, and morally straight.

In the Master's name we pray.   Amen.

MONDAY, JULY 22, 1968

Fear not, for I am with you; be not dismayed, for I am your God; I will strengthen you; yea, I will help you.—Isaiah 41: 10.

ALMIGHTY GOD, source of all wisdom, power, and love, help us with increasing fidelity to come to Thee for light upon our way, for strength that sustains us in our way, and for love which brightens our hearts along our way, that we may now, and always, do justly, love mercy, and walk humbly with Thee.

Living under the glorious banner of the Stars and Stripes may we make sure that the people on this planet shall continue to see America with the lamp of liberty held aloft and with the flag of freedom flying from the masthead of our Nation.

As we face the unfinished tasks before us may it be with courage and faith that we may make decisions wisely, plan our procedures skillfully, and develop our policies soundly for the good of all. In our work keep our minds clear, our hearts confident, our spirits courageous, and our hands clean that together we may move forward to a stronger nation and a better world.

In the name of Christ, we pray.   Amen.

WEDNESDAY, JULY 24, 1968

God hath made of one blood all nations of men to dwell upon the face of the earth that they should seek the Lord and find Him.—Acts 17: 26, 27.

O GOD, OUR FATHER, who hast made of one blood all nations of men to dwell upon the face of the earth and who dost call us to live together as Thy children, cleanse our national life of the spirit of discord and division; our racial life of the spirit of discrimination and disunion; and our personal lives of the spirit of disbelief and disillusionment.

Let our opinions of others be as thoughtful as our opinions of ourselves, our attitudes toward others be as good as our attitudes toward ourselves, and our relationships with others be as wise as our relationship with ourselves lest in bitterness and ill will we destroy each other.

In the midst of so many tragedies beyond our control but not beyond our compassion, may we place the weight of our influence upon the side of life and liberty and the pursuit of happiness for all men. Lead us and the nations of our world into the paths of peace and unity for Thy name's sake. Amen.

FRIDAY, JULY 26, 1968

He that abideth in Me and I in him, the same bringeth forth much fruit.— John 15: 5.

MOST MERCIFUL GOD, in this midday moment of meditation we come to Thee knowing Thou wilt receive us and never send us away emptyhanded or emptyhearted.

Make our minds shrines of Thy truth, our hearts sanctuaries of Thy love, and send us out into this new day with the glorious spirit of those who build highways of peace and good will among the children of men.

Help us now and always to walk worthily in the ways of Thy word and when temptations and troubles come may we prove to be faithful to Thee and fruitful in all good works.

We pray for our beloved country that she may be Thine instrument of good will in bringing together in a deep unity of spirit all the members of the human race.

In the spirit of Christ, we pray. Amen.

WEDNESDAY, JULY 31, 1968

Be of one mind, live in peace; and the God of love and peace shall be with you.—II Corinthians 13: 11.

O God, who art the source of light and life and the spring from which comes all noble endeavors, direct with Thy wise and gracious spirit the work of this day.

Give to these Representatives of our people insight into the needs of our Nation, inspiration to do something about it, and insistence that it be done and done for the good of all.

Guide, we beseech Thee, our President, our Speaker, all Members of Congress, and those who work so untiringly with them. Grant unto them wisdom of mind, strength of spirit, and vigor of body that supporting what is true and following what is good they may fulfill Thy purpose for mankind.

We commend to Thy loving care the men and women in the Armed Forces of our country. Defend them with Thy grace, strengthen them when tempted, give them courage to face danger's hour unafraid, and protect them wheresoe'er they go. Thus, evermore, shall rise to Thee glad hymns of praise from land and sea. Amen.

THURSDAY, AUGUST 1, 1968

If any of you lacks wisdom, let him ask of God, who giveth to all men liberally; and it will be given him.—James 1: 5.

O Thou Seeking Shepherd of our striving spirits whose goodness and mercy follow us all our days, may the thoughts in our minds and the attitudes of our hearts and the words on the lips be acceptable in Thy sight as we face the tasks of this day.

Amid the shifting scenes of modern movements we pray for strength to carry our burdens, for wisdom to solve our problems, for understanding to relate ourselves affirmatively to others, and for the faith of the patriot dream—

> That sees beyond the years
> Thine alabaster cities gleam,
> Undimmed by human tears!
> America, America,
> God shed his grace on thee,
> And crown thy good with brotherhood
> From sea to shining sea.

             Amen.

FRIDAY, AUGUST 2, 1968

O give thanks unto the Lord, for He is good; for His mercy endureth forever.—Psalm 107: 1.

Eternal God, Our Father, as we bring to a close this portion of the 90th Congress and look forward to a recess of a few weeks we turn again to Thee in prayer, as we have every day of this year, to acknowledge our dependence upon Thee and to offer unto Thee the devotion of our hearts. Thou hast been wonderfully good to us and our spirits rejoice, our minds give thanks, and our hearts take courage.

We thank Thee for the high privilege which has been ours to walk together and to work together in the service of our beloved country. We pray that our efforts may strengthen our Nation, improve the moral fiber of our people, increase law and order in our land, and meet the needs of all our citizens.

Now may the Lord bless us and keep us and return us with new vigor, new strength, and new enthusiasm on September 4.

In the Master's name we pray. Amen.

WEDNESDAY, SEPTEMBER 4, 1968

The righteous shall be glad in the Lord and shall trust in Him.—Psalm 64: 10.

Eternal God, Our Father, returning from a brief recess we assemble again in this shrine of our national life and bow our heads at the altar of prayer. Look with Thy favor upon us, upon our Speaker, the Members of this House of Representatives and their loved ones, and all who labor with them. Grant unto them to be healthy in body, hopeful in mind, and harmonious in spirit that they may think clearly, plan wisely, and work diligently. In deed and in truth may they be instruments of Thy will in this troubled time.

As we face the crucial days that lie ahead:

> God be in our heads
> And in our understanding;
> God be in our eyes
> And in our looking;
> God be in our mouths
> And in our speaking;
> God be in our hearts,
> And in our thinking;
> God be at our end,
> And at our departing.

In the Master's name we pray. Amen.

THURSDAY, SEPTEMBER 5, 1968

Brethren, ye have been called unto liberty; only use not liberty for an occasion to the flesh, but by love serve one another.—Galatians 5: 13.

O GOD, OUR HEAVENLY FATHER, in the quiet of this moment of prayer and with all sincerity of mind and heart we come to Thee who art the source of all wisdom, of all goodness and of all love.

Thou hast called us to work with Thee on behalf of our Nation and for the good of the world. Quicken Thou our love for our country and our concern for all mankind. Now and always may we keep our dedication to freedom, our devotion to truth, our delight in our democratic ways and our desire to make the world a better place for all people.

Grant us courage to be faithful in the struggle to make liberty the law and the life of all lands.

In the name of Him who sets men free we pray.   Amen.

TUESDAY, SEPTEMBER 10, 1968

The kingdom of God is not in word, but in power.—I Corinthians 4: 20.

O THOU WHO ART SEEKING TO LEAD US ALONG THE PATHS OF FREEDOM AND RIGHTEOUSNESS AND GOOD WILL, grant that in these decisive days we, the leaders of our people, may make wise decisions, be strengthened by Thy spirit to stand for what is sacred in life, and be given insight to see Thy way and inspiration to walk in it.

May we keep extending to one another the handclasp of friendship as together we march forward to the great task of establishing peace on earth and good will among the people on this planet.

Give to the nations the spirit which shall turn their hearts to the right and their minds to the rights of all that the darkness may turn to dawning and the dawning to noonday bright and Thy great kingdom shall come on earth, the kingdom of love and light.

In the name of Him who makes real the kingdom we pray.   Amen.

WEDNESDAY, SEPTEMBER 11, 1968

My meat is to do the will of Him who sent me and to finish His work.—John 4: 34.

O LORD, OUR GOD, grant unto us the spirit to think and the mind to do what is right and good that we may live according to Thy will.

Make us truly aware of what we are doing from day to day. We feel that we have so many things to do, so many meetings to attend, so many letters to write that we fail at times to see some of the things we ought to do and know full well should be done. Help us to take time for those things that matter most and less time for those things that matter least.

May we learn again not to major in minors but to master the matters that mean most to the morale and the morals of our modern mood.

Help us to think clearly, to choose wisely, and to make wise use of our time for Thy glory, for the good of our Nation, and for the benefit of all mankind.

In the Master's name we pray. Amen.

THURSDAY, SEPTEMBER 12, 1968

Not everyone that saith unto me, Lord, Lord, shall enter into the kingdom of heaven; but he that doeth the will of my Father who is in heaven.— Matthew 7: 21.

O GOD OF GRACE AND GLORY, on us pour Thy power as humbly we turn our spirits unto Thee in this our morning prayer.

We are grateful that our land has been blest with creative and courageous souls who have built on these shores a great Nation in which all men shall have the right to life, liberty, and the pursuit of happiness. Inspire us to continue their great work that our country may ever be the land of the free and the home of the brave.

God send us men whose aim will be
Not to defend some ancient creed,
But to live out the laws of Thine
In every thought and word and deed.
God send us men of steadfast will,
Patient, courageous, strong, and true,
With vision clear and mind equipped
Thy will to learn, Thy work to do.
God send us men with hearts ablaze,
All truth to love, all wrong to hate;
These are the patriots nations need,
These are the bulwarks of the state.

Amen.

MONDAY, SEPTEMBER 16, 1968

He who pursues righteousness and kindness will find life and honor.—
Proverbs 21: 21.

O GOD, OUR FATHER, whose glory is in all the world and whose spirit lives
in every breast, look with Thy favor upon us as we unite in prayer. Come
Thou anew into our lives and arise afresh within us that this day may be a
great day because we know that Thou art with us, and we are with Thee.

Kindle in our hearts and in the hearts of all men a true love for peace
and for law and order that in a real sense Thy kingdom of good will may
begin to come and Thy way of truth and love be trod by all the children
of men.

We commend to Thy care all who are engaged in the government of our
country. Continue to grant unto them an integrity of mind, a sincerity
of heart and an unfailing devotion to the welfare of our people. May all
legislation be worthy of our noblest efforts and for the good of all.

In the Master's name, we pray. Amen.

WEDNESDAY, SEPTEMBER 18, 1968

Thou wilt show me the path of life: in Thy presence is fullness of joy.—
Psalm 16: 11.

ETERNAL SPIRIT OF GOD, amid the tumult of these troubled times and the
difficulties of these demanding days, we come to this shrine of Thy presence
seeking strength for the day and wisdom for the hours that we may make
worthy decisions for the good of our Nation and the welfare of our people.
At this altar of prayer give to us the assurance that behind the failures and
the frustrations that mark many of our endeavors standeth Thy spirit ever
striving to hold us true to noble purposes and generous ways.

Empower these servants of our people and these leaders of our Nation that
they may bring to their daily tasks and growing responsibilities, minds illu-
mined by Thy presence, hearts aglow with Thy love, and hands ready to lift
the fallen, to strengthen the weak, and to give peace to those who have no
peace.

In the Master's name we pray. Amen.

WEDNESDAY, SEPTEMBER 25, 1968

For I the Lord thy God will hold thy right hand, saying unto thee Fear not; I will help thee.—Isaiah 41: 13.

O LORD, OUR GOD, from the rest of the night and with strength restored and spirits refreshed we launch out into another day which Thou hast made. In this moment of prayer make us strong to stand steady amid the sinister forces, within and without, which would deny freedom and degrade the dignity of man. Though all else change, keep our faith in Thee firm with growing trust and increasing confidence.

Deliver us from petty concerns about little things and stand us in the center of great needs. Then, help us to open our hearts to our people that we may endeavor to meet their needs, share in their struggles, glory in their achievements, and to lead them to a better life in a better nation in a better world.

In the name of Him who sets men free we pray.   Amen.

THURSDAY, SEPTEMBER 26, 1968

Truly my soul waiteth upon God; from Him cometh my salvation.— Psalm 62: 1.

O THOU WHO ART THE CREATOR OF THE WORLD, the sustainer of life, and the goal of our noblest endeavors, teach us to pray that in our prayers Thou canst draw nigh unto us. By Thy grace enable us to live through these days without frustration and with a firm faith in Thee, without discouragement and with a decisive devotion to our beloved Nation.

Give us wisdom and strength that we may rise above the confusion of this age, see clearly the needs of our people, strike forcefully at the roots of our Nation's ills, and make strong and clear the highway to an intelligent, united citizenship. May we keep the wheels of progress turning and never allow any rule or ruler to displace or destroy our democracy.

Abide with every Member of Congress and when they depart this day dismiss them with Thy blessing.

In the Master's name, we pray.   Amen.

MONDAY, SEPTEMBER 30, 1968

Hear my prayer, O Lord, and give ear to my supplications.—Psalm 143: 1.

WE THANK THEE, OUR FATHER, for this moment of prayer when we turn our hearts unto Thee and in all sincerity of mind and heart receive the guidance of Thy good spirit.

Let not the glory of this day, nor the glow of good health, nor the glamour of our position blind us to the seriousness of our tasks and deceive us into thinking that we can depend upon ourselves alone. All we are and all we have is a trust, O Lord, from Thee. Help us to be wise stewards of Thy gifts and to use them for Thy glory and to make more secure the freedoms of our country.

Bless these Representatives with Thy gracious favor, our people with the fruits of Thy loving spirit and all of us together with the faith in democracy that never falters and never fails.

We pray in the name of Him for whose kingdom we labor. Amen.

TUESDAY, OCTOBER 1, 1968

Behold, God is my salvation; I will trust and not be afraid.—Isaiah 12: 2.

O GOD AND FATHER OF US ALL, who art closer than breathing and nearer than hands and feet, make us truly conscious of Thy presence as we bow in this circle of prayer.

We thank Thee for the refreshment of rest which restores our souls and we ask for strength and wisdom to do our work well this day. In quiet confidence may we keep our hearts with Thee as we face the problems that are presented to us and the perplexities that pursue us.

In spite of all the ill will in our world we pray that we may be the promoters of good will in a firm determination to cross all barriers of race and creed and thus make our contribution to the coming day when justice and peace shall encircle the earth, and in the word of the prophet, "They shall not hurt nor destroy; for the earth shall be full of the knowledge of the Lord."

In the Master's name, we pray. Amen.

WEDNESDAY, OCTOBER 2, 1968

Have mercy upon me, O God, according to Thy loving kindness and blot out my transgressions.—Psalm 51: 1.

O THOU WHO ART THE SOURCE OF LIGHT AND LIFE, be with the Members of this body this holy day. Prosper them in their work, guide them in their tasks, forgive their sins, and bless them as they endeavor to do justly, to love mercy, and to walk humbly with Thee.

Fervently do we invoke Thy blessing upon our country. Protect her, O God, from calamity, discord, and violence. Let not any adversary triumph over her but let the glories of a just and righteous people filled with good will increase from age to age.

Enlighten with Thy wisdom and sustain with Thy power those in authority, our President, our Speaker, every Member of Congress, every judge, every executive, and everyone who is entrusted with our safety and with the guardianship of our rights and liberties.

May peace and good will be present in the hearts of all our citizens and may our common faith spread its blessings among us and exalt our Nation in justice and righteousness. Amen.

TUESDAY, OCTOBER 8, 1968

Teach me to do Thy will for Thou art my God and Thy spirit is good.— Psalm 143: 10.

E TERNAL FATHER OF US ALL, breathe upon us Thy lifegiving spirit as we wait upon Thee in prayer. We come to Thee facing tasks that tower above our ability to handle well and living through days that disturb us with their demanding duties. In the midst of these responsibilities may the strengthening power of Thy presence keep our hearts clean, our minds clear, and our spirits courageous.

Help us to hear Thy still, small voice sounding through the thundering noise of these tumultuous times, and hearing it may we work together with Thee to fashion our beloved country into an instrument of good will through which Thy good will may be done on earth.

In the Master's name, we pray. Amen.

THURSDAY, OCTOBER 10, 1968

*The Lord shall preserve thy going out and thy coming in from this time forth and even forevermore.—*Psalm 121: 8.

O UR FATHER GOD, whose mercy is over all Thy works and whose will is ever directed to Thy children's good, grant unto us the assurance that behind the shadows of our earthy scene stands One who slumbers not and in the midst of our joys and sorrows lives One whose strength never fails, and whose love never falters.

Now as we draw near to the close of this 90th Congress and look forward to the days ahead keep us mindful of Thy favor, eager to do Thy will, and ready to support our country in every good and noble way.

Some of these Representatives will be leaving not to return and some will be leaving to return—bless them all with Thy spirit. Give to them wherever they are and wherever they go, strength for daily tasks, patience, particularly when others are impatient, and a loving heart even amid the bitterness of those who differ with them. May they walk worthily in Thy wonderful way for the welfare of our country and the well-being of all mankind.

In the spirit of the Master we pray. Amen.

FRIDAY, OCTOBER 11, 1968

The Lord bless thee and keep thee and give thee peace.—Numbers 6: 24, 26.

God of our fathers, who are above all, and in all, and through all, we pause in Thy presence invoking Thy blessing upon us and upon the work of this year. We confess that we have fallen short of our best but in spite of our shortcomings we are grateful that we have had the high honor and the priceless privilege of working together to keep the flag of freedom and the banner of the rights of man flying in a world where freedom is denied and the rights of man are destroyed.

Now as the time of departing draws near we commit ourselves anew unto Thee and pray that Thou wilt strengthen us and continue to lead us as we endeavor to walk worthily in Thy way.

We clasp our hands together waiting for Thy blessing. May the Lord bless us and keep us, the Lord make His face to shine upon us and be gracious unto us, the Lord lift up His countenance upon us and give us peace, peace in our own hearts, peace in our beloved land, and peace in our world.

In the Master's name we pray. Amen.

SATURDAY, OCTOBER 12, 1968

If ye love Me, keep My commandments.—John 14: 15.

Eternal Spirit of God, who art from everlasting to everlasting unto Thee in this our morning prayer. Grant unto us wisdom to know Thy way, courage to set out upon it, and strength to walk in it. Save us from being too content with our lives and too satisfied with what we have done. Keep us from tolerating in ourselves what we condemn in others and help us to be understanding and forgiving. If changes are to be made let them begin in us. Thus may we be a part of the world's solution and not a part of its problems.

Renew our minds and hearts that we may present to this day a life honest and sincere, dedicated to the highest we know, and devoted to the best good of our beloved country.

In the spirit of Christ we pray. Amen.

MONDAY, OCTOBER 14, 1968

Keep yourselves in the love of God.—Jude 21.

ALMIGHTY GOD, from whom all thoughts of justice and peace proceed, kindle in our hearts and in the hearts of all our people a real love for brotherhood that we may learn to live together in peace with liberty and justice for all.

Most heartily do we pray that Thou wilt bless our President, our Speaker, the Members of Congress, and all who labor for them and with them. So rule their hearts and so direct their endeavors that law and order, justice and peace may here and everywhere prevail for the good of man and the glory of Thy holy name.

May virtue live in every heart, health and happiness in every home, friendship and fellowship in all our relationships, justice in our land, and peace in our world.

May Thy blessing abide with us now and forever more. Amen.

NINETY-FIRST CONGRESS
First Session

FRIDAY, JANUARY 3, 1969

"Behold," saith the Lord, "I have set before thee an open door."—Revelation 3: 8.

Eternal God, Our Father, as we enter the door of a new year and of a new Congress we pause in Thy presence to offer unto Thee the devotion of our hearts and to pray for guidance, strength, and wisdom as we face the crucial days that lie ahead.

In this high hour of a new beginning give to us, the leaders of our people, a deep sense of humility, a broad spirit of understanding, a great attitude of good will, and a real faith in Thee that we may govern well for the good of all and that freedom and justice may live long in our land.

Bless Thou our President as he leaves office ere long and our President-elect as he assumes his responsibilities. In this time of transition may there be a spirit of unity among us and may we go forward together to a greater nation and a better world.

We pray in the name of Him who taught His disciples to pray:

Our Father, who art in heaven, hallowed be Thy name. Thy kingdom come. Thy will be done, on earth as it is in Heaven. Give us this day our daily bread. And forgive us our trespasses, as we forgive those who trespass against us. And lead us not into temptation, but deliver us from evil. For thine is the kingdom, and the power, and the glory, forever. Amen.

MONDAY, JANUARY 6, 1969

The Lord give thee wisdom and understanding . . . that thou mayest keep the law of the Lord, thy God.—I Chronicles 22: 12.

O Lord of Love and God of all Goodness, in this sacred moment we bow at the altar of prayer thanking Thee for this glorious land in which we live. May we now and always prove ourselves a people mindful of Thy presence, eager to do Thy will, and ready to serve our fellow men. Save us from violence and discord. Mold us into a people united in purpose and principle, in faith and fortitude.

Endue with Thy wisdom all Members of Congress, especially this House of Representatives, and particularly our beloved Speaker. Direct their decisions, prosper their planning, and expedite their efforts as they seek to promote the welfare of our country and the good of all our citizens.

As a result of our endeavors may peace come to our world, justice rise to new life in our Nation, and happiness live in every human heart.

In the Master's name we pray.   Amen.

TUESDAY, JANUARY 7, 1969

Lead me in Thy truth and teach me, for Thou art the God of my salvation.—Psalm 25: 5.

O LORD, OUR GOD, grant unto the Members of this body, and all who work with them and for them, a fresh sense of Thy presence as we take up the duties of this day. May we learn to think Thy thoughts after Thee and to keep our hearts open to our people that to us will come wisdom as we make decisions, good will as we relate ourselves to one another, and courage as we endeavor to do what is right and good for all.

In this moment of prayer do Thou—

> Breathe on us, breath of God,
>   Fill us with life anew,
> That we may love what Thou dost love,
>   And do what Thou wouldst do.

In the Master's name we pray.   Amen.

WEDNESDAY, JANUARY 8, 1969

Speaking the truth in love, we are to grow up in every way into Him who is the head.—Ephesians 4: 15.

OUR FATHER IN HEAVEN AND ON EARTH, whose spirit dwells in the hearts of all men, make us conscious of Thy presence as we bow in prayer before Thee.

We have been taught to walk the way of truth and to live the life of love. May truth so triumph in our minds that we may overcome low prejudices with high principles and may love so live in our hearts that we may relate ourselves affirmatively to our fellow men. With truth and love alive within us may we devote ourselves to the welfare of our beloved country.

In the name of Him whose truth and love keeps men free we pray.

Amen.

THURSDAY, JANUARY 9, 1969

In the beginning God created the heaven and the earth.—Genesis 1: 1.

ALMIGHTY GOD, creator and sustainer of this wonderful universe in which we live, hour after hour Thou art speaking to us and day after day Thou art seeking to lead us. Help us to hear and to heed Thy word and to so respond to the leading of Thy spirit that the paths to peace may become plain and the ways of working together for freedom and justice may be made known to us.

In this knowledge and by this faith may we lead our Nation to deeper depths of devotion, to higher heights of honesty, and to greater goals of genuine good for the children of men.

We thank Thee for courageous men who, under the banner of our country, reach out for knowledge of other planets. We pray for them, for their safety, and for continued success in our astronautical endeavors. May the knowledge gained be used for the good of all men.

Hear us and help us, we beseech Thee, O Lord. Amen.

MONDAY, JANUARY 13, 1969

Be ye steadfast, unmovable, always abounding in the work of the Lord, forasmuch as ye know that your labor is not in vain in the Lord.— I Corinthians 15: 58.

ALMIGHTY GOD, Father of all men, who amid the trials and triumphs of trying times hast set eternity in our hearts, we turn to Thee at the beginning of another week knowing that without Thee all our labor is in vain.

In this high hour give to us, the leaders of our people, a true devotion to the welfare of our country, an outreaching concern for the well-being of all our citizens, and faith in Thee which opens for us the unfailing resources of spirit, bridges the differences which separate us, and makes us one in the glory of good will.

We thank Thee for brave men and women who by courage and faith have brought our country to the place of leadership among the nations of the world. Help us to honor our heritage by walking the ways of liberty and law. Give worth to our words, courage to our hearts, and strength to our hands as we strive to make patriotism beautiful and bright with the lift of our loyalty and the light of our love.

In the Master's name, we pray. Amen.

TUESDAY, JANUARY 14, 1969

*Fear the Lord and serve him faithfully with all your heart; for consider what great things He has done for you.—*I Samuel 12: 24.

O LORD, grant unto us to so love Thee with all our minds, with all our hearts, with all our strength, and our neighbors as ourselves, that the grace of brotherly love may dwell in us, that all harshness and ill will may die and our hearts be filled with compassion and love. Thus may we rejoice in the happiness and good success of others by sympathizing with them in their sorrows, by ministering to them in their needs, and by helping them in their efforts for a greater life with dignity and self-respect.

Keep ever before us the shining goal of a greater nation and a better world seeking the way to peace and the road to freedom for all.

> Incline our hearts with godly fear
> To seek Thy face, Thy word revere;
> Cause Thou all wrongs, all strife to cease,
> And lead us in the paths of peace.

In the dear Redeemer's name we pray.   Amen.

WEDNESDAY, JANUARY 15, 1969

The Spirit of the Lord is upon me.—Luke 4: 18.

Eternal God, our Heavenly Father, we come to Thee at this noontide moment of prayer humbly and gratefully for in Thee is the answer to our questions, the solution of our problems, and the goal of our noblest endeavors.

May it be our aim, as we meet daily in this historic Chamber, to meet the needs of struggling humanity, to strengthen the ties that bind free men together, and to find the way to peace among the nations of the world.

God bless America. Unite our people in safeguarding our liberties, in defending our institutions, and in supporting all men everywhere who live and fight and die for freedom.

May we realize more than ever that Thy spirit must touch and transform our own spirits if we are to continue to be free for in Thee alone is the life and the light and the law of liberty.

We pray in the name of Him whose life never fails, whose light never fades, and whose law never falters.   Amen.

MONDAY, JANUARY 20, 1969

You shall keep all the commandments which I command you this day, that you may be strong.—Deuteronomy 11: 8.

Almighty and Eternal God, we pray humbly and sincerely for our country, the land we love with all our hearts. We thank Thee for the men who founded our Republic and for those who through the years have kept the flame of freedom aglow in our world.

Now we invoke Thy blessing upon our President and Vice President as they take the oath of office and pledge their allegiance to this free land of their birth. Bless them with creative minds, courageous hearts and constructive hands as they endeavor to meet the challenge of these critical days.

Give us, the Representatives of our people, patience, wisdom, and understanding during this time of transition. Make us great enough for this day, strong enough for this hour, and good enough for this moment.

Bless all our people and help us as a nation to accept the privileges and responsibilities of sound citizenship, walking in the way of Thy commandments and keeping our faith in Thee. So rule our hearts and so prosper our endeavors that law and order, justice and peace may here and everywhere prevail to the glory of Thy name and the good of our country. Amen.

THURSDAY, JANUARY 23, 1969

He that handleth a matter wisely shall find good; and who so trusteth in the Lord, happy is he.—Proverbs 16: 20.

ALMIGHTY AND EVERLASTING GOD, who art always more ready to hear than we are to pray, and are wont to give more than we desire or deserve, pour out upon us an abundance of Thy mercy, cleansing us, forgiving us, and empowering us to do what is right and good for our country and our world.

Grant that what we say with our lips we may believe in our hearts and what we believe in our hearts we may practice with our lives, that in deed and in truth we may be doers of the word and not hearers only. In Thy light may we see life clearly and in Thy straight path may we not stumble. Through Jesus Christ, our Lord. Amen.

MONDAY, JANUARY 27, 1969

Thou wilt show me the path of life: in Thy presence is fullness of joy.—Psalm 16: 11.

OUR HEAVENLY FATHER, we pray that Thou wilt fill this sacred moment with the reality of Thy presence. Restore our souls, refresh our spirits, and reinvigorate our bodies that we may be made ready for the responsibilities of this day.

Grant unto us sincerity that we may persistently seek the things that endure, refusing those which perish, and that, amid things vanishing and deceptive, we may see the truth steadily, follow the light faithfully, and grow ever richer in that love which is the life of men.

We pray for those nations sitting around the peace table. Lead them into the ways of justice and truth and establish among them that peace which is the fruit of righteousness.

We meet this day with sadness in our hearts as we remember our beloved colleague who walks with us no more. We thank Thee for his life of public service and pray that the comfort of Thy presence may abide in the hearts of all who loved him and worked with him.

In the spirit of love we pray. Amen.

THURSDAY, JANUARY 30, 1969

I have strength for anything through Him who gives me power.—Philippians 4: 13.

In Thy Presence, Our Father, we pause for a moment, lifting our hearts unto Thee in prayer. As we pray, our strength is renewed, our courage restored, and our path is made plain. What we felt we could not do, now we can do; what we thought hopeless, is now full of hope; what seemed impossible, now becomes possible. We are ready for anything through the strength of Thy spirit living in our hearts.

Bless our Nation with Thy favor and make her a channel for peace and good will in our world. In Thy name we pray.   Amen.

MONDAY, FEBRUARY 3, 1969

Our sufficiency is from God.—II Corinthians 3: 5.

Eternal Father of our spirits, whose grace makes us sufficient for every task and whose strength holds us steady as we live through troubled times, speak Thou Thy word to us this day and make known Thy will that we may now and always walk along the paths of righteousness and justice and love.

Unite us as a nation that we may continue to seek the release of the captives, give light to those who sit in darkness, bridge the gulf which separates our people, and support every endeavor which creates and maintains understanding and good will in our national life.

In the spirit of Christ we offer this our morning prayer.   Amen.

TUESDAY, FEBRUARY 4, 1969

This I command you, that you love one another.—John 15: 17.

Dear Lord and Father of mankind, our spirit's unseen friend, we pray for every effort which is being made for peace and justice, for brotherhood and good will in our Nation, and throughout the world.

Breathe Thy spirit into every human heart that men may brothers be, and learn to live together in love, with understanding, and for the benefit of all Thy creatures.

Bless Thou our President, our Speaker, the Members of this House of Representatives, and all who labor under the glowing dome of this glorious Capitol. Preserve their health, give them wisdom, broaden their vision, and guide their aspirations that together we may seek the good of all mankind.

In the Master's name we pray.   Amen.

THURSDAY, FEBRUARY 6, 1969

And the Lord went before them by day in a pillar of cloud to lead them along the way, and by night in a pillar of fire to give them light.—Exodus 13: 21.

O GOD, OUR FATHER, in generation after generation men have sought Thee and have found that Thy faithfulness never fails, Thy love never falters, and Thy strength never fades. Our fathers walked by the guidance of Thy spirit and rested in Thy mercy, so to us, their children, be Thou a pillar of cloud by day and a pillar of fire by night to give us light upon our way, strength to walk along it, and peace in our hearts.

Remove the veil from every heart and unite us into one people as we walk together toward the promised land where free men shall dwell together in peace and good will.

In the Master's name we pray. Amen.

FRIDAY, FEBRUARY 7, 1969

My brethren, be strong in the Lord and in the power of his might.— Ephesians 6: 10.

GOD OF OUR FATHERS, amid the tumult of troubled times may we keep within our hearts a calm and a quiet place where Thou dost dwell, where Thy power strengthens us, Thy wisdom makes us wise, and Thy goodness keeps us good.

At times may we withdraw from the loud hatred of the world and the noisy bitterness of men and silently lift our hearts unto Thee in prayer. Then alive with Thy spirit may we face our daily tasks with courage and faith and hope.

Bless Thou our country. Make her faithful in her devotion to truth, great in her desire for honor, strong in her willingness to serve, and wise in her dealings with other nations. By doing Thy will may we bring peace to our world, peace to our Nation, and peace to our hearts. In the Master's name we pray. Amen.

MONDAY, FEBRUARY 17, 1969

The Lord give thee wisdom and understanding, that thou mayest keep the law of the Lord, thy God.—I Chronicles 22: 12.

O LORD OF LOVE AND GOD OF ALL GOODNESS, in this sacred moment we bow at the altar of prayer thanking Thee for the recess we have had and praying for Thy guidance as we face the days that lie ahead.

With the wings of Thy wisdom and the strength of Thy spirit may we accept the heavy responsibilities placed upon us in this high hour of our national life. During these turbulent times filled with the bitter tones of angry hatred, help us to hear Thy still, small voice speaking the words of justice and freedom and peace:

> Be Thou our wisdom, O Thou our true word;
> We ever with Thee, and Thou with us, Lord;
> Thou our Great Father, we Thy true sons;
> Thou in us dwelling, and we with Thee one.

Amen.

THURSDAY, FEBRUARY 20, 1969

Blessed is the nation whose God is the Lord.—Psalm 33: 12.

OUR FATHERS' GOD, to Thee, author of liberty, to Thee we pray; long may our land be bright with freedom's holy light; protect us by Thy might, great God, our King.

In this temple of freedom we give Thee thanks for the spirit and the service of our first President whom we affectionately call the Father of Our Country. We remember his courage in times of crisis, his fidelity during periods of adversity, and his faith which made him bend his knees on frozen ground that he might find strength and confidence to continue the struggle for independence.

Grant that the remembrance of this great life may strengthen us and our people to live and to labor for the freedom of all mankind. Thus may we ever be one nation, under Thee, with liberty and justice for all.

We pray in the spirit of the Lord of Life. Amen.

TUESDAY, FEBRUARY 25, 1969

If you continue in My word, you are My disciples, and you will know the truth.—John 8: 31, 32.

O THOU WHO ART THE TRUTH THAT MAKES MEN FREE AND THE LOVE THAT GIVES THEM LIFE, strengthen us by Thy spirit that no danger may overwhelm us and no discouragement overcome us. Make us one of that splendid company who find in Thy service perfect freedom and who in loyalty to Thee commit their lives to purposes greater than themselves.

Help us to make good use of this day, seeking always to know what Thou wouldst have us do. Beginning this hour with a vision of Thy presence, may we continue in dependence upon Thy spirit and come to rest at eventide knowing Thou art with us and that we have been with Thee all the day long.

Bless our President as he seeks peace and unity among the nations. Crown his efforts with enduring success and give him wisdom as he talks with the leaders and people of other lands. Grant him a safe return with greater ideas for the good of all and with a firmer faith in the goals of free men.

In the spirit of our Lord we pray. Amen.

WEDNESDAY, FEBRUARY 26, 1969

He who is of God hears the words of God.—John 8: 47.

O GOD, whose strength supports us in our labor and whose spirit sustains us in our work, give us a new and a fresh realization of Thy presence as we wait upon Thee in prayer. Grant unto us patience when we demand too much too soon and decisions do not go our way; courage in the face of apparent defeat that we may still believe in the ultimate victory of the good for the good of all; and love when we falter in fear and fail in faithfulness that we may have the steady assurance that Thou art with us loving us unto the very end and strengthening us for every noble endeavor.

Deliver our Nation from the spirit of discord and disunity and lead us in the paths of peace and prosperity, for Thy name's sake. Amen.

MONDAY, MARCH 3, 1969

O come, let us worship and bow down; let us kneel before the Lord, our Maker.—Psalm 95: 6.

O GOD, OUR FATHER, out of the confusion of the world we come with humble hearts to worship Thee. From the things that man has done we come into Thy presence to think of what Thou hast done for man. As we wait upon Thee, renew in us the spirit of wonder and joy and love.

From our worship send us out into this day to be better citizens of our beloved country. Put depth and devotion and dedication into our patriotism. May we not simply salute our Nation's flag and sing our country's songs, but may we shoulder some burden of useful and redeeming service for this land we love with all our hearts. Enlist each one of us in the ranks of those who serve their community and who lift the level of our public life. Thus may we make of our land a fairer place in which our children may live and grow.

In the spirit of Christ we pray. Amen.

TUESDAY, MARCH 4, 1969

The Lord is my defence: and God is the rock of my refuge.—Psalm 94: 22.

O GOD AND FATHER OF US ALL, who art the creator and the sustainer of all mankind, we pray that our lives may be built not upon the shifting sands of superficial spirits but upon the firm foundation of a fruitful faith in Thee.

As we pray, reveal to us Thy glory, make known Thy wisdom, and awaken in us a greater desire for goodness, truth, and love that our affections may be purified, our ambitions refined, our minds cleansed, and a right spirit be renewed within us. Ennobled by Thy presence, may we be, for our generation, channels through which Thy kingdom may come and Thy will be done on earth.

We pray for our Nation that our people may grow in a sense of responsibility, may cultivate the spirit of good will, and may dare to be pioneers in brotherhood sustaining the hands and hearts of all who venture to end strife and to bring in peace.

In the name of Him who said, "Love one another," we pray. Amen.

THURSDAY, MARCH 6, 1969

To this end we toil and strive, because we have our hope set on the living God.—I Timothy 4: 10.

O God, Our Father, who hast called us to walk in Thy way and to live with love in our hearts, grant unto us the steady assurance that although we forget Thee Thou dost not forget us, and that notwithstanding the fact we let Thee down Thou dost never let us down. May Thy spirit abiding in us through all our changing moods sustain us in every right and good effort.

Bless Thou the young people of our land. Let not the undue license of a few limit the due liberty of the majority. Strengthen our youth that they may have full regard for the rights of all their fellows. Help them to use their freedom to discover themselves at their very best, to find creative channels for their restless endeavors, and to live and labor for justice by all, good will among all and liberty for all.

In the name of Him who was true to Himself, to others, and to Thee, we pray. Amen.

MONDAY, MARCH 10, 1969

Let us hear the conclusion of the whole matter: fear God and keep his commandments: for this is the whole duty of man.—Ecclesiastes 12: 13.

O Thou who hast made us and dost keep us day by day, we bow in Thy presence at the beginning of another week to offer unto Thee the devotion of our hearts. Grant unto each one of us inner resources of spiritual power that we may not be overcome by troubles, but rising above them make each day a pageant of triumph. Make us such radiant personalities and so filled with good will that we may commend to the world the faith we profess.

We pray for our Nation, our President, our Speaker, Members of our Congress, those who work with them, and all our people. Following the leading of Thy spirit and walking in the way of Thy commandments, may we here in America find a new unity in a common faith and a common endeavor, and living close to Thee find ourselves closer to each other; through Jesus Christ our Lord. Amen.

WEDNESDAY, MARCH 12, 1969

Now abideth faith, hope, love, these three: but the greatest of these is love.—I Corinthians 13: 13.

O THOU ETERNAL SOURCE OF WISDOM, power and love, lead us through changes of this life upon earth to rest our spirits upon Thee. Help us to see Thee more clearly, to think about Thee more frequently, to pray to Thee more earnestly, and to do Thy will more faithfully. In Thee may we find confidence and courage for the living of these days.

In our minds we name before Thee those near and dear to us, and others whose lives have blended with ours and bring to us a sense of privilege and responsibility. Do Thou bless them mightily and sustain them in Thy service. Lay Thou Thy hand upon all those who are sick, comfort those who are sad, give courage to the discouraged, strength to the weak, light to those who sit in darkness, and love to those who would keep bitterness in their hearts.

We pray for our beloved land that we as a nation of free people may choose wisely, live worthily, relate ourselves to others affirmatively, and dare to be pioneers in brotherhood, strengthening the hands of those who would lead us in the paths of peace. Together may we go forward to build the kingdom of justice and truth and love among the children of men.

In the Master's name we pray. Amen.

MONDAY, MARCH 17, 1969

Give ear, O Lord, unto my prayer; and attend to the voice of my supplications.—Psalm 86: 6.

BLESS US THIS DAY, OUR FATHER, with a fresh realization of Thy presence, and strengthen us to face our tasks with faith and with fortitude. As we meet at the beginning of another week, gird our lives that they may be armored with all Christ-like graces in the fight to set men free. Grant us wisdom, grant us courage, that we fail not man nor Thee.

Help us to keep our minds clear, our hearts clean, and our spirits confident. May we live so honestly and so hopefully that no disputes may discourage us, no failure cause us to falter, and no falsehood make us false to ourselves, to others, or to Thee.

Give to us Thy love and in all the changes of this life upon earth; keep us loyal and loving unto the very end. Then open wide to us the gates of life eternal, through Him who lives forever. Amen.

TUESDAY, MARCH 18, 1969

They that wait upon the Lord shall renew their strength; they shall walk and not faint.—Isaiah 40: 31.

Eternal God and Father of us all, as we live through the hours of this day may we be humble in spirit, helpful in attitude, faithful in service, and fruitful in all good works.

Deliver us from worries that wear us out, from resentments that tear us down, and from frustrations that weaken our morale. Help us to realize that though life may have for us many difficulties and some disagreements, we must not allow difficulties to become too discouraging, nor permit disagreements to make us too disagreeable, and certainly never allow them to weaken our faith or lower our ideals.

Grant wisdom and courage to our President, our Speaker, all Members of Congress, and those who work diligently with them as they set themselves to solve the problems that confront our Nation in these trying times.

Together may all of us walk in Thy way and not faint.

In the Master's name we pray. Amen.

MONDAY, MARCH 24, 1969

Be not deceived; God is not mocked: for whatsoever a man soweth, that shall he also reap.—Galatians 6: 7.

Our Heavenly Father, grant unto us once again the assurance of Thy sustaining presence as we bow in this circle of prayer. Inspire us with a firmer trust in Thee and with a sympathetic outreach of good will toward all the children of men.

Give to each one of us the realization that Thy power is at work in the world moving in the direction of justice, peace, and love among all nations and in the hearts of all men. Thou art always with us—do Thou help us always to be with Thee.

Bless our Nation with Thy favor and as a people make us mindful of Thy presence and ever eager to do Thy will.

In the spirit of Christ we pray.   Amen.

TUESDAY, MARCH 25, 1969

My defense is of God, who saveth the upright in heart.—Psalm 7: 10.

O GOD, who art a strong tower of defense to those who put their trust in Thee, have mercy upon us as we bow in prayer before Thee and gird us for the experiences of this day. Grant that in moments of low moods and in minutes of high moods we may keep our faith in Thee in whom alone true life is to be found.

Forgive the ways we have placed shackles about ourselves and others, the intolerance we have shown when others differed from us, the envy we have revealed when some have received what we thought we deserved, the prejudices we have mistaken for principles, and the ill will generated at the success of others. May we pray not only to be forgiven but to learn to be forgiving.

Amid the perplexities of this period may we always remember to be kind and generous, understanding and upright in heart, knowing that he who lives in Thy spirit and who keeps Thy commandments is walking in the way of truth and love—the best defense our Nation can ever have.

We pray in the spirit of Him who walked the way of the loving heart.

Amen.

WEDNESDAY, MARCH 26, 1969

Finally, brethren, be of one mind, live in peace: and the God of love and peace shall be with you.—II Corinthians 13: 11.

ETERNAL SPIRIT, who art ever speaking to man and always seeking to lead Thy children into the ways of peace, we pray for our country.

Strengthen our leaders that they may walk with Thee as they carry their responsibilities. Sustain our people that in true service and with humble hearts they may usher in a new day of peace by doing Thy will.

So unite us in our love for Thee and by our confidence in one another that together we may hasten the day when "Nation shall not lift up sword against nation, neither shall they learn war any more."

With this creative faith and this courageous spirit may we march forward together toward a greater nation and a better world.

In the name of the Prince of Peace we pray.   Amen.

MONDAY, MARCH 31, 1969

Yea, though I walk through the valley of the shadow of death, I will fear no evil: for Thou art with me.—Psalm 23: 4.

ALMIGHTY AND ETERNAL GOD, the comforter of Thy children and the strength of those who put their trust in Thee, we assemble this day with sorrow in our hearts at the passing of General of the Army Dwight David Eisenhower, our beloved 34th President. Even in the sadness of farewell we think fondly of him who walked so worthily in our midst and who served so well as the leader of our country.

We mourn his passing because he reflected in his own personality the tradition of a free people and revealed in his life the shrine of our Nation's faith and hope.

We thank Thee for him, for his courage of mind and heart, for his strength of character, for his desire to do what he firmly believed to be right and for his devotion to his family and to his country. Certainly our United States is a better nation—stronger and freer—because he lived and led us in war and in peace.

So we honor the memory of this great and good man, "who more than self his country loved," and in so doing we dedicate ourselves anew to Thee and to our Nation in the global struggle between democracy and dictatorship.

Comfort the family with Thy sustaining spirit and strengthen them for these hours and for the days to come. Keep them and us, steady and strong, this day and forever more. Amen.

TUESDAY, APRIL 1, 1969

He that giveth, let him do it with simplicity; he that ruleth with diligence; he that showeth mercy with cheerfulness.—Romans 12: 8.

O GOD, OUR FATHER, in whose love is our life, in whose service is our strength, and in whose will is our work, grant unto us increasing power that we may labor unceasingly for the welfare of our country and the well-being of all mankind.

Save us from discord and disunity, from pride and prejudice, from vice and violence. Fashion us into a people united in purpose and program to promote justice, to proclaim freedom, and to provide food for the hungry, housing for the ill housed, and jobs for men who will work.

May the spirit of wisdom abide in all our hearts that we may make decisions daringly, plan procedures patiently, and live with love the light in our lives.

In times of trouble let not our faith in Thee falter and in periods of prosperity let our faith find its fulfillment in humble service and a grateful spirit.

In the name of Christ we pray. Amen.

WEDNESDAY, APRIL 2, 1969

Herein is my Father glorified, that ye bear much fruit.—John 15: 8.

ALMIGHTY GOD, by whose spirit men of old were guided in their decisions, direct, we beseech Thee, the deliberations of Congress this day. Help us to do well the work we have to do and may it be for the good of all.

To our President, our Speaker, and to all who share with them the responsibility of planning the program for our beloved country, grant spiritual strength, wise counsel, and an adventurous faith that they may continue to lead our people toward the high goal of one nation, under Thee, indivisible, with liberty and justice for all.

In the spirit of Christ we pray. Amen.

THURSDAY, APRIL 3, 1969

A new commandment I give unto you, that you love one another.—John 13: 34.

OUR FATHER GOD, as we continue our pilgrim way this holy week, entering an upper room, climbing the hill called Calvary, and realizing anew the glory of the Easter morn, we pause in Thy presence to lift our hearts unto Thee in praise and thanksgiving.

We thank Thee for Thy love revealed in the experiences of these days, for Thy forgiving love made known in the way of the cross, and for Thy strengthening power received in our response to Thy love and Thy forgiving mercy.

Bless us and our Nation in these crucial days that we may continue to be crusaders in the cause of human freedom, workers for an enduring peace, and cultivators of good will in the hearts of all people.

> Draw Thou my soul, O God, closer to Thine;
> Breathe into every wish Thy will divine.
> Raise my low self above, won by Thy deathless love;
> Ever, O God, through mine let Thy life shine.
> In the spirit of Christ, we pray.

Amen.

TUESDAY, APRIL 15, 1969

God has not given us the spirit of fear; but of power, and of love, and of a sound mind.—II Timothy 1: 7.

Most Gracious and Loving God, the strength of all who put their trust in Thee and the light of those who walk in Thy way, make us truly conscious of Thy presence as we enter this new day fresh from Thy hand. Grant that in the stress and strain of these troubled times we may never lose heart or hope.

We pray that our President, our Speaker, and all the Members of this House of Representatives may be abundantly blessed with the strengthening presence of Thy spirit as they labor earnestly for good will in our Nation, for peace in our world, and for the good of all mankind.

In all our endeavors on behalf of our country may we be ever mindful that our highest resources are spiritual, and upon the foundation of justice, righteousness, and good will may we build our life as a nation, and seek to build our lives together on this planet.

In the spirit of Christ we pray.   Amen.

WEDNESDAY, APRIL 16, 1969

By grace you have been saved through faith, and this is not your own doing, it is the gift of God.—Ephesians 2: 8.

Our Father God, in whom we live and move and have our being, we humbly pray Thee so to guide and govern us by Thy spirit that in all the procedures of these hours we may never forget that Thou art with us. Send us out into this new day sustained by—

> A faith that shines more bright and clear
> When tempest rage without;
> That when in danger knows no fear,
> In darkness feels no doubt.

Into Thy keeping we commit our country and all who live and fight and die for her that freedom may continue to be gloriously alive in our world. Strengthen them in danger; comfort them in sorrow; keep them steadfast in the performance of duty and ever loyal to this Nation we love with all our hearts.

Lead us, our Father, in the paths of right; blindly we stumble when we walk alone, only with Thee do we journey safely on.

In the name of Him who is the way, we pray. Amen.

THURSDAY, APRIL 17, 1969

I must work the works of Him that sent Me, while it is day.—John 9: 4.

GOD OF OUR FATHERS AND OUR GOD, cleanse the thoughts of our hearts by the inspiration of Thy Holy Spirit that we may truly love Thee and worthily serve Thee this day.

May our hearts be with Thee as we seek solutions to the grave and global problems that confront us and our Nation.

In this dear land of our birth, help us to close ranks in a greater unity of spirit as principalities and powers without seek to destroy our heritage of freedom, with liberty and justice for all.

Make us great enough in spirit that we may be equal to every experience, ready for every responsibility, and adequate for every activity.

In the name of the Master Workman, we pray. Amen.

MONDAY, APRIL 21, 1969

The Lord thy God bless thee in all the work of thine hand which thou doest.—Deuteronomy 14: 29.

O LORD, OUR GOD, whose glory is in all the world and whose goodness shines in all that is fair, we commit ourselves and our country to Thy merciful care: that being guided by Thy spirit we may learn to dwell together in Thy peace and to live by Thy laws.

Grant that the work of this day may be in accordance with Thy will. Give to us health of body, clarity of mind and strength of spirit that we may do what we have to do with all our hearts.

Deliver us from the fear that destroys, from the futility that deadens, and from the frustration that discourages us. Do Thou help us to work to make our dreams come true and to dream to make our work worth doing.

Keep our Nation strong in Thee. Let us walk and work together humbly and in all good will that in faith and freedom Thy glory shall be revealed in every effort we make to share in the work of the world: through Jesus Christ by whose life we have been redeemed. Amen.

TUESDAY, APRIL 22, 1969

My beloved brethren, be ye steadfast, unmovable, always abounding in the work of the Lord, for as much as ye know that your labor is not in vain in the Lord.—I Corinthians 15: 58.

O THOU GIVER OF EVERY GOOD AND PERFECT GIFT, we are grateful for the opportunities for good which have been ours; for the love in our homes; for the fellowship of friends; for the freedom to worship as we desire, and for the happy experience of serving our country in this House of Representatives. Keep us ever alive with gratitude for Thy goodness to us.

Do Thou forgive our mishandling of some of Thy gifts—the opportunity neglected, the untruth accepted, the shallow judgment made, and the cynicism enjoyed. Forgive the unkind word, the unjust criticism, the false ambition, and every unworthy spirit which has reigned in our hearts.

May the light of Thy love and the triumph of Thy truth purify us and send us out into this day to be true to Thee, loyal to our country, and in love with our fellow men.

In the name of Him who reveals life to us we pray.   Amen.

MONDAY, APRIL 28, 1969

Fear God and keep His commandments; for this is the whole duty of man.—Ecclesiastes 12: 13.

O GOD OF LOVE AND FATHER OF MERCY, we rejoice and our hearts take courage when we realize that Thou art always with us, available for every need and ready to help when we turn to Thee.

Each day at this noontide moment of prayer we seek Thy sustaining presence because we are meeting problems beyond our wisdom and managing responsibilities beyond our strength to carry.

Give to our President, our Speaker, every Member of this body, and those who work with them a clear sense of Thy guiding spirit as they endeavor to master the difficulties that beset our country.

In all our efforts to do what is right and good for all may we maintain a faith that never falters, a courage that never fails, and a good will that never fades.

Bless our Nation with Thy favor and make us ever eager to participate in the adventure of leading man and nations into the glorious light and life of liberty.

In the Master's name we pray.   Amen.

WEDNESDAY, APRIL 30, 1969

Beloved, follow not that which is evil, but that which is good. He that doeth good is of God.—III John 1: 11.

O Thou who hearest prayer and answereth according to Thy wisdom, to Thee we come in this silent moment of quiet devotion. We humble ourselves in Thy presence confessing that we have done that which we ought not to have done and left undone that which we should have done. Do Thou have mercy upon us, forgive us and send us out into this day with creative minds to think clearly, with hearts warm with love to spread good will, and with hands ready to serve Thee more fully and our country more faithfully.

Help us to bridge the chasms which separate men, to heal the festering sores which infect our national life, to foster unity among our people, and to promote cooperation between the nations of the world.

Breathe upon us Thy spirit, reveal to us Thy way and give us courage to walk in it to the glory of Thy holy name. Amen.

MONDAY, MAY 5, 1969

If My people humble themselves, and pray, and seek My face, and turn from their wicked ways, then will I hear from heaven, and will forgive their sin and heal their land.—II Chronicles 7: 14.

A lmighty Father, at this sacred moment of prayer we pause in silence before Thee, seeking the wise guidance of Thy worthy spirit as we face the problems that beset us and think of the decisions we must make.

In these critical days of our national life help us to see the way and give us the courage to walk in it, that we may promote the values which have made our Nation great and possess the virtues which have kept her strong.

During this time of turmoil when the spirit of revolution is in the air, when wrong seems at times triumphant and goodness so feeble, may we be sure of Thee and know that behind the shadows standeth Thy presence which never fails. May we realize anew that—

> This is my Father's world, and let me ne'er forget
> That though the wrong seems oft so strong,
> Thou art the ruler yet.

In Thy name we pray. Amen.

WEDNESDAY, MAY 7, 1969

Watch ye, stand fast in the faith, quit you like men, be strong.—I Corinthians 16: 13.

ALL PRAISE, honor and glory be unto Thee, O Father Almighty, for Thy loving kindness and Thy tender mercies which have been ours all the days of our lives. Protect us in our freedom and preserve us in our faith by Thy spirit of truth made known to us as we pray.

Cleanse the strivings of our hearts and clear our minds of stress and strain that inner peace may be ours and enduring peace may come to our world.

In this dark day may we as a nation not curse the darkness but keep the candles of faith and hope and love alight that all may see the way to life with liberty and justice and peace for all.

> "Dear Lord and Father of mankind,
> Forgive our foolish ways;
> Reclothe us in our rightful minds,
> In purer lives Thy service find,
> In deeper reverence, praise."

Amen.

THURSDAY, MAY 8, 1969

Continue steadfastly in prayer, being watchful in it with thanksgiving.—Colossians 4: 2.

O GOD, who art above us and yet within us in all reverence of mind and heart, we bow before Thee, acknowledging our dependence upon Thee and offering unto Thee the loyalty and love of our hearts. In this day when pagan forces would overwhelm us and a secular spirit would engulf our world, keep our honor bright, our hearts pure, our minds clean, and our devotion to Thee and our country steadfast and sure.

During these trying times when decisions are made which will determine the direction our Nation takes, help us to maintain our integrity, to rise above personal ambition and to put first that which is first, the welfare of our country and the good of our people.

Give to us the inspiration and the industry to continue to work for justice and peace and freedom both at home and abroad.

In the spirit of Christ we pray.   Amen.

MONDAY, MAY 12, 1969

Holy Father, protect by the power of Thy name those whom Thou hast given Me, that they may be one.—John 17: 11.

ALMIGHTY GOD, OUR FATHER, we come to Thee in earnest prayer that Thou wilt keep our country under Thy divine protection; that Thou wilt incline our citizens to live by the laws of our land; and that Thou wilt help our people to so cultivate a spirit of good will that they may learn to live together in peace and without fear.

We cannot all be of the same mind nor can we think alike, but we pray that Thou wilt make us one in our loyalty to our Nation, one in our love for liberty, and one in our search for justice and peace.

Deliver us from pride and prejudice, from intolerance, and from every evil way. By the might of Thy spirit within us may we show forth in our lives the fruit of our faith and the power of our principles.

In the Master's name we pray. Amen.

TUESDAY, MAY 13, 1969

Let us draw near with a true heart in full assurance of faith.—Hebrews 10: 22.

GOD OF OUR FATHERS AND OUR FATHER GOD, who art sending Thy spirit into the hearts of men seeking to bring justice and peace to our world, may we with open minds and receptive hearts receive Thy spirit and with Thee strive to make justice and peace a reality in our day.

Give us grace to take to heart the dangers involved in our unhappy divisions and our unhallowed differences. Remove from us all that hurts our unity of spirit and all that hinders our forward march together. Kindle in us the fire of Thy redeeming love, strengthen us by Thy power and draw us closer to one another.

To Thee and to our country we consecrate the work of this day.

In the Master's name we pray. Amen.

THURSDAY, MAY 15, 1969

You will seek Me and find Me; when you seek Me with all your heart.— Jeremiah 29: 13.

O LORD, OUR GOD, who art ever calling upon us to walk in Thy way, to try Thy truth and to live Thy life, grant that the spirit of our prayer this moment may be acceptable to Thee and our hearts be in harmony with Thy holy will.

Help us to consider carefully our pilgrimage upon this planet, to measure the deeds of the past by our devotion to the present and our dedication for the future. When we think of what we could have done had we given ourselves wholly to Thee we feel humble and are heartily sorry for our misdoings.

In reverence we come to Thee again and lay our supplications before Thee. Help us to right the wrongs we have done to others and give us grace to forgive those who wrong us. Enlighten our minds with truth, enlarge our hearts with love and enlist us in the struggle for justice in our Nation and peace in our world.

In the spirit of Christ we pray.　Amen.

MONDAY, MAY 19, 1969

I urge that supplications, prayers, intercessions, and thanksgivings be made for all men.—I Timothy 2: 1.

ALMIGHTY GOD, OUR HEAVENLY FATHER, who art with our astronauts flying through space and who art with us walking on this planet, make us positive factors in the world's fields of endeavors as we seek to extend our knowledge of the universe, to cultivate justice among men, peace between nations, and good will in the hearts of all men.

Make plain Thy path, help us to see it clearly and then give us courage to walk in it knowing Thou art with us all the way.

In this troubled time save us from the hot fever of foolish action and from the cold fear which would make futile any activity on our part. May Thy spirit live in us and in so doing lead us to a life together where men may live with dignity, self respect, and understanding love.

Bless our astronauts, bless Thou the men and women in our Armed Forces; may their contribution and ours become a blessing to our Nation and to all mankind.　Amen.

THURSDAY, MAY 22, 1969

Eye hath not seen, nor ear heard, the things which God hath prepared for them that love Him.—I Corinthians 2: 9.

ALMIGHTY AND EVERLASTING GOD, from whom all thoughts of truth and love proceed; kindle in our hearts and in the hearts of all men a real love for the truth and a deep concern for peace.

Guide with Thy wisdom those who lead our Nation, our President, our Speaker, the Members of this House of Representatives, and all who work with them under the dome of this Capitol, that in all good will Thy kingdom may go forward and Thy will be done on earth.

Make real in our hearts the spirit of Thy love; strengthen us by Thy power; draw us closer to Thee and, in so doing, bind us together in a firm and a faithful bond of unity, through Jesus Christ our Lord. Amen.

WEDNESDAY, MAY 28, 1969

Let us follow after the things which make for peace.—Romans 14: 19.

ETERNAL GOD, OUR FATHER, in whom our fathers trusted and were never let down, bless us this day as we bow before Thee in loving memory of those who laid down their lives for our country.

We thank Thee for men and women in time past who gave themselves that freedom may have fresh air in our Nation, and we are grateful for those in time present who are giving themselves that liberty may continue to live in our land.

That these may not have lived and died in vain we pray Thee to unite our people in one great purpose to preserve the principles of freedom, justice, and good will, and by Thy grace may we learn to live together in the spirit of true brotherhood.

Pour out Thy spirit upon us in such measure that we may turn from war to peace, from poverty to plenty, and from hate to love, through Jesus Christ our Lord. Amen.

MONDAY, JUNE 2, 1969

From the rising of the sun unto the going down of the same the Lord's name is to be praised.—Psalm 113: 3.

ALMIGHTY GOD, our loving Heavenly Father, who art clothing the world with beauty and throwing a mantle of green across the shoulders of the hills, by whose law the planets keep their courses and by whose creative thought life has risen on this planet, make us conscious of Thy presence and help us to be patient and strong in Thee.

May the thoughts of our minds be channels for Thy way. May the dreams in our hearts fulfill Thy purposes for our Nation and for mankind. May the work of our hands weed out injustice and war and cultivate the seeds that flower into justice for all and peace in our world. By Thy spirit may we have courage enough to be pioneers in brotherhood, sustaining the hands and hearts of all who seek to end strife and to bring peace to the hearts of men.

To this end guide Thou our President, our Speaker, the Members of this body and all who labor with them. Ennoble their lives by the sense of Thy presence that they may be for this generation channels through which Thy kingdom may come and Thy will be done on earth.

In the Master's name, we pray. Amen.

WEDNESDAY, JUNE 4, 1969

God be merciful unto us and bless us; and cause His face to shine upon us.—Psalm 67: 1.

O THOU WHO ART THE BRIGHT SUN OF THE WORLD SENDING THY LIGHT UNTO ALL THY CREATION, shine Thou upon our hearts as we pray this moment, driving away the darkness of evil and enabling us to walk without stumbling, to live without soiling our lives or the lives of others, and to serve our country without fear and with fidelity.

Consecrate with Thy presence the way our feet may go, the way our minds may think, and the way our hearts may feel, that our work may be well done and our lives be filled with the glory of Thy spirit.

Bless our Nation with the grace of Thy favor, our leaders with the greatness of Thy wisdom, and our people with the goodness of Thy love.

In the spirit of Christ we pray. Amen.

THURSDAY, JUNE 5, 1969

Let the people praise Thee, O God; let all the people praise Thee.— Psalm 67: 3.

BLESSED ART THOU, O LORD, OUR GOD, who turneth the shadow of night into the light of the morning and giveth to us the glory of another day; we lift our hearts unto Thee in praise and thanksgiving.

Thanks be to Thee for the revelation of Thyself in the light of Thy word, in the beauty of nature, in the orderliness of the universe, and in the splendor of triumphant spirits. Thanks be to Thee for the revelation of Thyself in our own hearts, for moments when Thy presence has been real and we have known Thou art with us and we are with Thee.

Grateful for this day, send us out to do our work as best we can, touching the lives of our fellow men for good. Help us to look at others with the eyes of a brother and endeavor to meet the needs of our people with sympathetic hearts and understanding minds. May we be walking centers of good will in a world of ill will to the glory of Thy name, for the welfare of our Nation, and for the well-being of all mankind. In the name of Him who went about doing good. Amen.

MONDAY, JUNE 9, 1969

Let not mercy and truth forsake thee; bind them about thy neck; write them upon the table of thine heart.—Proverbs 3: 3

O God, almighty and eternal, supreme ruler of men, without whom no nation can be great, no people can be good, make us mindful of Thy presence, eager to do Thy will, and willing to walk in Thy way.

May the light of Thy spirit enlighten our spirits that we may see the truth clearly, follow it courageously, and live with it confidently, knowing that it is the truth which makes and keeps men free.

Guide Thou our President and all who confer with him that out of conferences may come plans for the ending of war and procedures for ushering in peace. So may it be for Thy glory and for the good of all mankind. Amen.

WEDNESDAY, JUNE 11, 1969

Thou shalt do that which is right and good in the sight of the Lord; that it may be well with thee.—Deuteronomy 6: 18.

Eternal God, Our Father, with reverent hearts we pause in the midst of the day's duties to lift our spirits to Thee, unto whom all hearts are open, all desires known, and from whom no secrets are hid. Cleanse the thoughts of our hearts by the inspiration of Thy Holy Spirit that we may love Thee more perfectly, serve our country more fully, and lead our people more diligently.

During these difficult days let us not add to the problems we face by our own ill will and our selfish endeavors, rather help us to become part of the solution by our own good will and our unselfish efforts to lead our people to wider areas of understanding, tolerance, and friendliness.

Direct the leaders of our Nation, our President, our beloved Speaker, and all the Members of Congress. Grant unto them wisdom and strength that, upholding what is right, and standing by what is true, they may follow Thy holy will and fulfill Thy purpose for mankind: through Jesus Christ our Lord. Amen.

THURSDAY, JUNE 12, 1969

Thou hast given a banner to them that fear Thee, that it may be displayed because of the truth.—Psalm 60: 4.

ALMIGHTY GOD, we thank Thee for our beloved Republic, for the heritage which is ours, for the traditions and the institutions of a free people which have come down to us through the sacrifices of our fathers, and for which we now must live and labor to keep alive in our day.

Our hearts are thrilled as we look upon the starry banner, the flag of our United States of America. It speaks of freedom and democracy. It stands for law and order, justice and liberty, for peace and good will to all. It serves to proclaim the good news of a government of the people, by the people, and for the people. May this flag continue to be the symbol of hope to the oppressed, the rainbow of promise to the downtrodden, and the banner of freedom to all men.

May we celebrate its birth not only with our lips but with the lives devoted to Thee and dedicated to our country.   Amen and Amen.

MONDAY, JUNE 16, 1969

The ways of the Lord are right and the just shall walk in them.—Hosea 14: 9.

O THOU WHOSE SPIRIT SUPPORTS US IN EVERY NOBLE ENDEAVOR AND WHOSE STRENGTH SUSTAINS US AS WE LABOR FOR THE GOOD OF OUR FELLOW MAN, bless us with a realization of Thy presence as we begin another week and enable us to walk in the way of Thy commandments and to live in the spirit of Thy Son.

Thou hast brought forth on this land a Nation conceived in liberty and dedicated to the good of all men. Help us to maintain our freedoms in the spirit of justice and good will. Save our Nation from further discord and violence. Guide our people that they may see the futility of fostering fear and may seek the path that produces more unity and promotes mutual understanding.

Strengthen our leaders that they may walk with Thee as they make decisions and carry responsibilities. Together may leaders and people endeavor by honorable service and humble spirits to bring peace to our land and to our world. In the spirit of Christ, we pray.   Amen.

TUESDAY, JUNE 17, 1969

Happy is the man that findeth wisdom, and the man that getteth understanding.—Proverbs 3: 13.

ALMIGHTY AND MOST MERCIFUL FATHER, from whom cometh wisdom and understanding, make us aware of Thy presence as we seek to provide for the welfare of our people. May we be guided in all our consultations to find the more excellent way and be given strength to walk in it that the safety and honor of our Nation may be preserved, freedom be fortified, and Thy purposes be promoted on this planet.

Grant, O Lord, that we may do only that which is right and wise and good for all. Give to us a calmness of mind and a steadiness of spirit that we may fulfill Thy will in this all too short life and find happiness in walking in Thy ways and working for Thy way.

In the Master's name, we pray. Amen.

WEDNESDAY, JUNE 18, 1969

Be kindly affectioned one to another with brotherly love; in honor preferring one another.—Romans 12: 10.

OUR HEAVENLY FATHER, as we enter the gate of another day may it be in the faith that we are working for Thee and with our fellow Representatives on behalf of our beloved country.

May Thy spirit have full sway in our hearts and in the hearts of our people. Let discord and division be removed, all dissension and discrimination be erased. Make us mindful that we are dependent upon each other, that we need each other and that we must learn to live together on these shores. Help us to respect the rights of others and help others to respect our rights.

Above all remind us that we are here only for a little while and one day will lay down our tools and stand before Thee. At that time may we be unafraid and unashamed because we have been faithful in our stewardship.

In the spirit of Christ we pray. Amen.

MONDAY, JUNE 23, 1969

Bear ye one another's burdens and so fulfill the law of Christ.—Galatians 6: 2.

ETERNAL GOD, who hast called us to pray and to work, sustain us with Thy power that we may be daily mindful of Thy presence and ready to help bear the burdens of others.

Guide us with Thy spirit that we may understand this troubled time in which we live and so lead us that we may use our talents to bring forth the fruit of faithful living.

Grant unto us the wisdom to order the life of our Nation upon the principles of justice, righteousness, and good will.

Give us the readiness to render real service to Thee, our country, and our fellow man, that out of our efforts may come peace to our world, peace to our Nation, and peace to our own hearts.

Again death has invaded this Chamber. In the prime of his life our colleague has entered the life immortal. We thank Thee for his presence in our midst and for the contribution he made to our country through this body. Bless his family with the strength of Thy spirit and the comfort of Thy love: through Jesus Christ, our Lord, in whose name we pray. Amen.

WEDNESDAY, JUNE 25, 1969

In every nation he who fears God and does what is right is acceptable to Him.—Acts 10: 35.

O God, Our Father, who hast bidden us to let our light so shine before men that they may see our good works and glorify Thee, grant us grace to be faithful leaders of our people, thoughtful in our thinking, wise in our wisdom, genuine in our goodness, and with hearts ever open to Thee. Weave our lives and the life of our Nation into the struggle for freedom and justice and peace in our world.

Guide Thou our President, our Speaker, and these Members of Congress in their endeavor to find a just basis for the ending of war and in their efforts to discover a strong foundation for international cooperation and peace.

Awaken in our people an abounding good will and tie it to an adventurous willingness to work with Thee for the good of all.

To this end we commit our lives in the spirit of Jesus Christ, our Lord. Amen.

FRIDAY, JUNE 27, 1969

All things come from Thee, O Lord, and of Thine own have we given Thee.—I Chronicles 29: 14.

O Thou whose wisdom is so wise that we often doubt it, whose love is so loving we often deny it, and whose truth is so true we often fear it, grant unto us such a full measure of Thy spirit that we many never doubt Thy wisdom, never deny Thy love, and never fear Thy truth.

Thou hast called us to live together in peace and good will. Let Thy presence so move in men that the leaders of the world may find support for peaceful procedures in their endeavor to establish justice, to maintain order, to develop understanding, and to build bridges between nations and people.

Teach us to unite what we ought to do with what we will do, that walking in the way of Thy word and obeying Thy commandments, we may have life more abundant, liberty more abounding, and love more abiding—all to the glory of Thy holy name. Amen.

TUESDAY, JULY 1, 1969

He who is faithful in a very little is faithful also in much.—Luke 16: 10.

O LORD AND MASTER OF US ALL, who hast called us to be workers with Thee in the advancement of Thy kingdom, teach us to understand the meaning of this time in which we live with all its troubles and its triumphs. With this understanding may there come the spirit to deal with the demanding duties of this day courageously, handling ourselves well in trouble and handling trouble for the well-being of our people.

Sustain with Thy strength those who are in need. Inspire our people to be compassionate and helpful in their endeavor to provide assistance to those who seek work and who will work.

Grant unto us, the leaders of this free land, the will and the wisdom to continue to build the life of our Nation upon the strong foundation of justice and truth and good will. To this end may we be found faithful in our stewardship.

In the name of Him, who was always faithful, we pray. Amen.

WEDNESDAY, JULY 2, 1969

The fruit of the spirit is love, joy, peace, patience, kindness, goodness and faithfulness.—Galatians 5: 22.

ALMIGHTY GOD, Father of all men and ruler of nations, without whom no country can be great and no people can be good, we thank Thee for the blessings bestowed so abundantly upon us as a nation of free people. By our faith in Thee and Thy faith in us may we keep the spirit of freedom alive in our day realizing that it is a gift to be earned by just and good men of every generation.

Make us as the representatives of our Nation more responsive to Thee and more responsible to our people that we may sincerely seek the good of all and endeavor to maintain our freedom in righteousness and peace.

Awaken in our citizens a willingness to make sacrifices for peace as well as for war. To this end we pray that they and we may think clearly, plan courageously, decide confidently, and by Thy grace achieve creatively for the good of man and the glory of Thy holy name.   Amen.

MONDAY, JULY 7, 1969

Rest in the Lord, and wait patiently for him.—Psalm 37: 7.

O GOD, OUR FATHER, grant that we may have so enjoyed our holiday that our bodies have been renewed and our spirits restored, making us ready for the responsibilities of these days.

Give us steadfast hearts that no trouble may overcome, strong spirits that no temptation may overwhelm, and steady minds that worthy thoughts may keep wholesome.

Teach us to serve Thee and our Nation faithfully and fully, to give and not to count the cost, to fight and not to heed the wounds, to labor and not seek for rewards, save that of doing Thy will and seeking the best for our people.

In the Master's name we pray.   Amen.

WEDNESDAY, JULY 9, 1969

God is our refuge and strength, a very present help in trouble.—Psalm 46: 1.

ALMIGHTY GOD AND FATHER OF ALL MANKIND, whose love is the light of life and whose law is the litany of liberty, grant us wisdom to use in right ways the freedom which is our heritage by keeping ourselves dedicated to Thee and devoted to our country.

Give us the faith to go out into this day with courage not always knowing where we are going but with the assurance that Thou art with us, Thy hand is sustaining us and Thy spirit supporting us all the way.

Strengthen Thou the men and women in our Armed Forces throughout the world who are risking their lives on our behalf and seeking to keep freedom alive on this planet. By Thy grace may they be temperate in all things and may their homes be kept steadfast in loyalty during these days of separation.

Bless those of our number into whose homes sorrow has come. Comfort them with Thy presence and give them strength as they live through these days.

In life and death, may they and we realize that Thou art our refuge and strength and underneath are Thine everlasting arms.

In the Master's name we pray.   Amen.

WEDNESDAY, JULY 16, 1969

Prepare ye the way of the Lord, make straight in the desert a highway for our God.—Isaiah 40: 3.

O GOD AND FATHER OF US ALL, at this high moment in our national life we bow at the altar of prayer invoking Thy blessing upon us and upon our noble endeavors. Shine Thou upon our Nation as we launch out into a new day. Bless our astronauts as they wend their way to the moon, as they land on its surface, and as they find their way back. Grant them safety all the way and may they return with their mission accomplished and their aims achieved.

We thank Thee with glowing hearts that we live in an hour like this. May we play our part as participants in this crowning hour of our Nation's history.

In the spirit of the Pioneer of Life we pray.   Amen.

THURSDAY, JULY 17, 1969

Make Thy Face to shine upon Thy servants; and teach us Thy statutes.—Psalm 119: 135.

ETERNAL FATHER OF OUR SPIRITS, whose love never lets us go, whose strength never lets us down, and whose truth never lets us off, in the glory of a new day we lift our hearts unto Thee seeking guidance as we face the trying tasks of this turbulent time.

We quiet our spirits in Thy presence and rest in the assurance that Thy strength makes us strong, Thy wisdom makes us wise, and Thy love makes us loving.

Grant that in this hour we and our Nation may be messengers of hope to the nations of the world, particularly to those who sit in darkness without freedom but with faith in the coming day when liberty shall be the life of all.

Bless us in our endeavors to lift humanity to the heights from whence cometh our help.

In the spirit of Christ we pray.   Amen.

MONDAY, JULY 21, 1969

The heavens declare the glory of God; and the firmament showeth His handiwork.—Psalm 19: 1.

ETERNAL GOD, OUR FATHER, as we come to Thee in prayer may Thy spirit expand our hearts with the life of Thy love, our minds with the wonder of Thy wisdom and our spirits with the security of Thy strength.

On this glorious day when our astronauts have landed on the moon and walked on its surface the heart of our Nation rejoices and together we are filled with joy at the achievements of man in cooperation with Thee.

Grant that we may wisely interpret the meaning of this event and be given insight into Thy great and gracious purpose for all mankind.

While we look at the moon and are moved by the magnificence of this mission may we also look at the miseries of men on this planet and seek to master them that all may live with dignity, respect, and good will. Thus may every heart rejoice at what man can do when he walks with Thee.

In the spirit of Him who went about doing good we pray. Amen.

TUESDAY, JULY 22, 1969

Because Thou art my God, Thy gentle spirit shall lead me into the way of life.—Psalm 143: 10.

ALMIGHTY GOD, may this day be radiant with the reality of Thy presence as we address ourselves to the tasks before us. Bless Thou our President, our Speaker, all Members of Congress, and all who work with them that they may set themselves to meet the challenges of this hour with confidence and courage.

We do not pray to escape responsibilities, but to be made equal to them; not for removal of tasks, but to be made ready for them; not for burdens to be lifted from our hands, but to be lightened by the strength of Thy spirit.

We pray for our country. May this beloved land of ours be the channel through which the blessings of freedom may come to the oppressed, light may shine upon those who sit in darkness, strength may come to the weak, weights be lifted from the weary, and the joy of liberty dwell in every heart.

In the Master's name, we pray. Amen.

THURSDAY, JULY 24, 1969

The Lord is my light and my salvation; whom shall I fear?—Psalm 27: 1.

O GOD, OUR FATHER, in a world filled with the noise of those who put their faith in violence and whose loud clamor would drown out the efforts of those who seek the rights of men in the right way, we come praying to be kept steady in a world of change and to be made strong in a swiftly moving age.

Grant unto us a vision of Thy greatness and an experience of Thy presence that we may lead our Nation in the good paths of righteousness and peace.

Help us to meet this hard day with high courage, to do our demanding duties with undying devotion and to practice what we profess lest our professions be proven impractical.

Give to these leaders of our people the insight and the inspiration to lead our beloved Republic in making the American dream a reality in our day.

In the Master's name we pray. Amen.

MONDAY, JULY 28, 1969

Let us hold fast the profession of our faith without wavering.—Hebrews 10: 23.

MOST MERCIFUL GOD, who hast made us for Thyself so that our hearts are restless until they find rest in Thee, in this moment of prayer we renew our faith, we reaffirm the fact that Thou art with us, and we reenforce our desire to be of real service to our country and to our fellow man.

May the splendor of Thy spirit and the strength of Thy presence be revealed in us and through us, particularly when we are assailed by the moods of frustration and futility and feel that all our endeavors are in vain.

Bless the leaders of our land, these men and women of Congress and all who labor with them to creatively meet the demands of this distracting day. May their faith in Thee hold them up, keep them strong, and help them guide our Nation on the way to peace, justice, and good will. In the spirit of Christ we pray. Amen.

WEDNESDAY, JULY 30, 1969

As we have opportunity let us do good unto all men.—Galatians 6: 10.

ALMIGHTY GOD, on this first day of the rest of our lives, we pause in Thy presence uniting our hearts in prayer unto Thee. Fill us with the power of

Thy spirit that we may do our duties and carry our responsibilities with patient confidence and persistent courage.

As we seek cooperation among the nations of the world in an effort to bring peace on earth and good will to man may Thy truth be in our minds and Thy love in our hearts. Bless our President in his journey as he works toward this end.

Let us never be weary in well doing, let us always do good to all men, and let us forever seek the best even in the worst times.

In the name of Him who lived the good life we pray.   Amen.

FRIDAY, AUGUST 1, 1969

Where two or three are gathered together in My name, there am I in the midst of them.—Matthew 18: 20.

O GOD AND FATHER OF US ALL, at this noontide hour we pray that Thou wilt touch our spirits and transform our souls by Thy grace that we may have strength for the day, courage with each hour, and peace in every moment.

Kindle within us the fire of Thy spirit and warm our hearts with the power of Thy presence that in the time of trouble we may be equal to every experience, ready for every responsibility, and adequate for every task.

Grant that we may see Thy way more clearly and be given wisdom to work with Thee in making the world a better place in which Thy children can live together in abundant happiness, in abounding harmony, and in abiding hope.

In the Master's name, we pray.   Amen.

MONDAY, AUGUST 4, 1969

Ask, and it shall be given; seek, and ye shall find; knock, and it shall be opened unto you.—Matthew 7: 7.

O SPIRIT OF THE LIVING GOD, arise within us as we bow at the altar of prayer and lift our hearts into Thy presence. In this troubled time lead us beside the still waters where our souls can be restored and our faith renewed. In the quiet of this moment help us to hear Thy still, small voice and hearing it, obey it; and obeying it be led in right paths for Thy name's sake.

Direct and bless these leaders of our Nation that, in seeking to find solutions for the problems of this hour and endeavoring to discover a cure for the distress of our day, they first cleanse their own hearts and then may they see clearly to plan wisely and to move forward to the time when our people shall live together in good will and the nations shall dwell together in peace.

O God, make us good enough for this great day.

In the spirit of Christ we pray. Amen.

WEDNESDAY, AUGUST 6, 1969

The Lord is good; His mercy is everlasting; and His truth endureth to all generations.—Psalm 100: 5.

O God, who art the Lord of heaven and earth, whose love lives forever and whose truth endureth through all generations, hear us as we pray lifting our hearts unto Thee.

Thou hast called us to live together as brothers and has taught us that we belong to each other. Do Thou bless all endeavors leading toward peace in our world, justice in our Nation, and good will in all our hearts.

Let Thy spirit so live in men and so move among them that the leaders of our Nation and of every nation may seek peaceful means to settle disputes, to maintain order, and to establish justice.

Help us all to learn that peace depends upon understanding love; that law and order must be built upon righteousness and truth; and that justice can live only in the hearts of men of good will.

In the spirit of Christ we pray. Amen.

MONDAY, AUGUST 11, 1969

We take courage and say "the Lord is my helper, I will not fear what man shall do unto me."—Hebrews 13: 6.

Our Heavenly Father, we thank Thee for this new day fresh from Thy hand and pray Thou wilt help us to live it well. Cleanse our hearts and clear our minds that we may walk the upward way with Thee and with our fellow men.

Grant that we may always be on the side of justice and peace and good will. In so doing may we seek to make this earth a finer planet in which men can dwell together safely and securely.

We pray for our country, gratefully for the heritage of faith and freedom which is ours, humbly that we may prove ourselves worthy of this heritage, and positively that we may be given wisdom, understanding, and a concern to lead our Nation in right paths with true faith for the good of all.

In the spirit of Christ we pray. Amen.

WEDNESDAY, AUGUST 13, 1969

Now let Thy servant depart in peace.—Luke 2: 29.

O GOD AND FATHER OF US ALL, who dost reveal Thyself in all that is good and true and beautiful, make in our hearts a quiet place and come and dwell therein.

May the days ahead be a period of rest and relaxation for us and may we return ready in body and spirit for the tasks that lie before us.

As we separate may Thy blessing be upon us to keep us healthy and strong, ever ready to serve our beloved country and always being about our Father's business.

> God be in our heads and in our understanding;
> God be in our eyes and in our looking;
> God be in our mouths and in our speaking;
> God be in our minds and in our thinking;
> God be at our end—and at our departing.

In the Master's name we pray.   Amen.

MONDAY, SEPTEMBER 8, 1969

And thou shalt do that which is right and good in the sight of the Lord, that it may be well with thee.—Deuteronomy 6: 18.

O GOD, OUR FATHER, the light of all that is true, the life of all that is good, and the love of all that is beautiful, we lift our hearts unto Thee that we may find wisdom, strength, and love sufficient for all our needs.

Help us to walk in the light of truth, to live the life of goodness, and to share the love of the beautiful that we may play our part and do our full duty in this high hour of our national life.

We pray that Thy spirit may enter the hearts of all people that our Nation, and all nations, may be free from malice and bitterness and be filled with goodness and good will. To this end and by Thy grace may we do justly, love mercy, and walk humbly with Thee.

Bless the family of our beloved Senate colleague with the comfort of Thy presence as they walk through the valley of the shadow of death.

In the spirit of Christ we pray.   Amen.

WEDNESDAY, SEPTEMBER 10, 1969

Unto Thee, O Lord, do I lift up my soul.—Psalm 25: 1.

O GOD, OUR FATHER, who art the truth that keeps men free and the love that makes them good, give to us the faith to see life as it is, the strength to change for good what we can change for good, and the serenity to accept calmly and courageously what we cannot change at this time.

We pass through this world but once. Any good we can do, any kindness we can show, any help we can give do Thou help us to do it now, for we shall not pass this way nor live through this day again.

May we the representatives of our people in loyalty to Thee and our country keep our lives committed to goals great enough for free men.

In the spirit of Christ, we pray. Amen.

THURSDAY, SEPTEMBER 11, 1969

Let us have grace, whereby we may serve God acceptably with reverence and godly fear.—Hebrews 12: 28.

A LMIGHTY GOD, OUR HEAVENLY FATHER, we pause before the altar of prayer to lift our hearts unto Thee, praying for a fresh vision of Thy presence, seeking guidance for this day and strength for our tasks.

Increase our desire for clear thinking and honest dealing. Decrease in us any inclination for deceit and pretense. Stimulate us in our efforts to rise above the common level of life, to choose the hard right rather than the easy wrong, to live ever in the light and to serve Thee with all our might.

Bless our Nation with Thy favor. Keep her free; and in her freedom enable her to foster in the hearts of men a true love for peace with justice and good will for all.

In the Master's name we pray. Amen.

MONDAY, SEPTEMBER 15, 1969

He who gives heed to the word will prosper, and happy is he who trusts in the Lord.—Proverbs 16: 20.

O GOD, OUR FATHER, once more in this historic Chamber we respond to the call to prayer and in the quiet of this moment draw near to Thee. Make us aware of Thy presence as a quickening spirit, a sustaining power, a refuge, and a strength in the time of trouble.

We pray for our country that she may be guided and governed by Thy good spirit. Grant that all who call themselves Americans may be led in the way of truth, along the path of good will, and may hold the faith of our democratic life in a deep unity of steadfast purpose.

Bless our President, our Speaker, the Members of this body, and all who labor with them. Keep them calm and steady, full of faith in Thee and in the power of our Nation to be a leading light among the nations of the world.

In the spirit of Christ we pray. Amen.

WEDNESDAY, SEPTEMBER 17, 1969

And He hath put a new song in my mouth, even praise unto our God.— Psalm 40: 3.

O Thou Creator of the world and the Sustainer of life everywhere, hear the song of our hearts as we sing with gratitude for the accomplishments of our astronauts whom we delighted to honor yesterday. We thank Thee for their achievements in landing on the moon, for their safe return, and for the doors to a new future they have opened for us. May we have the courage and the faith to continue our technical and astronautical research for our own good and for the good of all.

God bless our country, the land we love with all our hearts. Lead her into the new unity of a common faith and a common endeavor that we may be makers of goodness in men even more than makers of goods for men. Grant that our gratitude to Thee for Thy goodness to us may find its fruit in good will for one another.

In the Master's name we pray. Amen.

THURSDAY, SEPTEMBER 18, 1969

O magnify the Lord with me and let us exalt His name together.—Psalm 34: 3.

Almighty God, who are the source of all our blessings and the fountain of flowing love, help us to realize that Thou art always with us—seeking our good, forgiving our sins, and endeavoring to lead us in the ways of justice and peace. Prosper us in our work, guide us through our difficulties, and reward with the joy of living those who extend a helping hand to others who have lost their way in the world.

We invoke Thy blessing upon us as we labor for the good of our people and upon our Nation in these crucial times. Let not our adversaries triumph over us but let the glory of a just people increase from year to year.

Sustain with Thy power those whom our people have placed in positions of authority and all who are entrusted with our safety and with the guardianship of our rights and our freedom. May peace and good will live in the hearts of our citizens and may our faith exalt our Nation in righteousness; to the glory of Thy holy name. Amen.

FRIDAY, SEPTEMBER 19, 1969

*Let not your heart be troubled; believe in God.—*John 14: 1.

O LORD, OUR GOD, who art truth and love and who dost give Thyself to men to lead them in Thy way, grant unto us Thy spirit that we may give ourselves in service to our fellow men.

May nations and races feel their kinship with each other since we are Thy children and may we learn to work together for the good of all.

Bless those who are in need, all who are oppressed in mind and body and all who suffer. Particularly do we pray for our prisoners of war. Strengthen them and their families here at home, give them patience in suffering and a happy issue out of their affliction. May the day soon come when those now separated can be home together and enjoy their freedom in peace.

In the spirit of Christ we pray. Amen.

WEDNESDAY, SEPTEMBER 24, 1969

*With Thee is the fountain of life; in Thy light shall we see light.—*Psalm 36: 9.

O THOU ETERNAL SPIRIT WHOSE WILL FOR US IS PEACE AND WHOSE PURPOSES NEVER FAIL, we come to Thee seeking to know Thy will and praying for strength to do it as we enter this new day fresh from Thy hand.

Amid the demanding duties of these disturbing days may we discover adequate resources in Thee and find our souls restored and renewed as we walk in right paths.

We pray for our country—that all malice and misery, all narrow exclusiveness may be swept away by Thy spirit and that honor, justice, and good will may be established among us. Thus may every person be given the opportunity to live a full, a free, and a fruitful life to the glory of Thy name and for the good of all mankind. Amen.

THURSDAY, SEPTEMBER 25, 1969

See that none render evil for evil unto any man; but ever follow that which is good, both among yourselves, and to all men.—I Thessalonians 5: 15.

God of grace and God of glory, in the midst of the troubles of this time we would find in the living water of prayer the spirit which can restore our souls, renew our bodies, and make us ready for the tasks of this new day.

We are disturbed by the divisions in our world and in our Nation, weighed down by many worries, tempted to lose hope, and to give up because peace and justice seem so long in coming. We confess that we do so little when there is so much to be done.

We pray for our country and for ourselves, the leaders of our people. May we not increase our divisions by any ill will but take advantage of every opportunity to spread good will so that our influence shall always be for the good of all.

Give us courage to carry on, knowing Thou art always with us and believing that with Thee we cannot fail.

In the spirit of Him whose truth is marching on, we pray. Amen.

MONDAY, SEPTEMBER 29, 1969

The Lord bless thee and keep thee.—Numbers 6: 24.

We come to the Altar of prayer, our Father, with grateful hearts as we remember the loving care with which Thou didst watch over our fathers as they founded and built our country. Time and again they found shelter under the shadow of Thy protecting love. Thou didst make of them bearers of Thy truth, champions of Thy law, and supporters of Thy kingdom. Give to us, their children, the courage and the strength to be true to our sacred trust.

In days of distress and in times of trouble fortify our spirits with a deep faith in Thee who never slumbers nor sleeps. Keep alive with us the great memories of the past, the good experiences of the present, and the grand visions of the future. May we always labor for that spiritual harvest when all Thy children shall be gathered under the banner of truth and love, and stand united in a common brotherhood.

In Thy holy name we pray. Amen.

WEDNESDAY, OCTOBER 1, 1969

Great peace have they who love Thy law; nothing can make them stumble.—Psalm 119: 165.

ALMIGHTY AND MOST MERCIFUL FATHER, who are ever coming to Thy children with strengthening spirit, make us strong in Thee that we may serve our country with great and genuine devotion.

Give us steadfast minds with no room for unworthy thoughts, serene hearts which no trouble can disturb, and strong hands with which to do Thy will in lifting our Nation to higher patriotic living.

We commend to Thy loving care all who are giving their lives for our country, that living or dying they may win for our world the fruits of justice and peace.

In the spirit of Christ we pray.   Amen.

THURSDAY, OCTOBER 2, 1969

Teach me, O Lord, the way of Thy statutes; and I will keep it unto the end.—Psalm 119: 33.

O THOU WHO DOST REVEAL THYSELF TO MAN IN ENDLESS WAYS, deepen within us the sense of Thy presence as we lift our hearts unto Thee in this our morning prayer. As our fathers came to this altar to worship Thee, so do we bow before Thee humbly and reverently.

With grateful hearts may we learn to labor in Thy spirit, to live in harmony with Thy laws, and to let love lighten and brighten our lives.

Turn Thou our strength to the tasks of justice, mercy, and peace that as we work for the common good we may find joy and satisfaction in useful living.

In Thy holy name we pray.   Amen.

FRIDAY, OCTOBER 3, 1969

God is love and he who abides in love abides in God, and God abides in him.—I John 4: 16.

O GOD, OUR FATHER, we the Representatives of the people of this Nation, bow before Thee seeking strength for this day and guidance for these hours. Make this moment of prayer a moment when we are aware of Thy presence, a moment when we hear Thy voice calling us to lead our people in the ways of justice, peace, and good will.

Give to us a higher faith and a greater courage to seek to lift the lowly, to strengthen the weak, to encourage the discouraged, and to make this Nation a nation in which men are concerned about their fellow men.

God bless this America of ours and help us to live together with respect for each other and with love in our hearts: through Jesus Christ our Lord. Amen.

MONDAY, OCTOBER 6, 1969

God loveth righteousness and justice; the earth is full of the goodness of the Lord.—Psalm 33: 5.

O Spirit of the Living God, who governs the world with righteousness and whose judgments are true and righteous altogether, grant that these Representatives of our people may be of one mind and of one heart as they seek to provide justice, to produce good will, to protect freedom, and to promote the welfare of all the citizens of our beloved land.

Endue them with Thy spirit that with clear understanding, clean motives, and creative principles they may rise above all self-seeking and through self-discipline be primarily concerned about the good of our country and the brotherhood of man.

Bless all the courts of justice in our Nation and particularly our Supreme Court opening on this day. Grant unto all Justices the spirit of wisdom that they may decide wisely and uphold the law as it is without fear or favor.

May the Lord give strength to His people and bless them with peace of mind, purity of heart, and power of spirit to work together for the good of all men.

In the Master's name we pray. Amen.

WEDNESDAY, OCTOBER 8, 1969

O give thanks unto the Lord; for He is good; for His mercy endureth forever.—Psalm 106: 1.

With grateful hearts, O God, we acknowledge that Thou art the creator of the world, the sustainer of life, and the rock upon which we can build securely. We thank Thee for Thy constant care and Thy abounding goodness which are ours day by day. Truly Thy mercies are everlasting, Thy faithfulness endures through all generations, and Thy love abides forever. Therefore we put our trust in Thee.

Bless our country with Thy guiding spirit and by Thy grace enable her to walk in the way of Thy commandments. May we as a free people always be the champion of peace and justice in our world. Strengthen the ties of fellowship within our borders that we may live together with understanding, respect, and good will and give to every man the opportunity to live a full and a free life. May the love of Thy dear name bless every heart and every home.

In the spirit of Christ we pray.   Amen.

THURSDAY, OCTOBER 9, 1969

They that wait upon the Lord shall renew their strength.—Isaiah 40: 31.

ALMIGHTY GOD, we thank Thee for all the blessings Thou hast so abundantly bestowed upon us. Do Thou help us to translate our thanksgiving into thanksliving and to live as Thy obedient and loving children. May we never forget who Thou art, who we are, and who our neighbor is.

Grant to the Members of this body the strength and the courage to do what they truly believe to be right and good for our Nation. Deliver them from pride and prejudice, from intolerance and every evil way, and bind them together in a faith which will enable them to labor unceasingly for the best interests of our people.

Look with Thy favor upon us, and may the words of our mouths and the meditations of our hearts be acceptable in Thy sight, O Lord, our strength and our Redeemer.   Amen.

MONDAY, OCTOBER 13, 1969

There will be glory and honor and peace for everyone who does good.—Romans 2: 10.

ETERNAL GOD, OUR FATHER, without whose blessing all our labor is in vain, grant that in the decisions we make we may be mindful of Thy presence and eager to do Thy will. Inspire us with a faith that never falters, a faithfulness that never fails, and a fidelity that never fades as we endeavor to do our duty for the good of our country.

Kindle in the hearts of all men a true love for peace, a sincere desire for the triumph of truth, and an increasing concern for the welfare of all mankind. So may Thy kingdom go forward, Thy will be done, and love live in the hearts of Thy children.

In the spirit of Christ we pray.   Amen.

WEDNESDAY, OCTOBER 15, 1969

Be strong and of good courage, for it is the Lord your God who goes with you; He will not fail you nor forsake you.—Deuteronomy 31: 6.

O GOD, OUR FATHER, who art acquainted with all our ways and who dost love us in spite of our shortcomings, we pause in Thy presence acknowledging our dependence upon Thee and offering unto Thee once again the devotion of our hearts. Confronting problems too difficult for us to solve and face to face with fears that frustrate us, we come to Thee for wisdom to rightly interpret the signs of this troubled time, for insight to see clearly the way we should take, and for strength to do what we ought to do for the good of our Nation.

May the blessing of Thy spirit rest upon our President, our Speaker, and these men and women called to lead our country in a day like this and upon all who work with them and for them. Give to them the assurance of Thy guiding spirit and the feeling that underneath are Thine everlasting arms.

O Thou who changest not, abide with us now and forevermore. Amen.

MONDAY, OCTOBER 20, 1969

The fruit of the spirit is in all goodness and righteousness and truth.— Ephesians 5: 9.

OUR FATHER, who art in heaven, we wait upon Thee with receptive minds and responsive hearts that the uplift of Thy spirit can be ours as we face the beginning of a new week. May we take up the work of these days with courage and confidence knowing Thou art with us and believing Thou art endeavoring to lead us in great and good ways. Grant that what we do may fulfill Thy purposes for us, for our Nation, and for our world.

Deepen the minds of men in truth and justice and mercy that order may prevail, laws be obeyed, good will be followed and people learn to live together with reverence before Thee, with respect for each other, and with a real faith in our beloved country.

In the Master's name we pray. Amen.

WEDNESDAY, OCTOBER 22, 1969

Blessed are they who observe justice and who do righteousness at all times.—Psalm 106: 3.

We come to Thee, Our Father, voicing the aspirations of our hearts in prayer, endeavoring to become aware of Thy presence, and seeking strength and wisdom for the tasks of this troubled time. During the pressure of daily duties we often forget Thee and in so doing we stifle the nobler impulses of our human nature. In this moment of prayer we would regain the feeling of our kinship with Thee. Help us to keep alive the sense of Thy spirit amid the labors of this day.

Enrich the life of our Nation with righteousness and truth. Make us equal to our high tasks, reverent in the use of freedom, just in the exercise of power, generous in the protection of weakness, and genuine in the spreading of good will: to the glory of Thy holy name. Amen.

MONDAY, OCTOBER 27, 1969

The Lord will give strength to His people; the Lord will bless His people with peace.—Psalm 29: 11.

O Thou who art the Shepherd of our human hearts, restore our minds and renew our spirits as we wait upon Thee in this our morning prayer. We would linger silently and reverently in Thy presence until Thy spirit comes to new life within us. Then with courage, strength, and wisdom we would face the trying duties of this turbulent day.

To Thy loving care we commend our Nation. So guide our President, so bless our Speaker, so direct these Members of Congress that filled with Thy spirit they may lead our people in right paths, by just ways, and along the solid road that ultimately brings us to an honorable peace, an enduring good will, and a willingness to work for the welfare of all mankind.

> "O Thou who dost the vision send
> And givest each his task,
> And with the task sufficient strength;
> Show us Thy will we ask;
> Give us a conscience bold and good;
> Give us a purpose true,
> That it may be our highest joy,
> Our Father's work to do."

Amen.

TUESDAY, OCTOBER 28, 1969

All the paths of the Lord are mercy and truth unto such as keep His covenant and His testimonies.—Psalm 25: 10.

Eternal Spirit, we pause with bowed heads at the opening of another day, lifting our spirits unto Thee, unto whom all hearts are open and all desires known. Teach us so to pray that Thy presence becomes real to us, that we endeavor more earnestly to do Thy will and to walk in Thy paths of peace.

We come disturbed by the problems of this period, burdened by many anxieties, tempted to feel our labor is in vain, and wondering what the future holds for us and for our Nation. We pray for ourselves in these trying times that we may not add to the divisions that divide us by giving way to petty prejudices but by our dedication to Thee and our devotion to our country may increase our unity by an ever-widening spirit of good will.

Give us strength to walk in Thy way, to travel in Thy truth, and to live in Thy light.

We pray in the spirit of Him whose life is the light of men.   Amen.

FRIDAY, OCTOBER 31, 1969

Come ye and let us go up to the mountain of the Lord; that He may teach us His ways and that we may walk in His paths.—Isaiah 2: 3.

Eternal God, who art our refuge and strength, our present help in every hour of need, we would begin this day with Thee, we would continue it with Thee, and we would end it with Thee. May this be a day when we truly adventure with Thy spirit and in so doing increase in faith, advance in hope, and extend good will in our Nation and in our world.

We pray for our country that our people may learn to be one in spirit, one in purpose, and one in a desire to live together harmoniously. As a result may we endeavor to bring peace to our world, understanding between nations, and a new sense of responsibility for the welfare of all mankind.

In Thy holy name we pray.   Amen.

MONDAY, NOVEMBER 3, 1969

He that dwelleth in the secret place of the Most High shall abide under the shadow of the Almighty.—Psalm 91: 1.

Almighty and Everlasting God, above the disturbances of our busy days and the disorders of our troubled times we would come to Thee seeking the calm of Thy holy presence. In the secret place of the Most High we would dwell, lifting our hearts unto Thee, praying for the guidance of Thy spirit and the direction of Thy wisdom as we face the experiences of another day.

Help us to serve our country with persistent faithfulness and patient fidelity that we may keep our Nation the hope of the world and the channel of peace for our generation. By Thy grace may we continue to work for the day when nation shall not lift up sword against nation, neither shall they learn war any more.

In the spirit of the Prince of Peace we pray.   Amen.

WEDNESDAY, NOVEMBER 5, 1969

He that doeth the will of God abideth forever.—I John 2: 17.

ETERNAL FATHER OF OUR SPIRITS, grant that in the worship of this moment and in the work of this day we may bear witness to the fact that we are Thy children. In our relationship with each other may we be generous in our criticism, just in our judgments, lavish in our praise, and loyal to the best in all of us.

Give us insight into the needs of our generation, inspiration to do something about them, and the confident assurance that Thou art with us, sustaining us, and supporting us, as we endeavor to keep our Nation great in goodness and good in greatness.

Unite us with all who are striving to safeguard our heritage of liberty and to keep our country forever the land of the free, the home of the brave, and the place where dwells justice and peace and good will.

In the spirit of Christ we offer our morning prayer.   Amen.

THURSDAY, NOVEMBER 6, 1969

Whatsoever ye would that men should do to you, do ye even so to them.—Matthew 7: 12.

ALMIGHTY GOD, who art the light and life of those who with true faith and hearty repentance turn unto Thee, have mercy upon us as we bow in this circle of prayer. Pardon and deliver us from all our sins, confirm and strengthen us in all goodness, and bring new life to us as we wait upon Thee.

With us is a deep weariness of body and within us is a disturbing unrest of spirit. We wonder what can be done, when we can do it, and who will help us do what ought to be done. Grant unto us the realization that with Thee all good things are possible and that we can be equal to every experience through the strength of Thy spirit living in our hearts.

Make us the kind of persons who can be trusted with Thy design for human brotherhood, with Thy determination for peace in our world, and with Thy desire for good will in the hearts of all people.

In Thy holy name we pray.   Amen.

THURSDAY, NOVEMBER 13, 1969

The salvation of the righteous is of the Lord: He is their strength in the time of trouble.—Psalm 37: 39.

O God and Father of us all, from whom all thoughts of truth and peace proceed, kindle in our hearts and in the hearts of all men a true love for peace. Guide with Thy wisdom all who are leading our Nation in these critical days, that justice may be our rule, good will our spirit, peace our aim, and liberty our very life. Breathe upon us, Breath of God, revealing Thy way and giving us courage to walk in it.

We pray for those in the Armed Forces of our country and for our veterans everywhere. Particularly do we pray for our prisoners of war. In their loneliness make them aware of Thy presence, in their suffering give them to realize Thou art their refuge and strength, in their hopelessness may they find hope in Thee. With all our hearts we pray that ere long they may be released and find joy in a reunited family life and in living again in a free world.

In the spirit of the Master we pray.   Amen.

MONDAY, NOVEMBER 17, 1969

With my whole heart have I sought Thee: let me not wander from Thy commandments.—Psalm 119: 10.

O God, who art the loving Father of all mankind, make Thy presence known to us through the hours of this day. Merge our moods and our motives into Thine own mold that honesty, integrity, and uprightness shall mark all our endeavors. Grant unto us the peace of those who put their trust in Thee, the strength of those who obey Thy commandments, and the love of those who walk in Thy way.

Give our citizens everywhere the mind and heart to heed the call of patriotic duty, to love our country with undying devotion, and to so live that the accent of our actions shall be in the spirit of cooperation. While there may be dissent let there not be dissension; while there may be differences of opinion may there not be differences in relationships, and while there might be disagreements let them not develop divisions among us.

Out of the agitation of these days may there come into being a unity of spirit which will strengthen our efforts for peace with justice, peace with honor, and peace with freedom for all.

In the spirit of the Prince of Peace, we pray. Amen.

TUESDAY, NOVEMBER 18, 1969

Be strong and of good courage, fear not, be not dismayed.—I Chronicles 22: 13.

us conscious of Thy presence and which calls us to a rededication of our

Lord of our lives, whose light is truth and whose love is life, we thank Thee for the dawning of a new day, for this moment of prayer which makes talents as we seek to lead our Nation in these troubled times.

During the busy hours of this day help us to think clearly, to speak constructively, and to act courageously that we may prove ourselves worthy of the positions we hold in our national life.

Give us the steadfast faith to join all men of good will who follow the light which leads to an enduring peace and to the establishment of law and order where men of all colors and all creeds can live together safely and securely.

In the spirit of Him who is the light of the world we pray. Amen.

WEDNESDAY, NOVEMBER 19, 1969

We do not grow weary; for though our outward man perish, yet the inner man is renewed day by day.—II Corinthians 4: 16.

Our Father God, ever ready to strengthen the souls of Thy children, we pause at this noontide altar of prayer to lift our hearts unto Thee. Into our littleness breathe Thou the greatness of Thy power, into our misunderstandings bring Thou the understanding of Thy wisdom, and into our troubled hearts let there come the steadiness of Thy strong spirit. Lift us from lower levels of living that, loving Thee fervently and serving our fellowmen faithfully, we may find our true selves in Thee.

We pray for our country. May the people of this free land not miss the right path amid the confusion of these times. With courageous hearts, creative minds, and confident hands, help us to bring order into the disorders of this world, to expel ill will with good will and to replace low prejudices with high principles that we may leave behind us a better world, where men live together in peace.

In the spirit of Christ we pray. Amen.

MONDAY, NOVEMBER 24, 1969

He who would love life and see good days, let him turn away from evil and do right; let him seek peace and pursue it.—I Peter 3: 10, 11.

O GOD, creator and sustainer of the universe and of this planet we call the earth, we Thy children, created in Thine own image, turn to Thee seeking strength for these hours, guidance for our undertakings, and good will for our relationship with other people.

We are burdened by the distressing difficulties of our day and by the perplexing problems that permeate our persistent pursuit of peace. Particularly do we pray for those who, meeting in Finland, are seeking to halt the nuclear arms race and for those who, meeting in France, are searching for an honorable end to war. May real success crown these genuine endeavors.

Grant wisdom to us and to all who are responsible for our Nation's welfare. May peace come to our world with justice and freedom for all.

In the spirit of Christ we pray.   Amen.

TUESDAY, NOVEMBER 25, 1969

He leadeth me in the paths of righteousness for His name's sake.—Psalm 23: 3.

O THOU WHO ART THE LIGHT OF THE WORLD, the Life of the faithful, and the Love of those who put their trust in Thee, let Thy spirit shine in our hearts as we wait upon Thee in prayer. Grant unto us the will to do Thy will that with faith in Thee alive within us we may let our light of hope shine before men. By Thy grace may we reverently use our freedom to maintain justice, to establish liberty, and to promote understanding among men and nations.

Deepen our life as a nation in righteousness, truth, and good will. Mold us into one people, united in purpose and program, to keep our Nation free and to strengthen the bonds of fellowship between the citizens of our beloved Republic.

Plant virtue in every heart, love in every home, light in every church, and liberty in every country, for Thy name's sake.   Amen.

WEDNESDAY, NOVEMBER 26, 1969

It is good to give thanks unto the Lord, to show forth Thy loving-kindness in the morning and Thy faithfulness every night.—Psalm 92: 1, 2.

ALMIGHTY GOD, OUR HEAVENLY FATHER, on this Thanksgiving eve we come to give Thee the humble and hearty thanks of our hearts for Thy loving-kindness to us and to all men. Thy goodness has created us, Thy providence has sustained us, Thy patience has borne with us, and Thy love has redeemed us. May we reveal our gratitude to Thee and return Thy love by giving ourselves in greater service to our fellow men, in deeper devotion to our beloved country, and by cheerfully cooperating with Thee in all things.

In Thy holy name we pray. Amen.

MONDAY, DECEMBER 1, 1969

The Lord will give strength unto His people; the Lord will bless His people with peace.—Psalm 29: 11.

O THOU WHOSE MERCY IS EVERLASTING and whose truth endureth forever, direct us, we pray Thee, as we face the duties of another week. Grant unto us the wisdom of Thy wise spirit and the confidence of Thy creative mind that we may eagerly seek the best and the noblest in all things. Help us to be courageous when courage is needed, strong when strength is demanded, patient when patience is necessary, and kind when kindness is essential.

Bless our President, our Speaker, Members of Congress, and all who work with them. May they be strengthened by the assurance that Thy hand supports them as they endeavor to lead our country in the paths of righteousness and peace.

In Thy name we pray. Amen.

TUESDAY, DECEMBER 2, 1969

Only fear the Lord and serve Him in truth with all your heart: for consider what great things He has done for you.—I Samuel 12: 24.

OUR FATHER, we thank Thee for the inspiration for great living this moment of prayer brings to us and for the insight into the meaning of life which comes as we pray. Never in vain do we call upon Thee. Always art Thou strengthening us with a strength which never lets us down. Always art Thou loving us with a love which never lets us go. Always art Thou leading us in true paths with a spirit which never lets us off. Give us grace to respond to Thee and with reverent courage to walk in Thy ways.

Bless our Nation with Thy gracious favor and these Representatives of our people with Thy loving wisdom. Kneeling before the altar of truth may we be united in the codes of high moral living, deep religious faith, great patriotic fervor, and genuine desire for peace.

In the Master's name we pray. Amen.

THURSDAY, DECEMBER 4, 1969

Your faith should not stand in the wisdom of men, but in the power of God.—I Corinthians 2: 5.

O UR HEAVENLY FATHER, who art the source of all our being and the companion of our way, we thank Thee for the creative ideas which come to life within us and for the deeper experiences of daily existence which enable us to realize the power of Thy presence. We are grateful for every awakening of mind that comes helping us to see human need and bidding us to share with others what we ourselves so richly enjoy.

By Thy spirit may we learn to live unselfishly and be concerned about the welfare of our people and the future of our country. Walking with Thee may we go forward building that which is good and true that Thy kingdom of justice and love and brotherhood may come upon this earth.   Amen.

MONDAY, DECEMBER 8, 1969

The name of the Lord is a strong tower; the righteous man runs into it and is safe.—Proverbs 18: 10.

A LMIGHTY GOD, who art a strong tower of defense to all who put their trust in Thee, we, Thy children, come to Thee with gratitude for Thy steadfast love and praying that Thou wilt continue to be our refuge and strength in every hour of need. Grant us insight and courage to shun the voice of moral compromise and to shy away from all that is morally questionable.

In hours of decision, during times of temptation, through days of responsibility, and amid periods of suffering may we have the royalty of an inward peace that comes to those whose minds are stayed on Thee. Teach us to value a clear conscience, a clean mind, a pure heart, and a sense of Thy presence before all the honors earth can bring to us.

In thought, word, and deed may we glorify Thy holy name as we seek the good of all mankind. Amen.

TUESDAY, DECEMBER 9, 1969

May the Lord make you increase and abound in love to one another and to all men.—I Thessalonians 3: 12

A LMIGHTY AND ETERNAL GOD, conscious of our obligation to the historic past, aware of the opportunities of the present, and with faith in the beckoning future, we humbly join our fathers in the affirmation—"glory be to Thee, O Lord most high."

Thou hast been wonderfully good to us and we are grateful. Thy spirit has led us. Thy hand has supported us, and Thy love has filled our hearts with good will. Make us one with Thee, we pray, as we face the duties of this day.

Standing as Americans together may we lift high the banner of freedom, strengthen the arm of justice, build bridges between races, classes, and nations, and keep ourselves ever mindful of Thy presence and ready to do Thy will.

In the spirit of Christ we pray. Amen.

THURSDAY, DECEMBER 11, 1969

God is the strength of my heart.—Psalm 73: 26.

Eternal Father, from whom we come and unto whom our spirits return, we bow our heads in adoration and gratitude before Thee. We thank Thee for every gift of Thy grace which lifts us and guides us, making us better men and better women.

We need Thy strengthening presence to support us through these troubled days, to keep our hearts free from the bitter spirit of hate and resentment, and to keep them filled with the happy spirit of love and good will.

We pray for our Nation and for the nations of the world. May the angels' song of good will among men be heard again and may the earth send back the song which now the angels sing. Led by Thy spirit, help us to live together in peace and with good will in all our hearts; through Jesus Christ, our Lord. Amen.

FRIDAY, DECEMBER 12, 1969

Let Thy work appear unto Thy servants and Thy glory unto their children.—Psalm 90: 16.

Our Father in heaven and on earth, author of our being, sustainer of our lives, and the giver of every good gift, we lift our hearts unto Thee praying that Thy spirit may so possess us that it will crowd out all evil intentions and enable us to think great thoughts, to do generous deeds, and to live genuinely good lives. Thus may we hallow Thy presence this day and all through the Advent season.

We commend to Thy loving care the men and women in our Armed Forces. Keep them strong when tempted, steadfast when lonely, and steady in the performance of duty when in peril that they may serve Thee without stumbling and without stain. Bless their homes through these days of separation and keep them loyal to each other, to our country, and to Thee.

Crown with success, we pray Thee, the efforts of our conferences to end war and to mark the beginning of peace on this planet. To this end may we follow the leading of Thy spirit.   Amen.

MONDAY, DECEMBER 15, 1969

Fear not; for, behold, I bring you good tidings of great joy, which shall be to all people.—Luke 2: 10.

O THOU WHO ART THE SOURCE OF LIGHT AND LIFE, whose Glory is in all the world, without whom no one is good, no one is wise: we remember with joy that the universe is Thy creation, life is Thy gift, and Thy love is offered to all the children of men. Lift our thoughts from the littleness of our own works to the greatness and the goodness of Thine and help us so to behold Thy glory that we may grow into the likeness of Christ. Help us to worthily celebrate His nativity this Advent season with hearts of compassion, deeds of kindly service, and the spirit of good will toward all mankind. In the name of Him who gives life to men, we pray.   Amen.

WEDNESDAY, DECEMBER 17, 1969

Unto you is born this day in the city of David a Saviour, who is Christ the Lord.—Luke 2: 11.

O GOD, OUR FATHER, who has brought us again to the glad season when we commemorate the birth of Jesus Christ; grant that Thy spirit in Him may be born anew in all our hearts and that we may joyfully welcome Thee to rule over us. Open our ears that we may hear again the angelic chorus of old; open our eyes that we may see the star that shines forever in our sky; open our lips that we may sing with uplifted voices, "Glory to God in the highest and on earth peace, good will among men."

As we enter the portal of this new day help us to be faithful in the discharge of our duties, honorable in our dealings, and loving in mind and heart; to the glory of Thy holy name.   Amen.

THURSDAY, DECEMBER 18, 1969

Glory to God in the highest and on earth peace among men of good will.—Luke 2: 14.

OUR HEAVENLY FATHER, who hast come into this world of darkness to bring light, into this world of worry to bring peace, and into this world of fear to bring faith, may Thy blessing be upon us and upon each one of our homes this Advent season. Do Thou lead us as we seek earnestly to be worthy followers of Thy wholesome way.

Make our feet to walk along the road to Bethlehem where we may give due honor and praise to Thee whose love gave us Christmas Day. May we so make room for Thee in all our hearts that we may live at peace with one another and in good will with all Thy family.

In the spirit of Him whose birthday we celebrate we pray. Amen.

MONDAY, DECEMBER 22, 1969

Unto us a child is born, unto us a Son is given; and His name shall be called "Wonderful Counselor, Mighty God, Everlasting Father, Prince of Peace."—Isaiah 9: 6.

ETERNAL SPIRIT, who hast been our refuge and strength in every age and who art our help in this hour of need, grant unto us Thy blessing this Advent season and give to us the assurance of Thy presence as we draw near Christmas Day.

May the joy and good will that passes around the world at this time be ours and may we respond to Thy love by giving ourselves in greater devotion to the welfare of our people and in deeper dedication to cooperation among the nations. So may we learn to live at peace with ourselves and in good will with all Thy family.

> "We hear the Christmas angels
> The great glad tidings tell:
> O come to us, abide with us,
> Our Lord Immanuel."

Amen.

TUESDAY, DECEMBER 23, 1969

We have seen His star in the east and have come to worship Him.—Matthew 2: 2.

ETERNAL GOD, OUR FATHER, send Thou the light of Thy spirit into the darkness of this world and into the turmoil of these times.

Let the star of love shine upon every heart and upon every family that good will may live within us and in every home in our land.

Let the star of hope be seen by the eyes of men and may they continue to look up even in dark days and amid discouraging experiences for Thou art the hope of the world.

Let the star of truth shed its light into the spirits of men, cleansing them and empowering them to walk in Thy way and to live Thy life.

Led by Thy star may we walk the way revealed to us as did the shepherds of old and the wise men from distant lands and in Thee find light and life and love.

> "As with gladness men of old
> Did the guiding star behold;
> As with joy they hailed its light,
> Leading onward, beaming bright;
> So, most gracious Lord, may we
> Evermore be led to Thee."

May the Lord watch over us as we depart, and when we return may His spirit guide us and our Nation through another year.

In the Master's name we pray.   Amen.

NINETY-FIRST CONGRESS

Second Session

MONDAY, JANUARY 19, 1970

Be strong in the Lord and in the power of His might.—Ephesians 6: 10.

O GOD AND FATHER OF US ALL, may we follow the leading of Thy spirit as we face another year and enter another decade. Bless us with Thy presence and help us always to be receptive to Thee and responsive to the needs of our fellow men.

At this high altar of prayer, the center of the spiritual life of our Nation, we pray for our President, our Speaker, Members of Congress, and all who labor with them, that they may be strengthened to meet confidently the searching demands of this stirring day.

Keep ever before us the goal of a better world with justice alive in our world, with peace between nations, and with good will in the hearts of men.

Hear us as we unite in offering unto Thee the Prayer of our Lord:

Our Father, who art in Heaven, hallowed be Thy name. They kingdom come, Thy will be done on earth as it is in heaven. Give us this day our daily bread. Forgive us our trespasses as we forgive those who trespass against us. And lead us not into temptation, but deliver us from evil. For Thine is the kingdom, and the power, and the glory, forever.

Amen.

TUESDAY, JANUARY 20, 1970

Whosoever heareth these sayings of Mine and doeth them, will be like a wise man who built his house upon a rock.—Matthew 7: 24.

ETERNAL GOD, who are the refuge of the humble and the strength of the faithful, help us to realize more than ever that the only firm foundation upon which our Nation can build safely is a true faith in Thee and in a real devotion to moral and spiritual values.

May the security of our American way, the survival of our democratic spirit, and the support of our free institutions find inspiration in the assurance of Thy power, Thy wisdom, and Thy love.

Each day may we keep ourselves committed to Thee whose love never falters, whose light never fades, and whose life never fails. Thus may we face this day with courage and faith knowing Thou art with us always and all the way.

In the Master's name we pray.   Amen.

WEDNESDAY, JANUARY 21, 1970

I will lift up mine eyes unto the hills from whence cometh my help.—Psalm 121: 1.

O LORD, OUR GOD, take our impatient spirits into Thy patient hands and breathe into them the power and the peace of Thy presence. Lift us above the clamor which is about us and the confusion which is around us and lead us to the high hills from whence cometh our help for the present and our hope for the future. O spirit of the living God make Thyself real to us as we pray.

Unto Thy loving care we commit our Nation. Make us worthy of the sacrifices which established on these shores a free people. Save us from the folly of our own foolishness and by sterling character, strong integrity, and steadfast faith may our Nation become a real blessing to the nations of the world.

In the spirit of Christ we pray.   Amen.

THURSDAY, JANUARY 22, 1970

Thou shalt remember all the way the Lord thy God led thee.—Deuteronomy 8: 2.

ETERNAL GOD, who didst lead our fathers to these shores that they may bring forth a just and a free nation, give Thy grace to us their children that we may be ever mindful of Thy presence and ever eager to do Thy will, without whom people cannot prosper, races cannot reason reasonably, and nations cannot live together in peace.

Grant that by the aid of Thy spirit true democracy may come to new life in our land, that government and industry and labor shall faithfully serve our people, and that our people in a real spirit of unity shall love our country with undying devotion.

Bless our President as he speaks to us and to our Nation this day. Make him wise with Thy wisdom, strong in Thy strength, good through Thy goodness and may he lead us in the paths of peace.

Bless our Nation abundantly and make her a blessing to all the peoples of the world.

In the spirit of the Pioneer of Life we pray. Amen.

MONDAY, JANUARY 26, 1970

To this end we toil and strive, because we have our hope set on the living God.—I Timothy 4: 10.

O Thou Eternal Father of our spirits, in this quiet moment at the beginning of another week we lift our hearts unto Thee who art the source of all our being and the goal of our noblest endeavors. We pray for strength to carry our burdens, wisdom to see through the problems we face, insight to discover what is right, and courage to walk in right ways.

With all our hearts we pray for our country, for Members of Congress, all who work with them, and for our people scattered far and wide on this land of the free. By Thy spirit may we learn to live together with respect for others in our minds, with good will for others in our hearts, and crown our good with brotherhood from sea to shining sea. Amen.

WEDNESDAY, JANUARY 28, 1970

Happy is the man that findeth wisdom and the man that getteth understanding.—Proverbs 3: 13.

Almighty God, who art our light in darkness, our life in trouble, and our love in sorrow, bless us as with one mind we draw to Thee seeking the power of Thy presence and the guidance of Thy spirit.

Throughout this day keep our hearts with Thee that in quiet confidence we may solve the perplexing problems of these hours with a wisdom greater than our own.

In the midst of this divided world send us forth as heralds of good will crossing all barriers of class and creed that we may make our contribution to the glorious day when justice and freedom shall live in every heart and in every nation.

In the Master's name we pray. Amen.

THURSDAY, JANUARY 29, 1970

If you believe in goodness, if you value the approval of God, fix your mind on the things which are holy and right and pure and beautiful and good.— Philippians 4: 8 (Phillips).

OUR FATHER GOD, who hast taught us that only the pure in heart can see Thee, cleanse our hearts of all impurity, all impenitence, and all impatience. Give to us such a love for that which is good and true and beautiful that we may be made strong in temptation and give strength to those who are tempted as we are.

Let not our strength fail, our steps falter, or our spirits faint as we labor for the good of our beloved America.

This day, and every day, may we place our hands in Thine, look up to Thee, and face the hours with faith and fortitude knowing Thou art with us and we are with Thee as we endeavor to lead our people in the ways of justice and the nations in the paths of peace.

We pray in the spirit of Him whose life is the light of men. Amen.

MONDAY, FEBRUARY 2, 1970

Bless ye the Lord, all ye hosts; ye ministers of His, that do His pleasure.— Psalm 103: 21.

ALMIGHTY AND ETERNAL GOD, at the beginning of International Clergy Week, we pause in Thy presence to pray for the clergymen of our land and our world. Give them grace to walk worthily in the calling to which they have been called, to serve Thee with all humility and patience, to help our fellow men with all sympathy and love, to promote integrity and good will in our Nation with all eagerness and enthusiasm, and to pave the way to peace in our world with all earnestness and sincerity. In all they plan may Thy thoughts guide their thinking, Thy wisdom make wise their minds, Thy love warm their hearts, and Thy purposes purify their lives.

Our lives are richer by reason of the ministry of those who minister in Thy name. Accept our gratitude for their presence in our midst.

Our Father, another of our colleagues has gone home to be with Thee. Receive him into Thy heavenly glory and bless his family with the comfort of Thy presence and the love of Thy spirit. Strengthen them for this experience and guide them step by step as they face the days ahead.

In Thy holy name we pray. Amen.

WEDNESDAY, FEBRUARY 4, 1970

Behold, Thou desirest truth in the inward being; therefore teach me wisdom in my secret heart.—Psalm 51: 6.

O GOD, OUR FATHER, who desirest truth in the inward life, in this disturbing day when falsehoods wear the masks of truth as they appeal for the allegiance of men, grant unto us the spirit of discernment and the wisdom of the wise that we may not be deceived by the followers of evil who wear the flower of heaven on their lapels and seek to disguise their low motives by the lofty flavor of high sounding words.

Help us to keep looking at that which is good and true and excellent that we may keep in step with Thee as we move forward to a better day when our Nation shall be great in spirit, great in good will, and great in the brotherhood of men.

In the spirit of Him who is the way, the truth, and the life, we pray.

Amen.

MONDAY, FEBRUARY 16, 1970

Teach me to do Thy will; for Thou art my God; Thy spirit is good; lead me into the land of uprightness.—Psalm 143: 10.

O GOD, OUR FATHER, whose will is peace, whose nature is love, and whose desire is that we live in peace with Thee and in love with one another grant unto us a vision of Thy purpose for mankind as we lean on the windowsill of heaven and look up to Thee in prayer.

Deliver us from antagonisms that annoy us, from trifles that try us, from disagreements that make us disagreeable, and by Thy spirit make us great in goodness, good in our greatness, and genuine in all our endeavors on behalf of our beloved country.

Amid the problems that perplex us and the difficulties that dismay us do Thou strengthen and sustain our spirits and lead us in the paths of righteousness for Thy name's sake.   Amen.

MONDAY, FEBRUARY 23, 1970

The ways of the Lord are right and the just shall walk in them.—Hosea 14: 9.

O THOU GOD of all goodness and of all grace; we assemble here in this historic Chamber to call to mind once again the birthday of our first President, whom we acknowledge to be the Father of our Country.

We recall with pride his willingness to adventure, his courage amid difficulties, and his devotion to the high principles of righteousness and justice which led him to champion the cause of freedom in our land.

Above all we thank Thee for his faith—the faith which time and again sent him to his knees in prayer seeking guidance and strength and wisdom that he might keep in step with Thee.

May the memory of this great spirit spur us to greater efforts in the adventure of bringing peace, freedom, and justice to this troubled world.

In the Master's name we pray. Amen.

WEDNESDAY, FEBRUARY 25, 1970

And now abideth faith, hope, and love, these three; but the greatest of these is love.—I Corinthians 13: 13.

O God and Father of mankind we call to mind before Thee the men and women who come from other lands to visit our country and to study at our universities in an attempt to learn something about our way of living. Keep alive in them and in us the love of that which is good that goodness may live in all our hearts.

Particularly do we pray for the President of France who visits us this day. Guide his country and ours that together we may walk in Thy ways and make freedom, justice, and peace an increasing reality in our troubled world. Let no bitterness separate us, but may good will fill our hearts and bind us together in a fellowship of kindred minds seeking the good of all mankind.

In the spirit of the Prince of Peace we pray. Amen.

MONDAY, MARCH 2, 1970

He leadeth me in the paths of righteousness for His name's sake.—Psalm 23: 3.

Our Heavenly Father, mindful of our responsibilities as the leaders of our people we bow before Thee praying that we may be led in right paths for the sake of our beloved America. May Thy spirit guide us that we be saved from false choices and be lifted to new heights of creative endeavor and courageous action. Together as leaders and people may we be physically strong, mentally awake, morally straight, and religiously alive.

We pray for the family of our beloved colleague who has gone home to be with Thee. We are grateful for his devotion to the district he represented, for his dedication to our country he loved with all his heart, and for his faith in Thee which held him steady throughout his life. May the comfort of Thy presence abide with his family and may the strength of Thy spirit dwell in all our hearts.

In the Master's name we pray. Amen.

WEDNESDAY, MARCH 4, 1970

Why art thou cast down, O my soul? and why art thou disquieted within me? Hope thou in God.—Psalm 42: 5.

O Thou whose presence underlies all that we do, whose power overarches all that we say, and whose peace surrounds all that we think, we bow at the shrine our fathers founded and lift our spirits unto Thee in prayer. As we offer unto Thee the devotion of our hearts, may the fruits of Thy spirit—love and joy, gentleness and goodness, patience and peace—come to new life within us.

We pray for our country and for our people in every section of our land. May the hungry be fed, the ignorant receive knowledge, the fearful find faith, and the weary come to rest at eventide. Grant that we may do all we can that children be raised to walk in right and good paths, that youth discover high ideals for clean and creative living, and that adults in body become adults in mind.

Abundantly bless our President, our Speaker, Members of Congress, and direct them in all Thy ways—to the glory of Thy holy name. Amen.

MONDAY, MARCH 9, 1970

So we do not lose heart. Though our outer nature is wasting away, our inner nature is being renewed every day.—II Corinthians 4: 16.

Eternal God, whose paths are mercy and truth and who dost endeavor to lead Thy children to the heights of righteousness and peace, we come to Thee seeking light upon our way, strength for our tasks, wisdom to see clearly, and the courage to do what ought to be done for the well-being of our country.

Help us to live this day with joy and peace, without stumbling and without stain, because Thou art with us and we are with Thee. May the labor of these hours be in accordance with Thy holy will and for the good of all our people.

"Come, O Lord, like morning sunlight,
Making all life new and free;
For the daily task and challenge
May we rise renewed in Thee."

Amen.

WEDNESDAY, MARCH 11, 1970

Exalt the Lord our God, and worship at His holy hill; for the Lord our God is holy.—Psalm 99: 9.

O LORD, OUR GOD, whose glory is in all the world and whose goodness continues forever, we commend ourselves and our Nation to Thee that being conscious of Thy presence, governed by Thy spirit, and living in Thy love we may dwell secure in peace and good will.

Bless our land with wise government, sound learning, and vital religion. Save us from discord and disunity, from pride and prejudice, and from vice and violence. Strengthen the bonds of friendliness between the citizens of our beloved land and make strong the ties of fellowship between the nations of the world. Plant love in every heart, truth in every home, faith in every church, justice in every nation, and peace in all our world. And may the love of Thy dear name hallow every noble endeavor for good.

In the spirit of Christ we pray.   Amen.

MONDAY, MARCH 16, 1970

Be of good courage and He shall strengthen your heart, all ye that hope in the Lord.—Psalm 31: 24.

O GRACIOUS FATHER OF MANKIND, our spirits' unseen friend, to Thee our prayer ascends at the beginning of another week. Help us to live through these troubled times with faith and hope and love. Let not our strength fail, nor our vision fade, nor our trust in Thee falter in the heat and burden of the day. Make us patient with one another and understanding, remembering that each one faces demanding duties and each one walks a lonely road.

Sustain us, O God, as we endeavor to do our duty, to seek the best for our country, and to lead our people in right and good paths. Day by day, whatever befalls us, may we hold Thy hand, look up to Thy face, and endeavor to walk with Thee until our work is done and our day comes to a close. In Thy name we pray.   Amen.

TUESDAY, MARCH 17, 1970

Blessed is the man who endures trial, for when he has stood the test he will receive the crown of life which God has promised to those who love Him.—James 1: 12.

O GOD OUR FATHER, who opens the gates of the morning and calls us to a new day, we commit our lives and our work unto Thee in the glad assurance that Thou art with us within the shadows and behind them working out Thy purpose for mankind.

In these trying times when our souls are troubled as we seek the good of man, when so much is demanded of us who would serve this present age, grant unto us insight and inspiration together with courage and confidence that we may prove ourselves worthy of the tasks our country has placed in our hands.

Confronted by problems too great for us to solve by ourselves we are driven to Thee for wisdom to see what must be done, for courage to set out to do it, and for strength to complete it.

O God, make us great enough and good enough for these challenging days. In the spirit of Christ we pray.   Amen.

WEDNESDAY, MARCH 18, 1970

Behold, God is my salvation; I will trust and not be afraid.—Isaiah 12: 2.

ETERNAL SPIRIT, who art the hope of the world and the help of all who put their trust in Thee, be Thou our hope and our help as we come to Thee in this our morning prayer. Lead us to the rock that is higher than we, and there may we find strength for each day, courage for each hour, confidence for each minute, and faith for each second. Thus may we defeat the foes that would conquer our spirits by being strong in Thee.

Our prayer leaps across the boundaries of color, creed, and culture to include the world in which we live. In spite of differences, bind us together in a common obedience to the moral law and make our faith real enough and strong enough to unite mankind in a fellowship of kindred minds. While it is yet day may we choose light and not darkness, love and not hate, truth and not falsehood, peace and not war—to the glory of Thy holy name.

Amen.

MONDAY, MARCH 23, 1970

All the paths of the Lord are steadfast love and faithfulness for those who keep His covenant and His testimonies.—Psalm 25: 10.

O GOD, OUR FATHER, whose power is without measure and whose judgments are true and righteous altogether, from the busy world about us and at the beginning of another day we would quiet our hearts in Thy presence and wait for Thy still, small voice.

Grant unto us the wisdom to know what we should do and the strength to do it Thy way. Undergird our lives that we may make decisions wisely, walk the high road of noble purpose faithfully, and with outreaching sympathy seek to heal the wounds of our human family.

We may move along an unknown path but we go forward with a firm faith in the reality of goodness, truth, and love and with the abiding assurance that Thou art with us.

In the name of the Master of men we pray. Amen.

THURSDAY, MARCH 26, 1970

This do in remembrance of Me.—Luke 22: 19.

As WE CONTINUE OUR WAY THROUGH HOLY WEEK, OUR FATHER, we would climb the stairs that lead to the upper room where we may be still and know that Thou art God, and from Thee receive forgiveness for our sins, love for our hearts, wisdom for our minds, and humility for our spirits.

Here we pray for our families whose affection and understanding make life worth living, for our friends whose faithfulness and friendliness make our existence a joy, for our Nation where freedom is a rich blessing and in whose heart we seek good will with justice for all, for the nations of the world, asking that we learn to treat them as we want them to treat us.

From this upper room of prayer send us out into the world to do justly, to love mercy, and to walk humbly with Thee.

In the spirit of the Master we pray. Amen.

MONDAY, APRIL 6, 1970

Choose you this day whom ye will serve: as for me and my house we will serve the Lord.—Joshua 24: 15.

O LORD, OUR GOD, who art the light of the world and the life of men, let Thy light shine upon us and Thy presence come to new life within as we pray in spirit and in truth. Strengthen our hearts that we may now and always be reverent in thought, word, and deed.

Bless our country with Thy gracious favor and make our people one in spirit, one in purpose, and one in steadfast good will. Whatever our differences, may we realize that we are one in Thee and may this bond of unity be increasingly strengthened until we learn to live together as good Americans in our great America.

In the spirit of the Master we pray. Amen.

WEDNESDAY, APRIL 8, 1970

O worship the Lord in the beauty of holiness: fear before Him, all the earth, for He shall judge the world with righteousness.—Psalm 96: 9, 13.

O GOD AND FATHER OF MANKIND, who hast preserved us as a nation and hast given us this good land for our heritage, grant unto us, who lead the people of this country, an unfailing and unfaltering devotion to Thee and to the welfare of our citizens.

Give us insight to see clearly what must be done to meet the needs of our countrymen, feeding the hungry, strengthening the weak, establishing justice, and building good will.

With this insight give us the inspiration to do it Thy way until justice and righteousness shall rule our Nation and peace and good will shall reign in the hearts of all nations.

In Thy holy name we pray. Amen.

THURSDAY, APRIL 16, 1970

He who is faithful in a very little is faithful also in much.—Luke 16: 10.

ETERNAL GOD, we pray for our Nation set today amid the perplexities of a changing order and face to face with great new tasks. We remember with pride how our leaders in times past arose to the occasion defending our liberties and preserving our unity. We recall with love the influence of dedicated spirits who devoted themselves to the welfare of our people.

Now we come to Thee in this challenging day praying that we may have courage to meet our tasks with clarity of purpose, strength to carry our responsibilities with high honor and faith to serve our people with fine fidelity.

God bless America. Let Your healing, cleansing, and strengthening power move in our hearts as a nation and bring us together who belong together, who need each other, who can help each other and who would enjoy each other.

Bless our astronauts. Grant unto them the peace of Thy presence, unto their families the strength of Thy spirit and unto us all the assurance that Thou art with us as they safely return to earth. Amen.

MONDAY, APRIL 20, 1970

Remember the day in which you came out of the land of slavery; for it was by a strong hand that the Lord brought you out.—Exodus 13: 3.

O Lord Our God, and God of our fathers, we greet Thee at the beginning of another week and on the eve of the Passover of our Hebrew brethren. As Thou didst lead the children of Israel out of the house of bondage into the promised land of liberty, so do Thou lead us into a new day of greater justice, of larger freedom, and of a finer spirit on the part of all our people.

Cleanse the hearts of men of the passions of hate and strife, of greed and lust for power, and fill them with faith and hope and love. Speed the Passover of the future when injustice shall cease, intolerance shall vanish, and freedom and peace shall reign forever. Hasten the day when all men shall learn that they are brothers and with joy proclaim Thee the God and Father of us all.

And we thank Thee for the safe return of our astronauts.

In Thy holy name we pray. Amen.

MONDAY, MAY 4, 1970

Be strong in the Lord and in the power of His might.—Ephesians 6: 10.

Almighty God, infinite in wisdom, power and love, whose mercy is over all Thy works and whose will is ever directed to Thy children's good, humbly we bow in Thy presence as we pray for those in the service of our country, particularly those who are prisoners of war—absent from their loved ones yet always present with Thee. Protect them from all dangers of body and spirit, grant unto them humane treatment, help them to be patient with themselves good to their fellowmen, and strong in Thee who art the strength of all Thy children.

Bless their families with the assurance of Thy presence and the comfort of Thy spirit. May they look forward with faith and hope to a safe return of their loved ones and to the end of the war.

We pray for the family of our beloved colleague who has gone home to be with Thee. Grant them Thy comfort and the strength of Thy spirit as they live through these days.

In the Master's name we pray. Amen.

WEDNESDAY, MAY 6, 1970

Thou shalt do that which is right and good in the sight of the Lord.—
Deuteronomy 6: 18.

ALMIGHTY GOD, who knowest our needs before we ask and who art endeavoring to lead us in right and good paths, we turn to Thee in this fellowship of prayer seeking light for our lives, hope for our hearts, and strength for our spirits.

We come to Thee in the midst of the problems and perplexities of daily living praying for greater faith, for higher wisdom, for broader sympathies, and for deeper good will. We are tempted to doubt, to yield to moods of depression, and to become cynical. By the might of Thy spirit restore our souls and lead us into the green paths of righteousness, peace, and love for Thy name's sake and for the good of all mankind.

Guide our Nation in these troubled times. Bless our President, our Speaker, Members of Congress, and all who work under the dome of this glorious Capitol. Increase our influence for good in the world by our genuine reliance upon Thee and by our generous response to the needs of our fellow men. In the spirit of Christ we pray. Amen.

MONDAY, MAY 11, 1970

*God is not far from each one of us, for in Him we live and move and have our being.—*Acts 17: 27, 28.

O GOD AND FATHER OF US ALL, we bow before Thee reverently and humbly as we begin the work of another week. Thou art with us every moment of every day. Help us, we pray Thee, to be aware of Thy presence as we endeavor to lead our people in right and just and good paths.

We thank Thee for brave words and courageous deeds which have made our Nation great among the nations of the world. In this moment we pray for those who with word and deed are seeking to keep our Nation great in this day—our leaders in Congress, the men and women in the Armed Forces of our country, those who labor for peace and freedom, and all who strive for liberty in law and law in liberty.

Give truth to our minds, love to our hearts, courage to our spirits, and strength to our hands that we may make patriotism shine with loyalty and love and life.

In the Master's name we pray. Amen.

WEDNESDAY, MAY 13, 1970

If thou shalt seek the Lord thy God, thou shalt find Him, if thou seek Him with all thy heart and with all thy soul.—Deuteronomy 4: 29.

ALMIGHTY AND ETERNAL GOD, without whom no one can live wisely and well, reveal to us Thy will and show us Thy way amid the problems of this perplexing period. As we draw near to Thee in prayer, so do Thou draw near to us, that in all the decisions we make we may be mindful of Thy presence, eager to do Thy will, and ready to walk in Thy way for the good of our beloved United States of America. Enlighten our understanding, purify our desires, strengthen every noble purpose, and make us diligent among the demanding duties of this disquieting day.

Give to these Members of Congress the willingness to listen to the voices of our day and with that the greater willingness to listen to the voice of the ages as we seek what is right and good for our country and endeavor to lead our people in the ways of peace and good will. To this end may our lips praise Thee, our lives bless Thee, our works glorify Thee, for Thy name's sake. Amen.

TUESDAY, MAY 19, 1970

The peace of God, which passes all understanding, will keep your hearts and your minds.—Philippians 4: 7.

O GOD AND FATHER OF US ALL, Thou hast made us to live in faith with Thee and in love with one another, yet our world is worried by war, our Nation divided, and our own lives troubled. We confess our faults, our lack of faith, and our failure to love. Forgive us, we pray, and help us from this day forward to be more responsive to Thee and more ready to react affirmatively to the needs of our fellow men.

Bless our Nation, our President, our National and State leaders. Particularly do we pray for the Members of this House of Representatives, our Speaker, and all who work with them. May they take time to listen to Thee and, in so doing, be given insight to see clearly the way to take, courage to walk in that way, and patience to persist in pursuing peace at home and abroad. May they be channels through which justice and freedom and good will can come to greater life in our Nation and in our world.

In the spirit of Christ we pray. Amen.

THURSDAY, MAY 21, 1970

Blessed be the name of God forever and ever: for wisdom and might are His.—Daniel 2: 20.

OUR FATHER GOD, reveal to us Thy glory as we turn our thoughts upward and lift our hearts into Thy presence. May discernment and discretion with confidence and courage arise within us with new vigor as we open our minds to Thee who art always understanding, always merciful and always seeking our good and the good of our people.

Grant unto us as we pray such an awareness of Thy spirit that this day may be spent in Thy service and for the best interests of our country. Give to us the grace to ask what Thou wouldst have us do that in Thy wisdom we may be saved from false choices, in Thy light we may walk and not faint, and in Thy love we may live with true freedom, through Jesus Christ our Lord. Amen.

MONDAY, MAY 25, 1970

He that handleth a matter wisely shall find good: and who so trusteth in the Lord, happy is he.—Proverbs 16: 20.

O THOU WHOSE PRESENCE SURROUNDS US, whose Power supports us, and whose Peace sustains us, our minds and hearts widen with wonder when we consider how mindful Thou art of us and how eager to lead us in right and just and good paths.

Inspire us, we pray, with a deeper concern for the welfare of mankind and instill in us a greater desire to walk with Thee and to work together that Thy kingdom of righteousness and peace may come and Thy will be done on earth.

Bless these Members of Congress as they endeavor to maintain a free society which respects the dignity of the individual and where understanding and justice are established. May they be united in spirit as they seek to solve the problems that beset this challenging day.

We pray for the family of our beloved Architect who has gone home to be with Thee. May the comfort of Thy spirit abide in their hearts now and forever.

In the Master's name we pray. Amen.

WEDNESDAY, MAY 27, 1970

With the Lord is strength and wisdom.—Job 12: 16.

Dear Lord and Father of us all, as the quiet splendor of a new day dawns upon us we look up to Thee seeking the guidance of Thy spirit, the goodness of Thy presence and the greatness of Thy power. In the heat and burden of this day let not our spirits fail, our steps falter nor our strength fade. Help us to stand visibly and vitally for what is right and just and good.

Bless our beloved Speaker and his wife, Harriet. We thank Thee for his long and faithful service in this body and for his wise and sound leadership as the Speaker of the House of Representatives. Grant unto this wonderful couple health and strength for years to come.

Keep in our hearts the loving remembrance of those who across the years have given their lives for our country and for those who even now are giving their lives or have become prisoners of war that we may be one nation under Thee with liberty and justice for all.   Amen.

MONDAY, JUNE 1, 1970

Thou shalt guide me with Thy counsel.—Psalms 73: 24.

Almighty and Everlasting God, who hast created us in Thine own image and called us to live together in the spirit of brotherhood, grant unto us to fearlessly contend against evil, to make no peace with oppression and to use our freedom in the maintenance of justice between men, good will among our people, and peace in our world.

We pray for our Nation in these troubled times. Direct the decisions of these Members of Congress that they may be in accord with Thy will, seeking the welfare of our country and the well-being of all mankind.

Guide the nations of the world into the ways of justice and truth and establish among them the peace which is the fruit of righteousness and good will—to the glory of Thy holy name.   Amen.

WEDNESDAY, JUNE 3, 1970

Let all the ends of the earth remember and turn again to the Lord.—Psalms 22: 27.

Almighty and Eternal God, who exaltest the nations that follow the way of righteousness, we pray for our President, our Speaker, Members of Congress, and all to whom have been committed the government of this Nation. Grant unto them wisdom, understanding, and strength that, upholding what is right, supporting what is good, and following what is true, they may fulfill Thy purpose for mankind.

We pray for the President of Venezuela and the people of that great land. May we be one in spirit as we seek to promote peace in the world, cooperation between the nations, and good will among all people.

In the spirit of the Prince of Peace, we offer the morning prayer. Amen.

MONDAY, JULY 6, 1970

Trust ye in the Lord forever: for in the Lord God is everlasting strength.— Isaiah 26: 4.

OUR HEAVENLY FATHER, we thank Thee for our brief recess, for the rest of the nights, for the refreshment of the days, and for the beginning of another week. As we face the tasks and trials of these hours help us to trust Thee completely and strengthen us to do what we ought to do.

Bless these Representatives and protect our country, keeping them all in Thy love and peace, through Jesus Christ, our Lord. Amen.

WEDNESDAY, JULY 8, 1970

*Every good tree bringeth forth good fruit.—*Matthew 7: 17.

WE OPEN OUR MINDS UNTO THEE, OUR FATHER, and pray that Thy spirit may come anew into our hearts, giving us power for the living of these days. Remove from within us any bitterness that blights our lives, any resentment that ruins our dispositions, and any worry that wearies us and wears us out.

Help us to think cleanly and clearly, to speak forcefully and faithfully, to work heartily and hopefully, and to live trustfully and truly. In this spirit may we learn to do what is best for our country and good for our world.

In the spirit of Christ we pray. Amen.

THURSDAY, JULY 9, 1970

*Ye shall know the truth and the truth shall make you free.—*John 8: 32.

ETERNAL GOD, OUR FATHER, we come to Thee in this quiet moment praying that Thy spirit may shine into our hearts darkened so often by doubt and fear. Strengthen and guide us as we seek sincerely to lead our Nation in right paths, along peaceful roads, and make plain the ways we should take.

Help us to realize that freedom must be won by every generation. With Thy spirit may we keep the flag of the free flying in our land and ultimately, we pray, in our world.

Grant that all threats to liberty be met with courage and with confidence, assured that Thy power undergirds the struggle for freedom.

In Thy name we pray. Amen.

MONDAY, JULY 13, 1970

Thou art my rock and my fortress: Therefore for Thy name's sake lead me and guide me.—Psalm 31: 3.

Almighty and Everlasting God, who art the Father of all mankind, we turn from the activities of the day to lift our spirits unto Thee from whom all blessings flow. Keep us ever mindful of Thy presence for without Thee all our labor is in vain.

We pray for guidance as we face the duties of these hours, as we make our decisions, and as we plan for the welfare of our beloved America. For courage and faith we pray that through these difficult days we may do justly, love mercy, and walk humbly with Thee.

Bless those who serve under the flag of our country, these Members of Congress, the men and women in our Armed Forces, our prisoners of war, and those in civilian offices. Keep us all united in the common cause of life, liberty, and the pursuit of happiness for all men.

In the Master's name we pray. Amen.

TUESDAY, JULY 14, 1970

The Lord is my strength and my shield: my heart trusts in Him and I am helped.—Psalm 28: 7.

Eternal God and Father of us all, in whose presence our restless spirits find peace, by whose guidance we are led in the paths of righteousness, and under whose banner we find our souls renewed, we turn from the tumult of a troubled world, not to evade it, but to be given insight to face our perplexing problems with a courageous faith, a confident hope, and a creative spirit.

Bestow upon us an abundance of good, sound commonsense, season it with understanding, flavor it with love, stir it with truth, that out of our efforts on behalf of our country may come a greater unity of free men living together in good will striving for peace in our world.

In the spirit of Christ we pray. Amen.

WEDNESDAY, JULY 15, 1970

O give thanks unto the Lord, for He is good: for His mercy endureth forever.—Psalm 118: 29.

O THOU IN WHOM WE LIVE AND MOVE AND HAVE OUR BEING, and from whom flows the life that is in us all, we thank Thee for the mercies which daily attend our days. For family and friends, for homes in which love rules, for churches in which we can worship as we desire, and for a Nation that is free, we thank Thee. For tasks which make us strong, for truth which enforces our endeavors for justice, and for love which enfolds us in our search for peace, we thank Thee.

Strengthen us to struggle against every enemy of the human spirit, to stand valiantly for what is true, right, and good, and help us so to live our own lives that when night comes we may not only receive praise from Thee but may also have the inner assurance of having fought a good fight and having kept the faith.

Bless our dear ones with the gift of Thy grace, comfort the sorrowing, heal the sick, and give light to all who sit in darkness. Bless our Nation with Thy favor and bring peace to all the nations: So may Thy kingdom come and Thy will be done on earth, to the glory of Thy holy name. Amen.

MONDAY, JUNE 8, 1970

The spirit of the Lord is upon me because He hath sent me to heal the brokenhearted, to preach deliverance to the captives, and to set at liberty them that are bruised.—Luke 4: 18.

O GOD AND FATHER OF US ALL, whose concern for the welfare of Thy children never fails and who calls us to be concerned about the well being of our people, prosper, we pray Thee, the labors of those who seek to minister to the needs of our countrymen, especially our prisoners of war. For these prisoners we offer a special prayer. Comfort them with Thy heavenly grace, strengthen them in their trials, and keep alive in them the hope of release from capture and a reunion with their families.

May the replicas picturing the state of our prisoners in our Capitol crypt arouse our people to the need of doing all we can to relieve their suffering and may we not rest until it is done.

In the name of Him who is the strength of our lives, we pray. Amen.

TUESDAY, JUNE 9, 1970

Be doers of the word and not hearers only.—James 1: 22.

O GOD, OUR FATHER, who art the creator of the world and the sustainer of life, into Thine ennobling presence we lift our spirits this day. Awaken in us the realization that Thou hast a purpose for each one of us, that life is filled with meaning, and that Thou dost even now speak to us in a still, small voice. Hushed we stand in Thy presence, seeking Thy guidance, eager to do Thy will, and ready to make our land a safe place in which to live.

Somehow we have failed in many ways. This Nation is not what it ought to be. There is too much violence, too much ill will, too much division. We pray that through the power of Thy spirit we, the representatives of our people, may bring a new unity of purpose to our country, a higher value of true patriotism, a greater conception of what it means to be an American, and a more passionate concern for the welfare of our citizens.

May our example in maturity help bring maturity to those younger than we. In the Redeemer's name we pray. Amen.

THURSDAY, JUNE 11, 1970

He looked for a city which hath foundations, whose builder and maker is God.—Hebrew 11: 10.

O GOD OF GRACE AND GOODNESS, we thank Thee for America with her high mountains, her deep valleys, her broad plains; for her homes, her churches, her schools, her Government; above all, for her people dedicated to faith, to freedom, and to the fruits of democratic living. We thank Thee for the heritage which is ours—the good gifts of the past—and we pray that we may continue these good works in the present, taking steps which lead to the higher ground of a free and a just society.

Help us and our people to accept our responsibilities as citizens of this Republic we love—to vote intelligently, to pay our taxes readily, to obey the laws of our land fully, to give our influence to right and good causes heartily, and to live as free men ought to live, going beyond the requirements of justice and mercy.

Thus may we begin to feel a bit at home in Thy kingdom, through Jesus Christ our Lord. Amen.

MONDAY, JUNE 15, 1970

Lift ye up a banner upon the high mountain, that men may go into the gates of the nobles.—Isaiah 13: 2.

O GOD OF TRUTH AND LOVE, we come to Thee this day as we unfurl the starry banner of our life as a nation and celebrate its birth. Floating high in the air may it ever speak to men of liberty and justice, of peace and good will. Wherever it goes, whenever it is seen, may it bring hope to the oppressed, freedom to those in bondage, and light to all who sit in darkness.

Under this banner and by Thy grace may we keep moving forward toward the goal of a free world at peace, with liberty and justice for all. To the glory of Thy holy name. Amen.

WEDNESDAY, JUNE 17, 1970

Let integrity and uprightness preserve me; for I wait on Thee.—Psalm 25: 21.

ETERNAL GOD, OUR FATHER, who hast brought us to the beginning of a new day, grant that in all our ways and always we may remember that Thou art with us. Help us to do our duties, to carry our responsibilities, and to make our decisions with sincerity of mind and genuineness of heart. Remove from us all pretense, all deceit, all hypocrisy, and by Thy spirit may we do what we believe to be right for our country and good for our people.

Fill our lives with the mood of love and the motive of service that we may leap the boundaries of class, color, and creed and seek to minister to the needs of all Thy children.

In the Master's name we pray. Amen.

THURSDAY, JUNE 18, 1970

O keep my soul and deliver me; let me not be ashamed; for I put my trust in Thee.—Psalm 25: 20.

INFINITE AND ETERNAL GOD, whose way is life, whose work is truth, and whose will is love—let Thy presence abide in our hearts this day and all days, that seeking Thy life we may find it, searching for Thy truth we may discover it, and striving for Thy love we may possess it. Thus may we dwell together safely and securely, proving ourselves faithful to Thy trust in us.

We commend our country to Thy loving care and keeping. Guide our leaders in right paths and our people in true ways for Thy name's sake.

Particularly do we pray for the men and women in our Armed Forces and for our prisoners of war. Strengthen them to endure what must be endured and give them hope for the end of conflict, for peace, and for a safe return to their loved ones.

In the spirit of the Prince of Peace we pray.   Amen.

MONDAY, JUNE 22, 1970

Lead me in Thy truth and teach me: for Thou art the God of my salvation: on Thee do I wait all the day.—Psalm 25: 5.

O GOD AND FATHER OF ALL MEN, who changest not in a world of change, who art forever loving, forever forgiving, and forever patient, amid the tumult of these troubled times we would enter the peace of Thy presence, receive the strength of Thy spirit, and go forth to labor with Thee in making this planet a better place in which men can live together.

Help us to build on earth a rule of peace and good will, a reign of human rights where there shall be no hunger, no discrimination, no lack of education, and a realm where man can grow not only in body, but even more in mind and, best of all, in spirit.

> "Set our feet on lofty places:
>> Gird our lives that they may be
>> Armored with all Christ-like graces
>> In the fight to set men free,
>> Grant us wisdom, grant us courage,
>> That we fail not man nor Thee."

                                                Amen.

WEDNESDAY, JUNE 24, 1970

And ye shall proclaim liberty throughout all the land unto all the inhabitants thereof.—Leviticus 25: 10.

O GOD, OUR FATHER, in this sacred moment we would rise above the feverish activities of a seething world where we can be still and hear Thy voice seeking to guide us as we face the perplexing problems of this difficult day. During this hour of our national life, when the world's best hope for a bright tomorrow is largely in our frail hands, do Thou help us to preserve our heritage of freedom, to proclaim liberty to all the world, and to promote peace and good will among all people.

To this end bless our President, our Speaker, Members of Congress, and all who work with them that in this day of decision we may not lose the way.

"Cure Thy children's warring madness,
Bend our pride to Thy Control:
Shame our wanton, selfish gladness,
Rich in things and poor in soul,
Grant us wisdom, grant us courage,
Lest we miss Thy Kingdom's goal."

Amen.

MONDAY, JUNE 29, 1970

Say to them that are of a fearful heart, be strong, fear not: behold your God will come and save you.—Isaiah 35: 4.

ALMIGHTY AND EVERLASTING GOD, quiet our hearts and strengthen our spirits as we wait upon Thee in prayer. During trying times like these keep us steadfast and strong and renew in us the assurance that goodness never fades, truth never falters, love never fails. May there come to us the lift of life that is given to those whose talents are dedicated to noble purposes and whose lives are devoted to the welfare of our country.

We pray for our beloved America that in this day of decision she may be delivered from all envy and greed, all misunderstanding, and ill will which are the seeds of division and be led to a finer spirit of unity and a greater desire to serve which will make her quick to welcome every adventure in cooperation and open wide the doors of opportunity to all men: To the glory of Thy holy name. Amen.

WEDNESDAY, JULY 1, 1970

Behold, how good and how pleasant it is for brethren to dwell together in unity.—Psalm 133: 1.

GOD OF OUR FATHERS, as we draw near the day when we celebrate the birthday of our independence as a nation, we pause to acknowledge our dependence upon Thee, to thank Thee for Thy guiding spirit in the past, and to pray that the power of Thy presence may fit us fully for the future. Without Thee we can do nothing, but with Thee all good and great things are possible.

We remember with affection and honor those who have given and are giving their lives on behalf of our country and in the service of noble causes. By the power of every life usefully lived, by the spirit of every person worthily engaged, may we make our Nation great in moral character, great in religious faith, great in justice and in the brotherhood of man.

May the words of our mouths, the worship of our hearts, and the works of our hands be useful in ushering in the day when men and nations shall learn to live together peacefully, in freedom and with good will toward all. In the spirit of Christ we pray.   Amen.

MONDAY, JULY 20, 1970

Let the peace of God rule in your hearts and be ye thankful.—Colossians 3: 15.

O GOD OUR FATHER, we rejoice in the dawning of another week and pray that we may be so conscious of Thy presence and so receptive to the leading of Thy spirit that we may walk more worthily in Thy wholesome ways. We know that Thou art with us and we want to feel that we are with Thee.

Deepen our faith, increase our love, strengthen our hands that we may be faithful to Thee, devoted to our country, and true to the best within us. We do not ask Thee to remove our temptations but to give us power to meet them courageously, to manage them confidently, and to master them creatively. We do not pray for tasks equal to our strength but for strength equal to our tasks; not for responsibilities we can carry easily but for an inner spirit to carry our responsibilities, however heavy.

Grant unto us such greatness of soul, such gentleness of spirit, such goodness of heart that we may do our duties with due regard for the rights of others. So may we be just and kind in all our ways and honest and straightforward through all our days.

In the Master's name we pray.   Amen.

WEDNESDAY, JULY 22, 1970

True justice is the harvest reaped by peacemakers from seeds sown in a spirit of peace.—James 3: 18 (new English Bible).

O LORD, OUR GOD, who hast made this earth a grand place in which man can live, reveal to us Thy will and renew Thy love in us that responding to Thee we may learn to live together on this planet in peace and with good will.

Help us to feel Thy presence within us this day seeking to guide us as we determine our decisions and striving to assist us in leading our people along the roads to righteousness, our Nation along the ways of justice, and our world along the paths of peace.

"Incline our hearts with Godly fear
To seek Thy face, Thy word revere;

Cause Thou all wrongs, all strife to cease
And lead us in the paths of peace."
Through Jesus Christ, our Lord. Amen.

THURSDAY, JULY 23, 1970

Restore unto me the joy of Thy salvation: and uphold me with Thy free spirit.—Psalms 51: 12.

ALMIGHTY GOD, unto whom all hearts are open, all desires known, and from whom no secrets are hid, make Thy presence known to us throughout the hours of this day. Fill our minds with wisdom, our hearts with love, and our spirits with the desire to walk humbly in the way of Thy commandments.

We are glad that we are American citizens and that we live in this blessed land of liberty. Let no violence, no prejudice, no discord dim our vision of a free people living together harmoniously, working for peace in our world.

Bless our President, our Speaker, our Members of Congress, and all who work under the dome of this Capitol. Bless every individual citizen that the sacred rights of a free people may be ours forever.

In the name of Him who keeps men free we pray. Amen.

MONDAY, JULY 27, 1970

Let the beauty of the Lord our God be upon us.—Psalm 90: 17.

GOD OF GRACE AND GOD OF GOODNESS, in the glory of another day, throbbing with the loveliness of summer, we pause in Thy presence with hearts aflame with the beauty about us—the blue skies, the green fields, and the flowers in bloom. May this beauty be a sacrament in which we become more aware of the greatness of Thy spirit.

Bless these Representatives of our Nation. Give them wisdom and guidance in all their deliberations. Endow them with pure motives, patriotic endeavors, and unselfish service. Lead them in leading our people in the ways of righteousness and peace. So shall we, looking up to Thee, learn to laugh and love and live, to the glory of Thy holy name.

We pause in sorrow as we think of the passing of our beloved colleague, MIKE KIRWAN. We thank Thee for the great contribution he made to our country serving so well and so faithfully in Congress. May the memory of his grand spirit linger forever in our hearts. Comfort his family with Thy presence and strengthen us to carry on the work which now must be done without him.

In Thy holy name we pray. Amen.

WEDNESDAY, JULY 29, 1970

We are laborers together with God.—I Corinthians 3: 9.

Almighty God, from whom we come, with whom we live, and in whose fellowship is our true life, we bring our spirits to Thee in the quiet of this moment of prayer. From the tumult and turmoil of the world we enter the sanctuary of Thy presence seeking peace and strength and wisdom as we face the duties of this day.

Empower all within these hallowed and historic walls who labor for the good of our country and who endeavor to lead our people in just ways to bring to their tasks the very best that is within them, ever standing up for the truth, siding with justice, and strengthening the good will in our world.

In the spirit of the Master we pray. Amen.

FRIDAY, JULY 31, 1970

If we hope for what we do not see, we wait for it with patience.—Romans 8: 25.

O God, creater and preserver of all mankind, we commend to Thy loving care and wise guidance the men and women who lead our Nation in these troubled times. Support them and strengthen them, we beseech Thee, and so prosper their endeavors that our people may be led in the ways of justice, by the roads of righteousness, and along the paths of peace.

We pray for all who serve under the glorious banner of our great country. Particularly do we pray for those who struggle for freedom and more particularly do we pray for our prisoners of war. May they have faith and courage to endure what must be endured, patience amid suffering, a happy issue out of their affliction, and a glad reunion with their faithful families. Hasten the end of conflict and grant us peace in our time, O Lord.

We pray in the spirit of Him who came to bring us Thy peace. Amen.

MONDAY, AUGUST 3, 1970

Know ye that the Lord is God: It is He that hath made us and not we ourselves: We are His people and the sheep of His pasture.—Psalms 100: 3.

Almighty and Everlasting God, Shepherd of the seeking souls of men, at this noontide altar of prayer we bow in reverence and humility before Thee, praying for ourselves, for our Nation, and for peace in our world.

Grant unto us worthy intelligences and a willingness to use them for the welfare of all our people and the well being of the nations. Teach our people the futility of violence, the foolishness of prejudice, and the folly of bitterness. Under the guidance of Thy spirit lead us into the ways of understanding and cooperation, peace and good will.

To this end cleanse Thou our own hearts, purify the hearts of our people, and prepare us for the coming of the better day of Thy kingdom when men shall learn to live together in peace.

In the spirit of Christ we pray.   Amen.

TUESDAY, AUGUST 4, 1970

My flesh and my heart faileth: but God is the strength of my heart and my portion forever.—Psalm 73: 26.

O God, who hast given us minds to think, hearts to love, and hands to work, help us to use our minds to think Thy thoughts, our hearts to love in Thy spirit and our hands to do Thy work according to Thy will. Make us so conscious of Thy presence that amid trials and troubles we may put first things first, grow in sympathetic outreach in our concern for others, and become stronger within ourselves.

Bless the statesmen of our country who give nobility to life and purpose to human destiny; who seek faithfully to protect our land from mortal enemies without and moral weakness within; who make no peace with oppression but are ever seeking the way to justice and peace among the nations of the world.

So guide us and sustain us in all our ways this day and every day. In the spirit of Him who is the Lord of life we pray.   Amen.

THURSDAY, AUGUST 6, 1970

Be strong in the Lord and in the power of his might.—Ephesians 6: 10.

O God and Father of us all, we thank Thee for our homes and pray that Thou wilt bless all who live within our family circles. We are grateful for Thy mercies which daily attend our days, for food, clothing, and shelter, for the warmth of our affections and for the ties that bind us together.

Help us so to live each day and so to love one another that we may never be afraid or ashamed but always may our hearts be happy, our thoughts good, our words gentle, our deeds genuine, and our hands ready to help.

Daily renew our strength, replenish our love and restore our faith that we may face life bravely because we face it together. As we come to family reunion day this Sunday deepen our love for one another and for Thee that love may reign in every room in our hearts and rule in every room in our homes.

In Thy Holy Name we pray.   Amen.

MONDAY, AUGUST 10, 1970

Finally, brethren, be of one mind, live in peace: and the God of love and peace shall be with you.—II Corinthians 13: 11.

O GOD, who art the light of all who put their trust in Thee and the life of those who walk in Thy way, we draw near to Thee in the quiet of this moment of prayer seeking strength and wisdom for the tasks of this day.

We bring to Thee our responsibilities to ourselves, to one another, and to our country, and we would see them in the light of Thy will for us. Empowered by Thy spirit we would carry them with honor to Thee, to our Nation, and to ourselves.

Again we bow in sorrow at the remembrance of our beloved colleague who has gone to his eternal home. We thank Thee for his presence in our midst and for the contribution he made to our country as a Member of this body. Comfort his family with the assurance of Thy spirit and strengthen them for this experience and for the days that lie ahead.

In the Master's name we pray.   Amen.

THURSDAY, AUGUST 13, 1970

Let integrity and uprightness preserve me; for I wait on Thee.—Psalm 25: 21.

O GOD AND FATHER OF US ALL, who art a strong tower of defense to all who keep faith with Thee, we Thy children come before Thee in gratitude for Thy steadfast love and Thy enduring truth. In Thee alone is our hope and in Thee alone is the strength of our Nation.

In our restlessness may we know the peace of Thy presence, in our fears the faithfulness of Thy spirit and in our uncertainties the certainty of Thy creative love. May our little efforts for good be supported by the greatness of Thy power and the goodness of Thy grace.

We remember in Thy presence all those bound to us by the ties of family, friendship, and the fellowship of working together; all who work for our country at home and abroad; all who serve in our Armed Forces and for our prisoners of war. Give to us such a depth of social vision and such a width of social concern that we shall seek the release of the captives, the end of war, and the coming of peace.

In the spirit of Him who sought the good of all mankind, we pray. Amen.

FRIDAY, AUGUST 14, 1970

Rest in the Lord and wait patiently for Him.—Psalm 37: 7.

O GOD, whose spirit dwells in the heart of every man and who art seeking to lead Thy children in living happy and useful lives, grant that we may be strong of will, loyal in affection, and great with good thoughts as we endeavor to guide our Nation in these days of decision and destiny. Make us instruments through which justice and good will may come to our Nation and make our Nation a channel through which truth and love may flow into our world.

To this end bless our President, our Speaker, and these Representatives of our people. Lead them in finding the way to a lasting peace, an enduring justice, and an abiding good will in our Nation and among the nations of the world.

May our recess be a source of refreshment and recreation and may we return renewed in body and spirit to carry on the work for our beloved country.

In the spirit of Christ we pray. Amen.

WEDNESDAY, SEPTEMBER 9, 1970

The Lord is good, a great help in the day of trouble: And He knows those who trust in Him.—Nahum 1: 7.

RENEWED IN SPIRIT AND RESTORED IN MIND, OUR FATHER, we return from our recess ready for the responsibilities we face in these troubled and trying times. Give us strength to do our work well this day and all days. Let us not turn from its difficulties, nor evade its challenges, nor seek to escape its duties.

Help us to keep our minds clear, our hearts clean, and to live so faithfully that no failure can dishearten us, no frustration can discourage us, and no fear can take away from us the joy of an inner integrity.

God bless America, we pray Thee, and lead her and all nations in the paths of peace. By Thy grace alive within us may we remove all bitterness, reduce all misunderstanding, and learn to live together in the spirit of a genuine good will: through Jesus Christ our Lord. Amen.

THURSDAY, SEPTEMBER 10, 1970

I therefore beg you to live a life worthy of the calling to which you have been called.—Ephesians 4: 1.

Eternal Father of our spirits who in Thy word hast revealed to us the way, the truth, and the life, lead us, we pray Thee, to walk in Thy way, help us to believe Thy truth and give us courage to live Thy life. Strengthen our hearts that in the midst of doubts within and disturbances without we may hold fast to those things we believe to be right and good for all.

Grant Thy blessing to all who work under the dome of this Capitol and to all who serve our Nation around the world. May all of us be made strong to do what ought to be done and what must be done if law and order is to prevail, if justice is to be done, and if people are to live together in peace.

In the spirit of the Master Workman we pray. Amen.

MONDAY, SEPTEMBER 14, 1970

The just shall live by faith.—Romans 1: 17.

Almighty and Most Merciful Father, we begin the week conscious of our own need and yet aware of Thy great power to sustain us in our endeavors on behalf of our beloved land. Keep us faithful in the performance of our duties, loyal to every high and holy principle, responsive to the needs of our citizens, and above all receptive to the leading of Thy living spirit.

We pray for our country—that as a people we may be delivered from malice, bitterness, and ill will. Strengthen within us all a true sense of justice, a due regard for the rights of others, and a genuine spirit of good will. Together may we get in step with Thee and with one another as we go forward to one Nation with liberty and justice for all.

In the Master's name, we pray. Amen.

WEDNESDAY, SEPTEMBER 16, 1970

He that dwelleth in the secret place of the Most High shall abide under the shadow of the Almighty.—Psalm 91: 1.

O God of all Grace and Goodness, we thank Thee for this quiet moment of prayer when facing the duties that confront us and seeking to carry the heavy responsibilities committed to our care we can look from the seen to the unseen, from the temporal to the eternal, and in so doing gain courage for these minutes, wisdom for these hours, and strength for these days. In the secret place of the Most High may we tap the resources which make us adequate for our tasks, give us an unswerving devotion to the right, and keep us dedicated to the high purpose for which our Nation was founded.

Amid the confusion and chaos of this generation may we know that Thy truth is marching on and may we here highly resolve that we will walk with Thee and work for Thee in building a world where righteousness and justice and love shall reign and war shall be no more.

In the spirit of the Prince of Peace we pray. Amen.

THURSDAY, SEPTEMBER 17, 1970

I had fainted, unless I had believed to see the goodness of the Lord in the land of the living.—Psalm 27: 13.

Eternal Father, whose strength undergirds those who trust in Thee and whose love gives understanding to those who walk in Thy way, amid the shifting scenes of this earth help us to look up and to see the shining truth of Thine eternal presence. Forgive us when we forget that above our pride and prejudice Thou art calling us to higher principles, underneath our frailties and faults Thou art offering us the strength of Thy spirit and around our failures and frustrations Thou art summoning us to wider fields of human service.

Make our country worthy of Thy blessing and willing to be a channel through which the spirit of democracy may flow into our world. Grant us grace to heal the broken relationships of mankind, to give light to those who sit in darkness, and to lead the nations in the ways of peace.

In the spirit of Christ our Lord we pray. Amen.

MONDAY, SEPTEMBER 21, 1970

O satisfy us early with Thy mercy: that we may rejoice and be glad all our days.—Psalm 90: 14.

Almighty and Eternal God, Ruler of the heavens and the earth, yet who art mindful of a falling sparrow and a cup of cold water given to one in need, help us in this quiet moment to lift our hearts unto Thee, to feel Thy presence near and to make ourselves ready for the duties of this day.

Give to each one of us a mind free from narrowness and ever open to the light of truth, a heart sensitive to human need and always eager to do good, and a spirit standing in reverence before Thee resolved to do Thy will seeking what is true and honorable and gracious and just.

We pray for our country, that our people may be free from bigotry and bitterness and that by giving primary allegiance to Thee may reap the harvest of a common faith and a common brotherhood.

In the Master's name we pray. Amen.

TUESDAY, SEPTEMBER 22, 1970

Let us come boldly to the Throne of Grace, that we may obtain mercy and find grace to help in time of need.—Hebrews 4: 16.

O God and Father of us all, who hast taught us not only to think of ourselves but to think of others and to be concerned about them, we remember before Thee all who are burdened and oppressed, particularly our prisoners of war. Comfort them with the sense of Thy presence, strengthen them for the ordeal they are facing, give them patience in their suffering, keep the hope of deliverance alive within them, and grant a happy issue out of all their affliction—a safe return to their loved ones.

Bless their families, weary and heavy laden, living in dark uncertainty yet still hoping and praying and working for the return of those they love with all their hearts.

May we here highly resolve to continue to do our best to seek the release of the captives, the end of war, and the beginning of peace on earth: through Jesus Christ our Lord. Amen.

THURSDAY, SEPTEMBER 24, 1970

My meat is to do the will of Him who sent me and to finish His work.—John 4: 34.

O God of Truth and Love, who art worthy of a nobler praise than our lips can utter and of a greater love than our minds can understand and our hearts can give, in Thy presence we bow in all reverence and gratitude.

We thank Thee for people great and good, for homes where love and loyalty live, for friends tried and true, for everyone who has urged us to leave the valley of discontent and to climb the heights of devotion to the highest, and for every example of confidence and courage, given us by persons in high places and low. Our gratitude to Thee for the goodness of life and the greatness of love.

We commend our Nation to Thy providential care. Guide our people as they choose their leaders, increase our fellowship with one another, and make us one in spirit and one in purpose as we face the crucial days that lie ahead.

Through all of life make us mindful of Thy presence and eager to do Thy will.

In the Master's name we pray. Amen.

MONDAY, SEPTEMBER 28, 1970

We are laborers together with God.—I Corinthians 3: 9.

O LORD, OUR GOD, we thank Thee for the gift of another day and pray that through all its hours we may live with Thee as we labor for the life of this land of liberty. Strengthen us that we may stand steady in this shaken world and amid constant change keep our faith firm with a growing trust and a deepening confidence.

Deliver us from petty concerns about ourselves, place us in the center of great needs, and open our hearts to all that we may share the glory of our human endeavors and the goal of our human energies. Reveal the heights above us that we may be mindful of Thy presence in the common routine of daily living and so bless us that we may work with integrity for the good of our fellow men. Let the gentle power of the Great Spirit be our strength in all we think and say and do; for Thine is the kingdom and the power and the glory forever. Amen.

WEDNESDAY, SEPTEMBER 30, 1970

Thou shalt love the Lord thy God with all thine heart and with all thy soul and with all thy might.—Deuteronomy 6: 5.

ALMIGHTY AND EVER-LIVING GOD, by whose mercy we have come with our Hebrew brethren to the beginning of another year, grant that we may enter it together with humble and grateful hearts. Confirm our resolutions, we pray Thee, to walk more closely with Thee and to labor more faithfully for the good of our fellow men according to the teaching of our law and the example of our Lord.

We invoke Thy blessing upon our country. Enlighten with Thy wisdom and sustain with Thy power those whom the people have set in authority, our President, our Speaker, Members of Congress, and all who are entrusted with our safety and our freedom. May peace and good will live in the lives of our citizens and may religion spread its blessings among us, exalting our Nation in righteousness.

In Thy holy name we pray. Amen.

MONDAY, OCTOBER 5, 1970

Where two or three are gathered together in My name, there am I in the midst of them.—Matthew 18: 20.

O Merciful God, give to us quiet minds and loving hearts as we wait upon Thee in this our morning prayer. Grant us wisdom as we seek to solve the problems that confront us, courage to do what we believe to be right, and the faith to keep us faithful in the performance of our duties.

In these days when the souls of men are tried and tempted, when so much is demanded of those who would lead our Nation, grant us courage in serving this present age that we may prove worthy of the positions we hold and ready for the tasks committed to us.

Guide our Nation and all nations into the ways of justice and truth, and establish among us all that peace which is the fruit of righteousness: To the glory of Thy holy name. **Amen.**

WEDNESDAY, OCTOBER 7, 1970

Restore unto me the joy of Thy salvation; and uphold me with Thy free spirit.—Psalm 51: 12.

O God of Peace, who hast taught us that in returning and rest we shall be saved, in quietness and confidence shall be our strength: by the might of Thy spirit lift us, we pray Thee, to Thy presence, where we may be still and know that Thou art God.

Strengthen and sustain us that the tensions and trials of this tumultuous time may not break our spirits, nor cause us to give up the struggle for life, liberty, and the pursuit of happiness for all.

Bless these Members of Congress who represent our people, who would serve Thee faithfully, and who would maintain order in our land and peace in our world. Grant that they may prove to be true to every task committed to their care. We ask it in the name of Him for whose kingdom we pray. Amen.

WEDNESDAY, OCTOBER 14, 1970

Above all put on love which binds everything together in perfect harmony.—Colossians 3: 14.

Eternal God, Our Father, ere our recess begins we pause to pray for the coming of Thy kingdom of righteousness, peace, and good will. In the midst of a swiftly changing order may our faith in Thee and our obedience to Thy laws continue to move us as we seek to usher in a new day of human brother-hood.

Direct our people as they elect our leaders. Grant that their choices may promote Thy glory and the welfare of our Nation. To those elected give courage, wisdom, and good will that they may lead our citizens in the ways of life and liberty for all, and may those not elected continue to labor faith-fully for the good of our Republic.

Bless all those in the service of our country, particularly our prisoners of war. Strengthen them to meet each day with the realization that Thou art their refuge and underneath are the everlasting arms.

May Thy peace and Thy love abide in our hearts now and always.
Amen.

MONDAY, NOVEMBER 16, 1970

The Lord is good, a stronghold in the day of trouble: and He knoweth them that trust in Him.—Nahum 1: 7.

E TERNAL SPIRIT, returning from our recess of strenuous activity we come to Thee now as we endeavor to complete the tasks which are set before us. When the worry of work done and left undone takes its toll of our human energies help us to tap the spiritual resources which are found in Thee. Do Thou renew our spirits and restore our souls with the joyful assurance that Thou art with us and we are with Thee.

We pray that Thy comforting grace may abide in the hearts of those who grieve over the passing of our beloved colleague, WILLIAM L. DAWSON. We remember his long and faithful career in Congress marked by firm convic-tions, rugged honesty, a readiness to cooperate and an earnest desire for lib-erty for all men. Bless his family with Thy presence and bless us who mourn his departure from these Halls to continue his fine work in the life beyond.

Truly, our Father, life is short. By Thy Spirit may we make the most of it while we can, through Jesus Christ, our Lord. Amen.

TUESDAY, NOVEMBER 17, 1970

Be strong, not in yourselves but in the Lord, in the power of His bound-less resource.—Ephesians 6: 10.

O GOD AND FATHER OF US ALL, out of the differences and divisions of this world we come humbly to worship Thee. From things that man is doing to man we enter Thy presence to think of what Thou art doing for man. As we pray reveal to us Thy glory, bestow upon us Thy wisdom, make us equal to the tasks of these troubled times and ready always to walk the path of goodness, truth, and love. As we pray do Thou purify our affections, refine our ambitions, cleanse our minds, and strengthen our spirits that we may think clearly, plan wisely, and work diligently for the good of our beloved country.

We pray for our President, our Speaker, and every Member of Congress. We pray for those who serve our country at home and abroad, particularly our prisoners of war. May Thy spirit steady them and strengthen them for every experience.

Grant that Thy mighty energy may surge through the peoples and governments of the world that we may learn the art of living together on this planet.

In Thy holy name we pray. Amen.

WEDNESDAY, NOVEMBER 18, 1970

Thou art my rock and my fortress: therefore for Thy name's sake lead me and guide me.—Psalm 31: 3.

O God, Our Father, in this quiet moment of prayer we lift our hearts unto Thee, who art from everlasting to everlasting. In this capital of freedom do Thou guide with the spirit of understanding and good will these Members of Congress. By their words and deeds may they seek to bring healing to our Nation and peace to our world.

In these days when men are divided, nations differ, and the world is in danger, grant unto us the wisdom, the power, and the love to burn the barriers to brotherhood as we endeavor to do justly, to love mercy, and to walk humbly with Thee.

In the spirit of the Lord of Life we pray. Amen.

THURSDAY, NOVEMBER 19, 1970

Do not worry over things, but always by prayer and supplication with thanksgiving let your requests be made known to God.—Philippians 4: 6.

Almighty God, Our Heavenly Father, the source of all wisdom and the fountain of flowing love, bless, we pray Thee, all who work under the dome of this glorious Capitol and help them to do the work they have been given to do. Enable all of us to plan carefully, to labor confidently, to live creatively, and to lead our people courageously.

Keep us ever mindful of the fact that without Thee we can do nothing and that with Thee all great and good things are possible. Bless us with Thy presence this day and lead us and our Nation in the paths of righteousness for Thy name's sake. Amen.

MONDAY, NOVEMBER 23, 1970

The hand of our God is upon all them for good that seek Him.—Ezra 8: 22.

O GOD OUR HEAVENLY FATHER, whose power is infinite and whose love is eternal, we pray for the leading of Thy spirit as we work for the well-being of our country and endeavor to secure peace in our world. May Thy wisdom so move our minds and Thy love so motivate our hearts that in the crises we face daily we may think clearly, speak calmly, and act courageously. Unite us and our people in the principles of democracy upon which our fathers founded this Nation that as responsible citizens we may do our full part in seeking the good of all.

Direct and prosper the deliberations of this body that truth and justice and good will may be established here and among all people.

In the Master's name we pray. Amen.

WEDNESDAY, NOVEMBER 25, 1970

Be thankful unto Him and bless His name. For the Lord is good.—Psalm 100: 4, 5.

O LORD, OUR GOD, we bow in Thy presence with hearts overflowing with gratitude because Thou hast been so wonderfully good to us. Thy mercies come with the morning light, they stay with us through the day and the evening hours and continue to be ours during the night. So we lift our hearts unto Thee in thanksgiving and love.

We thank Thee for food and clothing and shelter: for homes where love dwells, for churches where we can worship as we desire, for our Nation flying the flag of freedom and for the opportunity to serve our people in these Halls of Congress.

As Thou didst lead our fathers to found on these shores a free nation, so lead us in this day to keep our country great in spirit, good in purpose, and genuine in seeking for peace in our world, peace in our land, and peace in our own hearts.

In gratitude we pledge our love and our loyalty anew to Thee and to our country in the spirit of Christ, our Lord. Amen.

MONDAY, NOVEMBER 30, 1970

Thou, Lord, art good, and ready to forgive; and plenteous in mercy unto all them that call upon Thee.—Psalm 86: 5.

O THOU WHOSE LOVE PASSES UNDERSTANDING, whose wisdom is beyond our highest thought, and whose power strengthens us for every noble endeavor, open our eyes that we may see the leading of Thy spirit across the years and in the present time may we trust Thy patient power and Thy gentle goodness to bring us out of the strife between men and out of the bitterness that blights the brotherhood of man. Confirm us in that greatness of spirit which will make us united in purpose, elevated in our sympathies, global in our outreach, and eager to minister to the needs of men.

In the work of this day may we be attentive to Thy voice and responsive to Thy call that we may walk the way of truth and love for the sake of our country and the peace of the world. In the spirit of Jesus Christ, our Lord.   Amen.

WEDNESDAY, DECEMBER 2, 1970

Restore unto me the joy of Thy salvation and uphold me with Thy free spirit.—Psalm 51: 12.

"We pray for this great land of ours
Founded by men who put their trust in Thee;
Help us again to find the mighty powers
Of truth and faith and hope, to set us free.
Inspire our leaders, give us grace to find
The people who can steer the ship of state
In troubled waters, men who are not blind
Through pettiness, self-interest or hate.
And may we pledge, as statesmen long ago,
Our sacred honor, lives and fortunes, too,
To keep our country free—for well we know
That freedom only comes through serving Thee."
In the spirit of the Master of men we pray.   Amen.

THURSDAY, DECEMBER 3, 1970

O praise the Lord, all ye nations; praise Him all ye people. For His merciful kindness is great toward us and the truth of the Lord endureth forever.—Psalm 117.

E TERNAL GOD AND FATHER OF US ALL, everywhere present and everywhere available, we wait upon Thee in this, our morning prayer. We come with humble hearts and in deep need, crying aloud for insight to see the way we should take, for courage to walk in it, and for the strength to endure even when endurance seems impossible.

As we face the trying tasks of these hurried hours, our thoughts are with those in the service of our country, particularly our prisoners of war. Grant that the sacrifices they are making for freedom may never be in vain.

Guide our Nation, our leaders, and our people through these critical and crucial times. May we learn the wisdom of the ages that only those who trust in Thee win the higher victories which will usher in the great day of justice and enduring peace.

In Thy holy name we pray. Amen.

WEDNESDAY, DECEMBER 9, 1970

Come, let us go up to the mountain of the Lord, that He may teach us His ways and that we may walk in His paths.—Isaiah 2: 3.

OUR FATHER, GOD, who hast called us to take time for prayer, help us so to pray that we may be conscious of Thy presence as we face the tasks of this day and every day. May these daily moments of quiet meditation keep alive within us the higher virtues and the happier values without which we cannot live honorably with ourselves nor lead our Nation with honest motives nor learn to be harmonious in our relationship with the nations of the world.

Let the light of Thy spirit shine upon us in such measure that the darkness of doubt and fear may be dispelled and confidence and courage may come to new life in us. Increase our faith in Thee, deepen our love for Thee, broaden our sympathies with Thee, and lift our souls to Thee that with the true spirit of Christmas in our hearts we may walk in Thy ways and minister to the needs of our fellow men.

In the spirit of Him whose coming brought life to men, we pray. Amen.

THURSDAY, DECEMBER 10, 1970

The law of God is in his heart: None of his steps shall slide.—Psalm 37: 31.

ALMIGHTY GOD, OUR FATHER, we thank Thee for the open door of a new day which makes available to us once again the steps that lead to a better and a brighter life. Guide us, we pray Thee, that in this generation we may find the way to good will toward men, freedom among men, justice between men, and peace in the hearts of men.

Bless every lover of liberty, every effort for the growth of free institutions, and every endeavor to make democracy work on our planet. This is our task and our mission. May we prove ourselves worthy of it, and play our full part in climbing the steps toward this glorious achievement.

> "Give me the heart, to hear Thy voice and will
> That without fault or fear I may fulfill
> Thy purpose with a glad and holy zest,
> Like one who would not bring less than his best."

In the spirit of Him who leads us from strength to strength, we pray.
Amen.

FRIDAY, DECEMBER 11, 1970

Make every effort to supplement your faith with virtue, and virtue with knowledge, and knowledge with self-control, and self-control with steadfastness, and steadfastness with godliness, and godliness with brotherly affection.—II Peter 1: 5, 6.

> "God bless our native land!
> Firm may she ever stand, through storm and night:
> When the wild tempests rave,
> Ruler of wind and wave,
> Do Thou our country save
> By Thy great might!
> For her our prayer shall rise
> To Thee above the skies, on Thee we wait;
> Thou who art ever nigh,
> Guarding with watchful eye,
> To Thee aloud we cry, God save the state!
> Not for this land alone,
> But be Thy mercies shown from shore to shore;
> And may the nations see
> That men should brothers be,
> And form one family the wide world o'er."

Amen.

MONDAY, DECEMBER 14, 1970

This is the day which the Lord hath made; let us rejoice and be glad in it.—Psalm 118: 24.

ALMIGHTY AND EVERLASTING GOD, as we bow at the altar of prayer do Thou breathe Thy spirit upon us, fill us with life anew that we may love what Thou dost love and do what Thou wouldst have us do.

While we pray for tomorrow, we also pray for today that this day may be so well lived that every yesterday may be a dream of happiness and every tomorrow be a vision of hope.

> "Lord for tomorrow and its needs
>   We do not pray;
> Keep us, our God, from stain of sin
>   Just for today.
> Help us to labor earnestly
>   And duly pray;
> Let us be kind in word and deed,
>   Father, today.
>
> Let us in season, Lord, be grave
>   In season gay;
> Let us be faithful to Thy grace,
>   Father, today.
> Lord, for tomorrow and its needs
>   We do not pray:
> Still keep us, guide us, love us, Lord,
>   Through each today."

Amen.

TUESDAY, DECEMBER 15, 1970

The people who walked in darkness have seen a great light.—Isaiah 9: 2.

ALMIGHTY GOD, who by the birth of the Babe of Bethlehem has given light to those who sit in darkness, love to those who would live with ill will in their hearts, and life to those who walk through the valley of the shadow of death: Grant that in Thy light we may see light clearly, in Thy love may we possess love fully, and in Thy life may we learn to live all our lives.

Guide the citizens of our Nation in the ways of righteousness and the people of the world in the paths of peace. May good will live in all our hearts binding us together in the bond of true brotherhood, to the glory of Thy holy name. Amen.

WEDNESDAY, DECEMBER 16, 1970

Lift up your heads, O ye gates; and be ye lifted up, ye everlasting doors; and the King of Glory shall come in.—Psalms 24: 7.

AS WE LIFT UP OUR HEADS, OUR FATHER, may we also open the doors of our hearts that the glory of Thy spirit may come in and dwell with us, helping us to render a true service to Thee and a faithful service to our fellow men. Working under the banner of truth, justice, and love, may we lead our people beyond the limits of differences and divisions to the heights of unity and peace. For Thine is the kingdom, the power, and the glory forever.   Amen.

THURSDAY, DECEMBER 17, 1970

Come ye and let us walk in the light of the Lord.—Isaiah 2: 5.

O GOD, who art the strength of all who put their trust in Thee and the joy of every loving heart, we thank Thee for the happiness and hope which pass around the world at Christmastime. Grant that no obsession with things may keep us from the values these advent days represent. In the midst of the commercialism of this season help us to lift our eyes to Thee and to become conscious of Thy presence without whom there would be no Christmas and with whom Christmas is always a reality.

This day may we put first things first, last things last, and thus serve Thee and our country with all our hearts, in the spirit of Jesus Christ our Lord.

Amen.

SATURDAY, DECEMBER 19, 1970

For God, who commanded the light to shine out of darkness, hath shined in our hearts, to give the light of the knowledge of the glory of God in the face of Jesus Christ.—II Corinthians 4: 6.

ALMIGHTY GOD, who hast declared Thy love to men by the birth of the Holy Child at Bethlehem: Help us to welcome Him with gladness and to make room for Him in all our common days, so that we may live at peace with one another and in good will with all Thy family: In His holy name we pray.   Amen.

MONDAY, DECEMBER 21, 1970

The steps of a good man are ordered by the Lord: And he delighteth in his way.—Psalm 37: 23.

ETERNAL GOD, OUR FATHER, for the joy of this Christmas season we thank Thee and pray that it may ever live in our hearts. For the joy of this day, the birthday of our beloved Speaker, we raise our hearts in loving gratitude to Thee. We thank Thee for him who has provided such capable, effective, and unselfish service for his country and ours. For his wise and understanding leadership in this House, for his nobility of mind, his gentleness of spirit, his fervent support of home, church, and Nation, and for his loving devotion to his lovely wife, we thank Thee.

May this day be a great day for him and may it be a great day for us as we pray for a genuinely great and good man.

In the spirit of his Lord and ours we pray. Amen.

TUESDAY, DECEMBER 22, 1970

Glory to God in the highest and on earth peace, good will toward men.— Luke 2: 14.

O GOD, to whom glory is sung in the highest, while on earth peace is proclaimed to men of good will, we bow before Thee with hearts overflowing with gratitude for the coming of Christ into our world. May He—

> "Cast out our sin and enter in.
> Be born in us today."

Like the shepherds may we in spirit kneel before the manger child in wonder, love, and praise. Like the wise men may we follow the star that shines forever in our sky and like them offer Him the gift of our love. In truth may we make room for Him in all our hearts through all our days.

In His holy name we pray. Amen.

TUESDAY, DECEMBER 29, 1970

*So, my brothers, do stand firmly in the Lord.—*Philippians 4: 1.

O UR FATHER GOD, who reveals Thyself in all that is good and true and beautiful, help us to make our hearts receptive to Thee, and our minds responsive to the leading of Thy Spirit, as we face the tasks of the last days of the old year. Now and always may we keep alive our faith in values that live forever and in virtues that never die. No matter what may be our lot in life—joy or sorrow, victory or defeat—may we be strengthened by Thy presence and sustained by Thy power as we labor for the good of our country and as we work for a better world in which men can live together with justice and in peace.

We mourn the passing of our beloved colleague, L. MENDEL RIVERS, "who more than self his country loved." For his devotion to our country, particularly our Armed Forces, we thank Thee. For the love in his home, the warmth of his friendship, the greatness of his heart, we are grateful. The passing of this highly trusted and great-spirited public servant reminds us again that in the midst of life we are in death. Bless his family with the comfort of Thy presence and strengthen them for the days ahead.

In Thy holy name we pray. Amen.

THURSDAY, DECEMBER 31, 1970

Let Thy work appear unto Thy servants and Thy glory unto their children.—Psalm 90: 16.

E TERNAL GOD, who hast been our dwelling place in all generations, our fathers prayed at this altar and trusting in Thee were sustained all their lives. Give to us the realization, as we pray at the same altar, that Thou art with us and so undergird us that we may be upheld all our days.

Strengthen us to resist temptation, deliver us from constant moods of ill will, help us to help others—to feed the hungry, to clothe the naked, to set free the captive, to give liberty to those who are oppressed, and to promote peace in our world, justice among men, and good will in all hearts.

So may our Nation be blessed and become a blessing to all mankind.

In the Master's name we pray. Amen.

SATURDAY, JANUARY 2, 1971

As I was with Moses, so I will be with you: I will not fail you or forsake you.—Joshua 1: 5.

O GOD, OUR FATHER, by whose mercy we have come to the portal of another year, grant that we may enter it with humble and grateful hearts. Confirm us in our resolution to walk more closely with Thee in Thy way and to labor more faithfully for the good of our country and the peace of the world. Thus may this year be a better year and our Nation a better nation because we live and work and pray during these coming months.

Bless Thou our beloved Speaker and his lovely wife. Looking forward, may they feel the support of Thy grace, be sustained by our affection, and find security in their faith in Thee and in our country. Guided by Thy Spirit, may they and we walk along the path that shineth more and more unto the perfect day of Thy heavenly kingdom.

May Thy blessing abide with us and our Nation now and forevermore.

Amen.

O

www.ingramcontent.com/pod-product-compliance
Lightning Source LLC
Chambersburg PA
CBHW030922090426
42737CB00007B/283